Sonia Livingstone

YOUNG PEOPLE AND NEW MEDIA

Childhood and the changing media environment

SAGE Publications
London • Thousand Oaks • New Delhi

First published 2002
Reprinted 2003, 2005

SAGE Publications Ltd
1 Oliver's Yard, 55 City Road
London EC1Y 1SP

SAGE Publications Inc
2455 Teller Road
Thousand Oaks, California 91320

SAGE Publications India Pvt Ltd
B-42 Panchsheel Enclave
Post Box 4109
New Delhi **100 017**

British Library Cataloguing in Publication data

A catalogue record for this book is available from
the British Library

ISBN 0 7619 6466 5

ISBN 0 7619 6467 3

Library of Congress Control Number available

Typeset by SIVA Math Setters, Chennai, India
Printed and bound in Great Britain by Athenaeum Press, Gateshead

CONTENTS

ACKNOWLEDGEMENTS

While writing is generally a solitary activity, the original empirical research on which this book is based rests on the efforts and support of many people. I am grateful to Jay Blumler for his consistent encouragement from the outset of the project onwards, to Andrea Millwood Hargrave and her colleagues at the Broadcasting Standards Commission for co-ordinating funding and supporting the research process, and especially to Moira Bovill for her enthusiasm, interest and commitment to the project. To Peter Lunt I owe much for his constructive and incisive criticism over the past five years, encompassing all stages of the work from research design to analysis and writing. I am also grateful to Rodney Livingstone and Maggie Scammell for undertaking the task of reading and advising on the draft manuscript, to Julia Hall at Sage for waiting so patiently for the manuscript to arrive on her desk, to George Gaskell for working with me in the early stages of this project and its associated European comparisons, and to the many colleagues and friends who have borne with me, offering advice, challenge and support, over the period during which I have been preoccupied with this research project and its publication. Warm thanks are also due to Cliff Christians, David Swanson and Andrea Press at the University of Illinois at Urbana-Champaign for hosting my sabbatical term and so greatly facilitating the writing of this book, and to my colleagues in the Department of Social Psychology and *Media@lse*, for whom this book is the explanation of why my attention was not always where they wished it to be.

The empirical research for this book was multiply funded and I wish to thank, for making the project possible at all, the Advertising Association, the British Broadcasting Corporation, British Telecommunications plc, the Broadcasting Standards Commission, the European Commission (Youth for Europe Programme, DGXXII), the European Parliament, the European Science Foundation, ITVA, ITV Network Limited, Independent Television Commission, The Leverhulme Trust, STICERD (The London School of Economics and Political Science) and Yorkshire/Tyne-Tees Television. I am also very grateful to the many children, young people, parents and teachers who agreed to be interviewed during the course of the empirical research discussed here. They were generous with their time and thoughts. I trust they find their experiences fairly represented in this book.

Lastly, my own children provided a host of observations while I was writing this book, their offers of help – for, as they pointed out, they knew a lot about children and television – challenging my commitment to reflect children's voices in my writing. While they noted the irony of my staring at a screen all day, apparently not hearing what they said, I thought about my daughter avidly collecting and then growing out of Barbie, watching *The Sound of Music* repeatedly, a point of safety after her adventures with things new, and now aged eight introducing me to the latest girl bands who inspire her to dance. I tried also to represent the experiences of my son, aged six at the start of this project, playing Teenage Mutant Ninja Turtles in the playground without having seen the programme, aged ten rebutting my complaint about time spent online by calculating how to reimburse me from his pocket money, aged eleven inviting and then scorning my view on whether Pokémon is 'good for kids'. So many of their comments kept my enthusiasm for this project alive, as when Anna hunted for the video remote control by saying, 'where's the mouse, I want to save the programme', or when Joe said, 'I can't really see the difference between the television and the computer, only with the computer, you're doing something'. To Joe and Anna, I dedicate this book.

Sonia Livingstone

London

A NOTE ON THE TEXT

- The original empirical material discussed in this book was collected as part of a project originally titled *Children, Young People and the Changing Media Environment*, directed by Sonia Livingstone, with Moira Bovill (research officer) and Kate Holden (research assistant), along with the advice and collaboration of George Gaskell and others. It was first reported in *Young People, New Media* (Livingstone and Bovill, 1999), an LSE report available at http://psych.lse.ac.uk/young_people and containing many of the quantitative and qualitative findings summarised here in greater technical detail.
- Earlier versions of some of the material published here can be found in Livingstone (1997, 1998a, 1999a, 2000) and Livingstone and Bovill (2001a).
- All statistical results are only reported if statistically significant ($p < 0.05$).
- Socio-economic status of households is measured using the standard, though not entirely satisfactory, market research segmentation (A–E) and paraphrased verbally through the contrast between middle-class (ABC1) and working-class (C2DE) households.
- All names of respondents have been changed to pseudonyms.

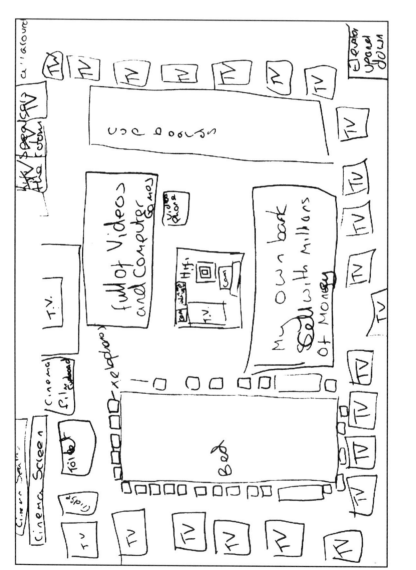

Bedroom of the future (10-year old boy)

1

CHILDHOOD, YOUTH AND THE CHANGING MEDIA ENVIRONMENT

FROM SPECULATION TO RESEARCH

A group of boys go to play with the friend who has a new computer game. A teenage girl checks out the web site of her favourite band. In the playground kids discuss the latest episode of an Australian soap opera. Parents buy a computer to support their children's education but are then unsure how to use it. Meanwhile teachers are faced with considerable inequalities in pupils' domestic experience of computers and the Internet. When kids ask their parents for a mobile phone for Christmas, telephones become more individual than household appliances. So too with television and, more recently, computers, as electronic screens of one kind or another multiply in bedrooms, living rooms and even hallways. Saturday morning means television time; music, cartoons and news are already available round the clock, and digital television further expands the options available.

We can no longer imagine living our daily lives – at leisure or at work, with family or friends – without media and communication technologies. Nor would we want to. As we enter the twenty-first century, the home is being transformed into the site of a multimedia culture, integrating audiovisual, information and telecommunications services. There is much discussion of the potential benefits of the ever-more significant, ever-more multifunctional electronic screen. Media headlines regularly focus on the possible consequences – e-commerce, the virtual classroom, global consumer culture, cyber-democracy, and so forth. And public anxieties keep pace, reflecting a widespread concern with the kind of society that today's children will grow up to live in as adults. Hence, there is speculation about 'the digital generation', children in the 'information age', 'computer nerds', 'innocents on the Net', the 'digital divide' and 'addicted surfers'.

In both public and academic domains, grand claims abound. Optimists foresee new opportunities for democratic and community participation, for creativity, self-expression and play, for the huge expansion of available knowledge, thereby also supporting diversity, difference and debate. Pessimists lament the end of childhood, innocence, traditional values and authority. Interactive media are seen to herald the rise of individualised and privatised lifestyles increasingly dependent on the economics of global consumerism, often iniquitous in their effects, tending to undermine national culture and national media regulation. Indeed, the potential impact of new forms of information and communication technologies (ICT) has been speculatively related to almost every aspect of society, from home to work, from education to leisure, from citizenship to consumerism, from the local to the global; perhaps their most radical impact appears to be the blurring of these traditionally important distinctions. The result is a flurry of hype and anxiety, a pressure on public and commercial bodies as well as on individuals to be seen to be responding, a fear of not 'keeping up'.

Behind the speculation lies a dearth of knowledge about the social meanings, uses and consequences of new information and communication technologies. How are children and young people using these rapidly developing new technologies? What do they think of them? And how important are they for their leisure and, as leisure provides the space for young people to experiment with identity and relationships, how important are they for their development and social relations? Will some be excluded from these opportunities while others live in an increasingly information-rich environment? How do the new forms of media affect uses of older, more familiar media, and vice versa? Will the greater variety of media contribute to the withdrawal from traditional leisure activities and even social and political participation? Will the media operate to strengthen local identities with locally-produced programming or will they support the emergence of transnational or global identities? And so forth.

We know from historical studies of past 'new' media that the outcome of ICT diffusion and appropriation is sometimes at odds with popular expectations, is often shaped by those expectations, and may be amenable to intervention if opportunities are recognised in time. Empirical research is essential if we are to understand the balance between the potential and the dangers of today's new media. Yet an exclusive focus on the latest media would be inappropriate. Not only do new media add to and, in the process, transform existing leisure options, but also existing practices mediate the appropriation of new media into daily life. Consequently, this book examines the state of current research on the diffusion, use and significance of new media and information technologies among children and young people by considering 'new' media in the context of older media, media use in the context of leisure, and leisure in the context of the rest of children and young people's lives.

Two trends make an academic volume on children and young people's media environments valuable at the present time. First, and as the empirical research to be discussed clearly shows, the media are playing an ever-greater role in children's daily lives, whether measured in terms of family income, use of time and space, or importance within the conduct of social relations. Secondly, and here too the evidence is convincing, the media are extending their influence throughout children's lives so that children's leisure can no longer be clearly separated from their education, their employment prospects, their participation in public activities, or their participation within the private realm of the family. Yet the key terms and frameworks for conducting such research – children and young people; audiences, users and contexts of use; the 'new' media; and social change – are widely contested. Before considering the empirical research base, we must therefore examine the nature of each of these concepts in order to understand what questions can be, and have been, pursued effectively. That is the task of this chapter.

YOUNG PEOPLE'S MEDIA CULTURE

I will begin by asking, why focus on children and young people? Curiously, there is a notable discrepancy between the high levels of public concern over children and young people's use of new media and the paucity of empirical research conducted thus far.[1] Although children are often left out of 'population' surveys, in Europe approximately half of all households contain parents and children, and some two-thirds of the population live in these households (Kelly, 1998). Beyond considerations of population size, their activities and interactions make children and young people distinctive in several ways.

First, children and young people are a distinctive and significant cultural grouping in their own right – a sizeable market segment, a sub-culture even, and one which often 'leads the way' in the use of new media.[2] Households with children generally own more ICT, and many media goods, especially those that are relatively cheap and portable, are targeted at and adopted by the youth market. Moreover, children and young people are at the point in their lives where they are most motivated to construct identities, to forge new social groupings, and to negotiate alternatives to given cultural meanings; in all of these the media play a central part.

Within the household, media of one form or another are often implicated in the sometimes fraught negotiations between children and adults. Crucially, one cannot be certain of children's ICT access and use, given only information at the level of the household, because traditionally, though perhaps decreasingly, they lacked the power to determine activities in the home. As explored in Chapter 2, for a variety of reasons children may not use media located in the home, and they may use media elsewhere which they lack at home. Moreover, children may diverge from adults in their perceptions of everyday practices precisely because their actions represent tactics to resist or reinvent the adult-created contexts in which they live (Graue and Walsh, 1998).

In *Kids' Media Culture*, Kinder (1999: 19) identifies significant differences between children and adults in their use of, and response to, diverse media products, seeking to rectify the way in which the meaning-making activities of children are often rendered invisible or inconsequential. Indeed, as she points out, not only are 'adult anxieties and fantasies about their own social realities, political agendas, and personal memories ... sometimes projected onto these texts', but also, as part of the everyday contexts of media reception and use, the conflict between adult and child responses to media texts 'can itself become a means of socialisation for children or a potential object of commodification for media producers with transgenerational marketing goals'. By linking production and consumption in this way, Kinder shows how, while adults struggle to resolve, or undermine, children's sometimes transgressive readings of media contents, producers structure media contents so as to appeal to both adults and children, thus exploiting generational differences in media culture.

In order to recognise how gender and generation subdivide the household, research must encompass both individual and household levels of analysis. In achieving this, it is no more acceptable to ask adults alone to speak for children than it is to ask husbands to speak for wives. Children's voices are indeed increasingly being heard in public, policy and commercial fora. Children and young people have long been the subject of specific policy intervention, premised on the assumption that they constitute a 'special audience' (Dorr, 1986), drawing on a well-established tradition of policy designed to protect children from potential harms. This tradition is now being rethought, as part of the move to recognise children's rights. For example, the internationally-endorsed

Children's Television Charter[3] not only specifies that children's programmes should be non-exploitative and free from gratuitous sex and violence, but also that children should have high-quality programmes made specifically for them, so as to support the development of their potential, and through which they can hear, see and express their experiences and their culture so as to affirm their sense of community and place.

It is also the case that children – as audiences for and users of new media – are distinctive because of the perennial social anxieties concerning children, childhood and youth. Indeed, the combination of children, new media and social change commonly arouses particularly strong views. However, as each new medium is introduced, similar hopes and fears – with the fears generally dominating the agenda – have arisen on each occasion.[4] Currently, these so-called 'moral panics' centre on the Internet, with questions typically being asked about violent, stereotyped, commercially exploitative or pornographic content and about the reinforcement of individualistic, lazy, prejudiced, uncritical or aggressive activities. Yet similar questions were asked about the introduction of video games before the Internet, about the VCR a couple of decades earlier, about the introduction of television before that, about radio, cinema, comics, and so on. As Drotner (1992) points out, it seems that as each new medium is introduced, through a kind of 'historical amnesia' about previous panics, we come to accept, or incorporate, the medium that preceded it. Predictably, she argues, each panic tends to move from 'pessimistic elitism' to a 'more optimistic pluralism'; in other words, initial calls for technocratic and legalistic measures such as censorship and direct social control give way to a tacit paternalism and the advocacy of moral education or media literacy.

This account is not meant to imply that these and related concerns are in principle improper or misguided. It may well be the case that the media do encourage a tolerance of aggression, stereotyping or prejudice, for example. Moreover, it is clear that these questions are of considerable concern to many parents. Why do adults keep harking back to their childhood? Not simply nostalgia, but a need to mark change and to understand it, an acknowledgement of the importance of thinking through the implications of change. As we shall see later, today's parents – like those of every generation – recognise that these are differences which are informative about the world they now live in, and which require a response from them. Indeed, asking yet again the old questions of new media can be seen as productive, inviting us as a society to rethink widespread assumptions or challenge long-held beliefs or give recognition to submerged problems.[5] Thus ICT provides a new opportunity to rethink familiar issues and to raise, once more, important questions about the place of communication and information – as mediated by technologies – in our everyday lives, as well as broader but still pertinent questions about the nature of childhood, family life, education, community, identity, and so forth. In short, both researchers and funding bodies appropriately derive some research questions from public imagination concerning ICT, asking, for example, whether cyber-friendships are 'real', whether children are becoming video games 'addicts', who are the 'information poor', will e-commerce alter the domestic gendered division of labour, how truly participatory are democratic fora on the Internet? However, it is crucial to examine such questions critically, being aware of who asks them, why, and in whose interest.

As Cohen (1972) argued, public anxieties or moral panics may present themselves as positive and wholesome, as 'respectable fears' (Pearson, 1983), establishing an image of children as vulnerable, innocent and in need of protection from the faults or poisons of society. Yet examined closely, these often transpire to represent middle-class concerns about the 'polluting' effect of working-class practices, and so rest on social division and conflicts of interest. The common claim that one worries less about one's own children and their media use but more about those of others is perhaps better read as a middle-class anxiety about the supposed failure of working-class parents to control their children. In short, behind the rhetoric of a moral panic lies the middle-class assertion of the right to define, and the struggle for the authority to legislate for, standards and values – to define good against bad, decent against criminal, culture against populism, quality against cheap pleasures, morality against depravity. For Cohen, the creation of 'youth' as a deviant and stigmatised image in 1950s Britain represented one such tactic. As children and young people have their own interests, desires and values, these panics may also be read as a struggle between current and upcoming generations, a struggle in which the definition of children as vulnerable further legitimates adult authority to regulate their interests and pleasures. Buckingham (1993) has noted more recently that focusing these debates on the latest new media offers the further benefit of displacing attention from other more complex social ills: the media, treated as scapegoat, can be blamed for social unrest, crime, breakdown of the family, political apathy, thereby simplifying and trivialising the underlying social problems (e.g. Putnam, 2000).

Moreover, or perhaps as a consequence, moral panic questions have generally not been productive of good research, tending to generate narrow and unimaginative hypotheses that even then are often not supported empirically. For instance, far from finding that teenagers are turned by computer games into lonely, isolated addicts unable to communicate with each other, it seems that teenagers are incorporating new media into their peer networks, using both face-to-face and online communication, visiting each others' houses to talk about and play computer games just as they visited and swapped comics a generation before, using new media to supplement rather than displace existing activities.[6] To take another example, when Schoenbach and Becker (1989) surveyed the impact on households of media introduced in the 1980s (VCR and cable/satellite television) across a variety of Western countries, they found little evidence of a reduction in time spent on non-media leisure and little evidence of reduction in time or money spent on print and auditory media. Rather, their claims were more modest, suggesting consistent evidence for increasing diversification and specialisation in uses of all media.

For a variety of reasons, it seems that to research children and young people – particularly in relation to the media – is to enter a domain that, for the adult population, arouses deep ambivalence. In arguing for a new, child-centred approach to the sociology of childhood, Qvortrup (1995: 9) identifies nine fundamental paradoxes in our culture's orientation to children and young people.[7]

- 'Adults want and like children, but are producing fewer and fewer of them, while society is providing less time and space for them;
- 'Adults believe it is good for children and parents to be together, but more and more they live their everyday lives apart from each other;
- 'Adults appreciate the spontaneity of children, but children's lives are more and more organised;
- 'Adults state that children be given first priority, but most economic and political decisions are made without having children in mind;
- 'Most adults believe that it is best for children that parents assume the major responsibility for them, but, structurally, parents' conditions for assuming this role are systematically eroded;
- 'Adults agree that children must be given the best start in life, but children belong to society's less affluent groups;
- 'Adults agree that children must be educated to freedom and democracy, but society's provision is given mostly in terms of control, discipline and management;
- 'Schools are generally seen by adults as important for society, but children's contribution to knowledge production is not recognised as valuable;
- 'In material terms, childhood is important for society rather than for parents themselves; nevertheless society leaves the bulk of expenses to parents and children.'

Each of these paradoxes tells us something about the locus of concern over young people, and each warns us of the traps into which we as adult researchers are liable to fall. Taken together, they also pinpoint key issues for a more balanced, less anxious or idealistic research agenda. In relation to the changing media environment, we may pose a specific set of questions concerning: the embedding of media within the temporal, spatial and social dimensions of children's lifeworld; questions about the management and regulation of children's leisure and the values which guide this; questions about opportunity, equality and marginality, especially as these differentiate among children; and questions of meaning, perspective and voice in so far as these distinguish children and adults. To pursue these questions, let us turn to research on audiences.

AUDIENCES, USERS AND EVERYDAY LIFE

There is no convenient term to describe people's relation to media. Different media are associated with different activities – communicating, viewing, reading, listening, writing, playing. The term 'audience' does not capture all these, although media research has traditionally used this term, being until recently heavily focused on broadcasting. Today the personal computer and other media compete with television for our attention, while audiences are becoming more fragmented in response to diversifying content both within and across media. Given such competition across media, the medium of television and, consequently, being part of a television audience, seems less central in our lives. Yet, as we shall see later, partly because television has moved more into the background it has also become more pervasive, its taken-for-granted presence permeating every aspect of our lives. Thus it is not only because of the diversification of media that the term 'audience' is becoming awkward. It is also that we no longer divide our time between media and other activities, but rather, for much of the time, we are both part of an audience and engaged with other activities. And it is children and young people especially who enjoy, and play with the possibilities of, such a simultaneous participation in multiple activities.

As 'audience' seems no longer to serve as well as before, some research is settling on the term 'users'. This perhaps seems narrow, being associated with the tradition of uses and gratifications research which, while enjoying a revival as media become more interactive and so more variable in their gratifications, is widely seen as reductive to the individual level of analysis (Blumler et al., 1985; Elliott, 1974). 'Users' can also seem too neutral a term, for it does not distinguish the use of media from the use of any other object and so fails to capture what is specific about media, namely their unique capacity to convey complex and meaningful texts. The term is useful, however, in so far as many pressing research questions are currently focused more on media as technologies, as consumer durables and as domestic products than they are concerned with how people engage with, typically, broadcast content. Consequently, people's relation to media is being construed not only in terms of viewing, reading or listening but also in terms of using, consuming, owning.

Silverstone (1996: 286) writes, 'television and other media and information technologies are doubly articulated into the culture of the household', as material, technological objects located in particular spatiotemporal settings and as texts, symbolic carriers of messages, located within particular sociocultural discourses. Given the present developments in ICT, it seems that media-as-objects appear more interesting than media-as-contents. Media goods are widely represented as technologically innovative, as symbolic of social status, and at the same time as expensive and difficult to use. Moreover, notwithstanding the proliferation of new media technologies, they have hitherto had the character of 'old wine in new bottles', for to a considerable degree new media goods have been carrying old media messages (McLuhan, 1994). Yet much of this is set to change further, with attention turning from delivery – itself becoming progressively more user-friendly and familiar – to content and, particularly, to the possibilities for new forms of content. Perhaps this will renew interest in audiences and in the primary question asked by audience researchers, a question still pertinent in the new media environment, namely what are the diverse, motivated, located, interpretative activities with which people make sense of media texts and, perhaps in consequence, make sense of the world around them and their place in it?

Pragmatically, given that in their daily lives people are both grappling with the media as technologically complex consumer goods and making sense of the meanings of media texts or contents, both 'audience' and 'user' retain a heuristic value. Theoretically, research debates over audiences continue, often with the aim of developing an alternative to Lasswell's (1948) challenge to the early communication researchers, namely that they should discover 'who says what in which channel to whom and with what effect'.[8] Problematically, Lasswell's model positioned ordinary people, whether as 'audiences' or 'users', only at the end-point of the communication process. Instead, the everyday activities through which people engage with media are increasingly seen to shape as well as to be shaped by the cultural context within which the media are embedded. However, Lasswell's linear approach remains an influential model of communication (Carey, 1989), it being the first of three metaphors which usefully capture contemporary thinking about the media:[9]

- *As a conduit* for the transmission of certain meanings. Often the metaphor behind public concern over undesirable or harmful contents, this places the audience at the end-point of the influence process, construing it as impinged upon rather than participating in a process of communication.
- *As a language.* Here technological and semiotic researchers may ask about media channels, codes or 'grammar', while rhetorical scholars consider its persuasive effects. With the growth of multimedia, these questions which, from the audience's viewpoint, centre on media literacy are again prominent.
- *As an environment.* This raises questions about the interactional, relational and ritual possibilities of different media, with the media seen as framing the social context for communication as well as transmitting content and so as contributing in both these ways to a mediated culture integral to everyday life.

In response to recent debates over audiences and users, this book begins with the third metaphor, emphasising the notion of the 'media environment' in order to consider how the media are involved in every part of children's lives, whether in the background or foreground. While questions arising from the conduit and language metaphors are also explored, the emphasis on environment, or context, is central. Most simply, media and leisure activities are made meaningful by their mutual relations with all others: watching television means something different for the child with nothing else to do compared with the child who has a PC at home or friends knocking on the door. Thus conditions of access and choice within the child's environment are central to an understanding of the meanings of media use. Moreover, without thorough contextualisation in the everyday lives of children and young people, media research tends to lose sight of the bigger picture, tending to transform the positives and negatives of people's lives into images of positive and negative children or young people, particularly negative ones. Similarly, without contextualisation research tends to pit 'old' media against 'new' media ('the end of print', the end of the 'mass audience', etc.), failing to recognise the complex ways in which they are mutually entangled in our daily lives.

However, there is some dispute over how far to take the argument for contextualisation. Most would agree that 'television's meanings for audiences – textual, technological, psychological, social – cannot be decided upon outside of the multidimensional intersubjective networks in which the object is inserted and made to mean in concrete contextual settings' (Ang, 1996: 250). Taking this a stage further, Janice Radway (1988: 366) has called for 'radical contextualism', namely 'the analytic displacement of the moment of text-reader reception by ethnographic studies of the everyday' and a focus on 'the kaleidoscope of daily life' or, as Paul Willis puts it, on 'the whole way of life' (1990). While a contextual approach is currently much in vogue, and rightly so, it is crucial for media researchers to retain a focus on the media (being media-centred, though not media-centric; Schroeder, 1994). Notably, during the practice of empirical research no natural boundaries to 'the context' arise, making it easy to become lost in ever-widening circles of contextualisation.

Consequently, research must tread a fine line between two pitfalls: first, the technologically-determinist, media-centric approach that attributes social change to technological innovation and underplays social and cultural contexts of use, thereby constructing, in their more extreme versions, such mythical objects of anxiety as the computer addict, the screen-zombie, the couch potato, the Net-nerd, the Nintendo-generation, the violent video fan, etc.; and secondly, a non-media-centric, cultural determinism (W.R. Neuman, 1991) that assumes, at least implicitly, a romantic view of childhood in which children are seen as too sophisticated to be taken in by the messages of consumer culture and too interested in hanging out with friends in a nearby park to waste time watching television in their bedrooms – too sensible, in short, to warrant public concern over media contents. In the course of the research discussed in this volume, we met few addicts or nerds, but nor did we meet many children for whom the media are unimportant or without influence. A dual focus is required for, as this book will argue, when one's starting point is a focus on the media, the story rapidly becomes one of 'it depends on the context', but when the starting point is a focus on family life or the home, the story instead becomes one of 'look how important the media are'.

A DUAL FOCUS ON YOUNG PEOPLE AND NEW MEDIA

If we reframe this dual focus in positive terms, research on children and young people's media environment can adopt a child-centred or a media-centred approach, seeing the media as figure and childhood as ground or vice versa. Ultimately, of course the contexts of childhood and youth shape the meanings, uses and impacts of media just as these, in turn, contribute to shaping the experience of childhood and youth.

The *child-centred* approach directs us towards the many parameters of young people's lifeworlds. After all, the media represent just some of the consumer goods available in the home, some of the competing options for leisure activities, and some of the sources of influence upon them.

This approach is valuable for putting the media in context, for playing down some of the hype, utopian and dystopian, surrounding new media by 'putting them in their place', and so for refusing to reify children in terms of media use (as addicts, nerds, fans, etc.). Within children's life-worlds, the home represents the primary location for media use for younger children as well as being an important location for teenagers, although contextualising domestic media use in relation to school, peer culture and community contexts is also vital.

Encompassing diverse aspects of children's lives requires an interdisci-plinary approach. Until recently, child-centred research has been predomi-nantly psychological, often wedded to a somewhat simplistic version of Piagetian theory and lacking in contextualisation. Since the psychological approach remains dominant, it is worth for a moment considering the dif-ficulties it has generated. For example, in *Children's Journeys through the Information Age* (1999), Calvert adopts a 'public health' model in which children are construed as willing or unwitting participants in their own downfall, surrounded by a media environment which variously threatens, harms or undermines their healthy development, engaging in self-destruc-tive activities of various kinds (watching television, playing computer games) because neither they nor their parents fully understand the harms which result, as revealed by experimental psychological research.

Although Calvert provides a clear and comprehensive review of an influential body of literature on the potential harms of the violent, gen-dered, commercial messages of media, little or no attention is paid in the book to the contexts of use. These children are not, in any meaningful sense, living their lives at home, with parents and siblings, with friends, or in a community: they are individuals in front of one screen or another, with before and after effects to be measured. This is not to say that the research is 'bad' or necessarily 'wrong-headed'; some of it is very useful, for example, when comparing girls and boys for their confidence in using computers at school, or interviewing children for their awareness of the persuasive messages in advertising. But repeatedly the experimental work produces contradictory findings, frustrating attempts to generate clear strategies for evaluation, advice or targeted intervention, as the public health model requires, because – implicitly and inevitably – context inter-venes. For example, one study shows that structuring girls' access to com-puters improves their confidence with them, another shows it decreases their confidence. We can only conclude that the type of computer use, the specific contexts of use and the cultural assumptions of the girls and their teachers all matter.

By contrast, and in attempting to broaden the research agenda on childhood so as to encompass 'the concentric circles of influence with which children interact' (Hill and Tisdall, 1997: 3), the sociology of childhood offers a new approach to childhood (e.g. James et al., 1998; see also Prout and James, 1990). The central argument of this approach is that children are active in the construction of their own lives, of those around them and thus of the society in which they live.[10] This implies the rejection of 'presociological' images of childhood – the evil child, the innocent child, the immanent child, the naturally developing child, the unconscious child. Qvortrup (1995) concurs, characterising the new sociology of childhood as stressing:

- the structural aspects of childhood, with its dynamics and determinants, rather than a naturalistic conception of the individual child and its development;
- the relational – neither 'the child' in isolation from others, nor 'the household' as sufficiently descriptive of its members, and these relationships are worthy of study in and of themselves;
- the present – children as people now, their relationships and cultures considered worthy of study in their own right, rather than forward looking – children as merely persons-to-be and so as indicative of the adults they will become;
- the normal or everyday rather than the atypical or problematic.

For example, through his contextualised analysis within the sociology of childhood of the micro-workings of peer culture, Corsaro (1997) shows how the everyday activities of children reveal their participation in the production and reproduction of society. Drawing on Goffman's (1961) notion of secondary adjustments, Corsaro stresses that through such daily actions, often invisible to adult eyes, children contribute to the construction of social structures which have consequences for both children and adults. This requires a methodological commitment to the social worlds of childhood and youth as real places where real meanings are generated, rather than regarding these as fantasy or imitations of the 'real', i.e. adult, world. Indeed, along with this stress on children as active rather than passive goes a politicisation of childhood – childhood is seen as not only a demographic but also a moral classification, central to the project of making children count when apportioning the resources of society (Qvortrup, 1995).

Given that 'childhood socialisation is not only about preparation for the future, but also about acquiring a sense of self as a child, belonging to peer-based groups and developing child-based norms and practices' (Hill and Tisdall, 1997: 116), it is curious that the sociology of childhood pays little attention to the media.[11] This may be because the stress is on recognising, celebrating even, the cultures children create for themselves, or because of a cultural assumption that face-to-face communication is more authentic or influential than mediated communication. Or it may be social influence is not seen to vary according to the channels, forms or contexts with which such symbolic representations are conveyed, or perhaps because of an implicitly elitist rejection of the media as uninteresting, unimportant or a distraction from more serious matters.[12] Whatever the reason, the rethought sociological child-as-agent (rather than child-as-object) lives a non-mediated childhood – a carefree child playing hopscotch with friends in a nearby park, not a child with music on the headphones watching television in her bedroom. Stronger links exist between youth studies and media studies although these are often narrowly focused on certain media (e.g. music) or certain aspects of audiences (e.g. counter-cultures, resistance) to the neglect of other, more widespread and more ordinary media uses.[13]

By contrast, the *media-centred* approach takes much of its lead from technological developments. For example, when LaFrance (1996) dubs 1960s children 'the TV generation', 1970s children 'the video generation', 1980s children 'the Nintendo generation' and 1990s children 'the Internet generation', he highlights a significant shift in the character of the electronic screen – from television-centred to computer-centred. The media-centred approach tends to be more sensitive to the medium- or content-specific characteristics of different media, tracing the chain of influence from innovation and marketing through diffusion into the home, then to actual use and, eventually, to consequences for children and young people. For example, such an approach asks about the significance of the recent transformation in the European audiovisual sector from 'channel austerity' (typically, one or few often public service channels) to 'channel abundance' (mainly growth in commercial, digital or global channels) (Curran and Gurevitch 1991a), with narrowcasting including specialist children's and youth channels, becoming a reality.

The changing media environment raises some interesting social questions. Significantly, access to the dominant leisure media of the twentieth century has for the most part been democratic, equally available to children of all social class and gender groups. Anyone could watch television, and almost anyone could work a VCR, and neither had direct implications for individuals' educational advantage and transferable workplace skills. This situation is changing as diverse information and communication technologies become a key feature of the modern home. What are the implications of the diversifying media environment for a common national culture? Further, what of the inequalities that result from such diversification, as households invest differentially in the new media? As we shall see, parents and children are investing heavily in domestic ICT; parents through their expenditure and efforts to support an informal learning environment for their children, children through the enormous leisure-time energy they put into learning and playing computer games, using the Internet and developing other computer skills – practical, creative, interactive, and critical. But such skills may have direct value for children's education and prospects in the workplace, raising the crucial question of whether and how investment in technology at home perpetuates social inequalities beyond the home?

Until fairly recently, however, the media-centred approach has tended to neglect the social contexts of use for media, including the ways in which media use is contextualised in relation to other media. This can result in non-commensurate images of children and young people. We hear of the oppositional youth culture of the music fan, the imaginative world of the reader, the aggressive world of the video game player, the mindless world of the television viewer, and so forth, ignoring the way that children and young people construct diverse lifestyles from a mix of different media, rarely if ever making use of just one medium. For this reason, the notion of the *media environment* is stressed throughout this book, precisely to avoid the problems of technological determinism which often face research on new media.[14]

Undoubtedly, as each new technological change emerges, there is a broad set of questions to be considered concerning the consequences and significance of these changes. Yet such research may seem to invite answers which simply attribute subsequent social and cultural changes to features of the technology itself, instead of leading one to ask what it is about a culture at a particular historical point that facilitates the adoption of one medium over another or that encourages the appropriation of that medium within a particular set of cultural meanings and practices. For example, rather than asking whether the Internet displaces television or how television displaces books, one might draw on the larger historical picture, which suggests that new media supplement rather than displace older media, and so ask how people cope with the increasing diversity, or how new forms of media transform or are transformed by patterns of use surrounding older forms of media. For, as socially meaningful phenomena, ICTs are not pre-given, fully-formed, automatically determining of the manner of their use, but rather their meanings depend on the complex, contingent ways in which they are, over time, inserted into specific contexts and practices of use. Hence, research must uncover the balance according to which social contexts both shape and are shaped by technology.

If we look beyond specific technologies, and beyond the cultural anxieties regarding children, more underlying changes, concerning post-war transformations in time, space and social relations, may be observed (Thompson, 1995; Ziehe, 1994). For example, in many countries children no longer walk to school or play in the streets as freely as they used to. Yet while their lives may be less locally-grounded, they are simultaneously becoming global citizens, increasingly in touch with other places and people in the world. This is particularly apparent once they reach adolescence, with transnational entertainment media now playing a key role in young people's identity formation and peer culture. In the family, too, larger changes are occurring. Comparing young people's lives with the childhood and youth of their parents, the divorce rate has escalated, more women engage in paid work and the structure of families has diversified. More children are better off but more, too, are poorer. More young people are going into further or higher education while entry into the workplace is more difficult, with the prospect of a job for life diminishing (Lagree, 1995). Even larger changes are also at work, as globalising economic, political and technological developments challenge the autonomy of the nation state. What are the consequences of such changes for children, young people and their use of media? Does lack of freedom to play outside influence time spent watching television? Do global media encourage consumerist values? And how does children's new-found expertise with computers affect parental authority?

These questions point to a third starting point for researching children and young people's changing media environment that goes beyond the child-centred and media-centred approaches. Specifically, debates about childhood and youth, and about media and information technologies, can be encompassed within the broader set of concerns commonly theorised as 'late modernity'.[15] Theorists of late modernity stress the convergence of several historically-linked processes, operating at both the institutional and individual level, which, while not necessarily constituting a break with the past, open up a new array of opportunities and dangers across diverse spheres of social life. Thus Giddens (1991: 1) argues that 'modern institutions differ from all preceding forms of social order in respect of their dynamism, the degree to which they undercut traditional habits and customs, and their global impact'.[16] Media and communications institutions represent prime examples of this, and so too do the family and school. From the point of view of children and young people, these historical processes of late modernity have resulted in a crucial reconsideration during the twentieth century of their status as citizens within Western society. Most notably, the UN Convention on the Rights of the Child ratified a wide range of children's rights, although this stress on children's rights is paralleled in other spheres by a growing perception of children as a market.

In short, this book takes the broad conceptual framework of late modernity as a means of holding together the child-centred and media-centred approaches so as to benefit from the strengths of each while overcoming their limitations by identifying not only how each provides a crucial part of the context for the other, but also the common processes of social change which affect both children and the media environment. Having argued for a historical and contextual approach, these broader questions of social change are addressed in some depth in the chapters to follow. In the remainder of this chapter, two themes are developed of particular importance for understanding young people and new media. First, we consider the nature of change in the media environment. Secondly, we consider how this relates to changes in childhood and the family context. In both cases, the time frame is the past fifty years or so, focusing on the change from the heyday of the mass broadcast television audience, shared by the nation, experienced with the nuclear family in the living room, to that of the individualised, multi-set, multichannel multimedia home. Methodologically, this new environment is less easy to research than before. Domestically, it is less easy to supervise than before. Nationally, it is less easy to regulate than before. And as the experience of the media becomes increasingly diverse, there is increased scope for social, psychological and cultural factors to influence who watches what, or uses what, and why.

WHAT'S NEW ABOUT NEW MEDIA?

Notwithstanding the excitement, and anxiety, experienced by those among the public, journalists, policy-makers, and business people who believe that society is on the edge of an information revolution analogous in scale and significance to the Industrial Revolution, social science is taking a cautious approach. It warns that social change is complex and that attributing social change to technological innovation is naïve. Moreover, change is not necessarily the same as progress, especially for those who are left out. In short, social change is generally evolutionary, not revolutionary. Moran and Hawisher (1998: 80) offer a useful analogy here, comparing new media with the sense in which we say a child is new. While obviously a distinct individual, 'the child, in some lights and at some moments, looks very much like her mother; in other lights and at other moments, she resembles her father; and sometimes she even reminds you of a grandparent'. The 'child' analogy is appropriate not only because of her heritage but also because of her youth: 'the e-child is still young, and other genes and influences are still waiting for the proper conditions for their expression. The e-child has been, and will be, shaped by her cultural contexts, and as an agent she will shape the culture that she joins' (1998: 81).

Empirical research is vital for evaluating the many claims for change. Key to this is investigating the activities of real audiences and users as they acquire, use and make sense of new media goods, particularly given the degree to which the 'implied audience' or implied user is presumed, imagined or mythologised in the discourses surrounding new media (Livingstone, 1998c). Indeed, a critical examination of claims, implicit and explicit, about audiences across new media theory, production and policy is required. Not only do anticipated audiences map poorly on to actual audiences, but also it appears that audiences themselves are becoming less predictable, more fragmented and more variable in their engagement with media. This is itself subject to debate. For Mackay (1995a: 311), new technologies change audiences: 'the mass basis of the television audience is being diluted as more delivery routes and reception devices become available'. By contrast, W.R. Neuman (1991: 168) argues that audiences shape the technological offer: 'both media habits and media economics … continue to involve strong incentives towards common-denominator mass-audience content'. With the struggle for both mass and specialised audiences underway in the market, an understanding of audiences in relation to both the social shaping of technologies and their appropriation, consumption and impact is needed.

In pursuing such an empirical project, what theory should one draw upon? Because of the historical coincidence of the expansion of twentieth-century social science with the dominance of national, public service, mass-market television, the grounding assumptions of most media theory have made it primarily television theory. How far do new media represent a new domain for old theories and to what extent are new frameworks and questions required?[17] Whether new media are defined in terms of technology (interactivity, digitalisation, convergence, etc.) or services (delivery of information, entertainment, political participation, education, commerce, etc.) or textual forms (genre hybridity, non-linearity, hypertextuality, multimedia, etc.), they raise different questions from those which have dominated the research agenda over recent decades, particularly when one pursues the relations among old and new media, within an account of the social contexts of their use. This broadening of the research agenda necessitates an interdisciplinary approach to the investigation of young people's changing media environment, including developmental and social psychology, cultural and sociological studies of childhood and youth, media uses and gratifications, the sociology of leisure/consumption, diffusion research and reception studies.

Yet it was noted earlier that an exclusive focus on the newest media would be inappropriate. Given that technologies are continually changing, what should be the time scale against which to define 'newness' or to evaluate change? Key questions concern long-term social consequences of the introduction of ICT – questions about social inequalities or the digital divide (the so-called 'info-rich' and 'info-poor'), about displacement, socialisation, education, and so forth. Crucially, these are the result of processes of diffusion and appropriation that can only begin when a new product has become widely available, by which time it is generally already technologically out of date. In other words, although policy-makers and the public are most interested in those technologies which are on the horizon, users are not yet using them and so researchers cannot research them, except perhaps for that unrepresentative group of users, the 'early adopters' (Rogers, 1995).

Several strategies are open to researchers of new media. One may indeed research the few who have gained access to the newest media – the early adopters, atypical of the population though they are. Or, one may draw on the history of previously new media, and argue by analogy to today's new media. To take the obvious case, if the personal computer is the radically new mass-market screen medium of the 1990s, forty years ago it was television that drew all the attention. So, rather than reinventing the wheel, we may argue that we know a lot about television viewing, so let us take the theories, methods, past findings from a well-researched medium and see how they apply to the PC and the Internet.[18] The difficulty here is that the very newness of the new medium is what tends to get left out, while the features in common with the older medium get researched. A further strategy is to define new media in social rather than purely technical terms, as media new to society, including new for some segments of the population even if familiar to others, and so new in the sense of awaiting – or still debating – a widespread cultural representation or established practices of use. To be sure, this means studying some technologically rather familiar media, but since many questions regarding these media are still pressing, this strategy has some value.

Since one can hardly wait for the lessons of history to learn about today's new media, all three strategies are employed in the present volume, with this inclusive conception of new media allowing a broad purview of what's new for audiences and users of ICT. Four themes suggest how new media contribute to the changing social environment.[19]

First and most simply, we are seeing a significant multiplication of personally owned media. Media familiar to us all are being used in new arrangements of space and time as households come to possess multiple televisions, telephones and radios, etc. Facilitated by the reduction in price for media goods and by the growth of mobile media (e.g. mobile phone, Walkman), what's new here is primarily to do with social contexts of use rather than the technologies themselves. These social contexts of use are themselves part of a wider reformulation of the relation between public and private. For example, the traditional notion of 'family television' (Morley, 1986), with its associated hierarchies of gender and generation, is rapidly becoming obsolete, for the very possibility of personal/private television viewing created by multi-set homes is transforming the meaning of both solitary and shared viewing.

Secondly, media are diversifying in form and contents, resulting in local and global, general and specialised television channels, in diverse kinds of computer and video game, and so forth. This further encourages the multiplication of familiar goods, for as new forms of media come on to the market, families upgrade their existing goods, and thus the older media are passed down, from parents to children, from living room to bedroom. Perhaps most important in social terms is the way that such diversification allows for increasing flexibility to combine different media in different ways, thereby facilitating the broader Western trends towards individualisation (Beck, 1992) and globalisation (Tomlinson, 1999), in which media use is becoming detached from traditional sociostructural determinants and construed within diverse – and often transnational – conceptions of 'lifestyle'.

Thirdly, the more technologically radical shift towards convergent forms of information services, as media, information, and telecommunications services become interconnected, raises the possibility that emerging screen technologies contribute to convergence across hitherto distinct social boundaries (home/work, entertainment/information, education/leisure, masculine/feminine, etc.). As the structures that have maintained these boundaries rest on, and sustain, traditional authority relations, such convergence may also facilitate a general trend towards democratisation (within the family, in terms of citizen participation, in the accessibility of once-expert knowledge, etc.).

Fourthly, the potentially most radical change of all is the shift from one-way, mass communication towards more interactive communication between medium and user. While the argument for the active audience of traditional media has probably been taken as far as it can go,[20] interactive technologies now coming on to the market increasingly put such interpretative activities at the very centre of both media design and media use. To use Eco's (1979) terms, the distinction between 'virtual' and 'realised' text is greater for interactive media, particularly for the flexible, impermanent, non-linear, hypertextual data structures of the Internet.[21] Through greater user participation, the blurred boundaries identified above in relation to contexts of media use are drawn into the very construction of texts. Thus ICT content supports 'edutainment', 'infotainment', 'glocalisation', etc., mixing print and audiovisual genres, high and low cultural forms, as well as perhaps inventing new forms of media content.

CHILDHOOD, MEDIA AND SOCIAL CHANGE

If the media have changed in the past fifty years, so too have the contexts of childhood, whether this is charted in terms of the social structures of family or community, of consumer and labour market expectations, or of values and identities. Parallel changes in media and in childhood must be considered in tandem if we are to avoid either technological or cultural determinism. Thus this book links changes in media and childhood over the past half-century. Not only was the post-war period the moment when the home gained its first and still dominant screen medium, television, but also it represents a golden era in the public image of family life, continually revived in popular discussion, whether of politics, gender relations, parenting advice or lifestyle aspirations. Such an idealisation was itself promoted by the images shown on television, television thus insinuating itself not only as the centre of the family home, but also as central to notions of family, home, childhood, nation.

But we must beware of over-simple, now-and-then comparisons. This picture now seems typical only of a certain period in the history of television and, moreover, atypical of the history of the media more generally. Similarly, it was argued above that comparisons between the introduction of television and that of the personal computer into the home offer a less productive lens than does locating the arrival of each within a longer historical process of innovation, diffusion and appropriation, and this is developed in Chapter 2. I note here that, for similar reasons, we should be wary of comparing childhood cross-sectionally – from the 1950s to the 1990s, for example – when the processes of social change encompassing the family, childhood and the home operate over a similarly lengthy time scale. For problematically, making now-and-then comparisons means picking out two points from the longer historical trends even though, given the fluctuations within most social processes, these two points may poorly capture the overall trend.

Such misleading comparisons are easily made in relation to both childhood and the media. As regards the former, and because of the coincidence of a variety of socio-economic trends, it seems that a particular model of the suburban nuclear family – breadwinner father, the housewife mother, the two children and the affluent consumer lifestyle – became a dominant one in the early post-war period. This resulted in what Coontz (1997) calls 'the 1950s family experiment', where for a time family life and gender roles became much more predictable and settled in the 1950s than was the case either twenty years earlier or twenty years later. She argues that although as a society we may look back nostalgically to that time, worrying about what has gone wrong, trying to recapture the proper family and home, such a nostalgic vision falsely constructs a temporary and historically specific moment as a permanent moral truth. On this view, the 1950s family is seen as traditional rather than experimental, as how things always were until the litany of supposed disasters – the rising divorce rate, the growth of crime, the diversification of family structures, the loss of consensual moral values – so consistently deplored in the popular press.

Undoubtedly, there is evidence that the 1950s family did not in fact match up to this ideal. But more significantly, Coontz shows how the 1950s family experiment was no more characteristic of the preceding decades than it was of those that followed. For example, she observes that 'today's dual-earner family represents a return to older norms, after a very short interlude that people mistakenly identify as "traditional"' (Coontz, 1997: 54). Rather, much longer-term trends – towards the urbanisation and education of the population, the emancipation of women, the growth of affluent individualism together with a dispossessed poor, the gradual inclusion of the diversity of the population in terms of ethnicity and sexuality and the decline in public participation and political commitment – have shaped the family during the twentieth century, along with a set of economic policies which have been, and still are, reshaping the relations between public and private, state and commerce, society and individual.

Coontz's analysis of the 1950s family experiment can also be applied to 'family television'. In other words, that period which Morley (1986) captured under the heading of 'family television' can be recognised as just as much an experiment, a moment in the history of the media, as was the 1950s family experiment. For several decades, television has been seen as – and for many people has been – what the family watched together, after father came home from work and while mother had finished tidying the house for the day. Television represented a key means by which father – by choosing to watch 'his' programmes – asserted his economic power, while mother – regulating the children's viewing while father was at work – showed her moral proficiency in managing her family. Coontz's twin critiques apply. First, as even Himmelweit et al. (1958) showed, 'family television' was more an ideal than actuality, for she found even in the

1950s that children stayed up 'too late' watching television, that they watched 'inappropriate' programmes, and so forth. And secondly, while for a time the arrival of television signalled a temporary but culturally significant grouping of the family around the living-room television, and the nation around the prime-time terrestrial schedules, the longer-term trends reveal this to be something of a temporary experiment. Over the twentieth century, the broader trend has been towards the multiplication and diversification of media that are largely used individually, according to particular tastes or lifestyles. But, in shifting the unit of analysis for media consumption from the individual or demographic segment – as had been typical of the press, of books and of the cinema – to the family, the dominance of mass terrestrial television bucked for several decades the longer trend of individualisation.

In other words, the signs of individualisation that we see today may well contrast with the 1950s image of family television, if one believes in it either as an ideal or as historical fact, but they are nothing new. On the other hand, just as Coontz, in writing about the 1950s experiment, takes seriously people's nostalgia for that period, we must see that nostalgic images for past media and past media practices are defining of the present. That post-war vision of suburban family life, rich in consumer goods, successful in its balance of work and leisure, clear in its gendered division of labour and its assignment of duties of care and respect to parents and children, and consensual in its moral values, lives on through its framing of the expectations held by many parents for their children, setting out a conception of family life and so providing criteria for evaluating the performance of parents and children. Within this, the media take their place. Often, it is through the lens of 'the 1950s family' that today's adult generation views as problematic the changing relation between media and childhood. As the media environment changes, parents balance their anxious sense of decline in the quality of childhood against the unknown but significant promise of the new information and communication technologies, and within this they chart their course for parenting. Children, on the other hand, are relatively unburdened by this sense of decline, by ideals of proper family life, of the moral superiority of reading or talking over viewing or surfing. For these and other reasons, their views do not always coincide.

THE *YOUNG PEOPLE NEW MEDIA* RESEARCH PROJECT

This book has its origins in the attempt to update, forty years on, Himmelweit et al.'s *Television and the Child* (1958), a key research project which established our understanding of the place of television, a new medium in the 1950s, in the lives of children. Himmelweit and her colleagues at the London School of Economics and Political Science took a comprehensive look at a new media technology entering children's lives, examining many of the putative effects of television on children's lives.[22] At the time, almost nothing was known about the likely impact of this new medium on children. Consequently, the design and findings of the study were integral in framing the new field of media research both in Britain and elsewhere, and played a key role in informing broadcasting policy for years to come (Himmelweit, 1996; Oswell, 1998a).[23] Contrary to some of the critical attention the project received subsequently, the guiding assumption of that project, which research both then and since has supported, was that television has a diverse range of moderate effects on children, and that these depend on children's age, ability, gender, social class and personality.

In designing the *Young People New Media* project,[24] again at the LSE but four decades later, it was immediately obvious that both childhood and the media environment had changed, making any direct replication of the earlier study inappropriate. To be sure, we once again face what feels like a defining moment, the introduction of significant new media into children and young people's lives. But the questions faced by that project were framed in relatively simple terms, asking what happens when one significant change is made, namely the introduction of one national, terrestrial, public service television channel in children's lives.[25] As we have seen, today a neat experiment such as Himmelweit et al.'s comparison of children before and after television is not possible for the computer or the Internet.[26] Not only is the definition of 'new media' far from obvious, but also understanding media access today means mapping complex combinations of diverse media – hence the stress here is not on a particular medium but on the media environment. There are a number of further changes made in the *Young People New Media* project (hereafter, YPNM), compared with those early days of research on children and the media, reflecting the changed research environment forty years on.

- In response to the sustained critique of the effects tradition (Livingstone, 1996) as well as to the practical impossibility of constructing a before-and-after research design, given that multiple forms of media are gradually diffusing through society, it is assumed that the concerns behind effects studies – themselves the most heavily researched but also highly vexed topic in the field of children and media – may be better addressed by a more contextualised analysis of the meanings and practices which constitute children and young people's lifeworlds, locating adoption of new media within this account.

- Rather than see children as the object of media effects, they are instead seen as actors in the household and community, co-constructors of the meanings and practices of their everyday lives. Indeed, if we forget to see young people as actors as well as acted upon, if we fail to listen to participants' voices as they speak for themselves (Morrow and Richards, 1996), we miss understanding their experience of the media, tending to succumb to our often nostalgic perspective on childhood and so missing the new skills and opportunities that these media may open up for them.

- Although Himmelweit et al. knew they were dealing with a dramatic change in the media environment they did not appear to grasp the historical specificity of the period. Nor did they see television as a cultural phenomenon and so did not recognise their research questions, or findings, as revealing more of the 1950s than of either television or the child in absolute terms. Of course, some continuities span the decades, and some of their findings still hold today, but this is a matter of historical and cultural contingency rather than a guarantee of the generality of their findings.

- When Himmelweit et al. began *Television and the Child*, the social segmentation between children, young people and adults was different. Then, she could say that 'in many ways a 13–14 year old does not differ much from an adult in his tastes and reactions' (Himmelweit et al., 1958: 10).[27] For this reason, studying 10–11 and 13–14 year olds was considered sufficient to capture a picture of 'the child', in the singular. Now we have children, teenagers and a semi-autonomous youth culture. Since childhood and youth have tended to be theorised separately, by distinct research literatures, there is a further challenge in accounting for media uses across the age range selected for our project, namely 6–17 years old.

In its empirical design, the *Young People New Media* project matched the theoretical commitment to contextualisation with a commitment to a multi-method design triangulating qualitative and quantitative data sources. In the final report of the project, the focus was on access, meanings and use of old and new media for children and young people (Livingstone and Bovill, 1999). In its sizeable collection of tables, summaries of findings, and illustrative use of children and young people's own views of their media use, the emphasis was firmly on mapping the current media environment, as a more or less factual slice through time. The present volume draws heavily on that report for the empirical framework – who has what and when they use it – but shifts the focus more towards the contextual and the interpretative. In exploring the significance of media in children and young people's lives, it is hoped that this book is 'quite as much about critique, problematizations, invention and imagination, about the changing shape of the thinkable, as it is about the "actually existing"' (Gordon, 1991: 7–8).

In what follows, after first mapping the diffusion of diverse media into the household, Chapter 2 investigates how far gaining access to media goods determines or frames their subsequent use, tracing the slippage between access and use, and arguing in consequence for an account of the meanings and contexts of media use within daily life. In pursuing this contextualisation, Chapters 3–5 explore the interrelations among three key overlapping but not necessarily identical terms used to think about 'context' – leisure, home, family. Although the terms 'media', 'leisure', 'home', 'family' are increasingly aligned, this alignment masks a series of tensions which characterise the underlying processes of social change in late modernity, particularly concerning the individualisation of leisure (Chapter 3), the loss of public leisure in tandem with the privatisation of everyday life even within the home (Chapter 4), and the democratisation of cross-generational relationships within the family (Chapter 5). If the contexts of media use are changing, so too are media contents changing as computer-based media become ever more central (Chapter 6). As we shall see, this too has implications for how children and young people engage with the media.

NOTES

1 Key early research, mainly focused on television, includes Dorr (1986), Hodge and Tripp (1986), Palmer (1986). More recent research on young people and ICT includes van den Bergh and van den Bulck (2000), Buckingham (1993), Buckingham et al. (1999), Calvert (1999), Durkin (1995), von Feilitzen and Carlsson (1999, 2000), Gunter and McAleer (1997), Howard (1997), Kinder (1999), Kline (1993), Lohr and Meyer (1999), Sefton-Green (1998), Seiter (1999), Singer and Singer (2001).

2 Although see Bingham et al. (1999) for a critique of the discourse of young people as pioneers with the 'frontier' technologies.

3 Reproduced in von Feilitzen and Carlsson (1999).

4 For discussions of the moral panics inspired by different media following their introduction, see Barker and Petley (1996), Buckingham (1993),

Drotner (1992), Pearson (1983), Wartella and Reeves (1985). While the commonalities are many, there are also some specificities. For example, Haddon (1993) analyses the moral panics induced by computer and video games. These were stimulated, he argues, by the combination of the hobbyist, toys-for-the-boys image of the early home computer games (i.e. the anoraks and hackers who arouse anxieties about masculinity and about vulnerable and isolated loners), and the sleazy image of the arcade games (with their addicts, gamblers and other antisocial or deviant characters).

5 As critical educationalist Quinn observes, with some asperity, 'many authors dismiss the re-invention of the wheel. Such people attend more to the importance of wheels than of re-invention, they think more of re-invention than of education, and ignore the point that re-invention is just a form of invention, of creativity' (1997: 122).

6 Durkin (1995), Livingstone and Bovill (1999), Pasquier et al. (1998).

7 See also Holland (1992).

8 See Livingstone (1998b and c).

9 See Meyrowitz (1993).

10 We might add a historical gloss on the recent emergence of this new sociology of childhood, seeing it as itself an outcome of the social trend through which children, traditionally subordinated by or excluded from civic society, are repositioned as citizens in a democratic society and as partners within the home.

11 Taking Qvortrup's *Childhood Matters* (1994), James et al.'s *Theorising Childhood* (1998) and Corsaro's *The Sociology of Childhood* (1997) as indicative of this new approach to childhood, it is notable that none considers the media in any detail, if at all. This is also the case for the sociology of the family, where again the media figure little if at all (e.g. Allan's *Family Life*, 1985; Brannen and O'Brien's *Childhood and Parenthood*, 1995; Hill and Tisdall's *Children and Society*, 1997; Muncie et al.'s *Understanding the family*, 1999). In these and other volumes, the media only make an occasional appearance as a transmitter of violent imagery or as central to deviant youth subcultures. The centrality of the media over the leisure spaces and timetables of family life – as we shall see in the chapter to follow – is consistently ignored, as are the new domestic computer-based media.

12 Child psychology does acknowledge the media, but mainly in relation to cognitive development, and much of it remains within the effects tradition.

13 For example, Drotner (2000), Fornäs and Bolin (1995), Frith (1978), Kellner (1995), Sefton-Green (1998).

14 See Willams (1974) for an early critique of technological determinism, elaborated subsequently by Smith and Marx (1994) and MacKenzie and Wajcman (1999) among others. Technological determinism takes it for granted that 'qualities inherent in the computer medium itself are responsible for changes in social and cultural practices' (Snyder, 1998a: 132), and that 'the relation between the technology and human beings is external, that is, where human beings are understood to manipulate the materials for ends that they impose upon the technology from a pre-constituted position of subjectivity' (Poster, 1997: 205). In making the case for an alternative, social shaping analysis, MacKenzie and Wajcman assert instead that 'the technological, instead of being a sphere separate from social life, is part of what makes society possible – in other words, it is constitutive of society' (1999: 23).

15 See Fornäs and Bolin (1995), Giddens (1991), Reimer (1995), Thompson (1995).

16 With the exception of Habermas's work on the public sphere (1969/89), Reimer notes that the main theorists of modernity pay rather little attention to the media (1995). See Thompson (1995) for a recent analysis of the media in late modernity.

17 See, for example, Gunkel and Gunkel (1997), Morris and Ogan (1996), Newhagen and Rafaeli (1996).

18 See the special issue of *Journal of Communication* (Vol. 46(1), 1996) and the first issue of *New Media and Society* (Vol. 1, 1999).

19 See Livingstone (1999a).

20 Audience research has mapped a diversity of modes of engagement between ordinary people and media texts, offering several dimensions with which to theorise these modes of engagement, for example in terms of popular pleasures or public information (Corner, 1991) or in terms of the reproduction of meanings common to a nation (Dayan and Katz, 1992) versus more individualised meanings (Eldridge, 1993). The research has shown that the interpretative and contextual activities of the audience play a crucial and often unanticipated mediating role in the reproduction of textual meanings (see Livingstone, 1998b).

21 In his *Role of the Reader*, Eco (1979) distinguishes the virtual text – that unread, singular, context-free, flexible content which is available for and open to interpretation – from the realised text, which is read and known but which therefore exists only in multiple, context-dependent versions or realisations.

22 The main findings of Himmelweit et al.'s (1958) substantial project can be summarised briefly as follows. (1) Television rapidly became children's main leisure activity, to some extent displacing reading and 'doing nothing', especially immediately after adoption, and providing functionally equivalent leisure with little detrimental effect on school work. (2) The effects on beliefs and behaviour were few, and in particular no negative effects on levels of aggression were found. Viewers tended to become more ambitious and more middle-class in their aspirations, having seen middle-class, comfortable situations being portrayed on television, while girls became more concerned to adopt feminine roles. (3) Children were found to watch, and to prefer all kinds of programmes, of which many or most were 'intended' for adults (notwithstanding the primary focus of parents, teachers and regulators on specifically children's broadcasting). Looking within the family, parental control and example proved important to mediating and even determining the viewing habits of their children. (4) The uses and impacts of television depended on children's ability and critical perspective (with less informed or less critical children being most affected by the new medium), as well as their gender, age and personality. In this the findings were broadly in line with a parallel study conducted in America (Schramm et al., 1961).

23 Himmelweit et al.'s *Television and the Child* (1958) was influential in policies which established a highly regulated, paternalistic children's broadcasting culture, with careful scheduling according to idealised notions of children's viewing habits, with the 'toddler's truce' in the early evening, heavily restricted advertising on the new independent channel and reassuring, 'parental' figures presenting the programmes.

24 The theory and background to the project are discussed in the full report, *Young People, New Media* (Livingstone and Bovill, 1999); see also Livingstone (1998a) and Livingstone and Gaskell (1997). For a brief summary, see the Appendix to the present volume.

25 In fact, during the conduct of the project, a second, commercial channel was introduced (ITV, in 1955) and so some of the research compares this to the BBC channel already available.

26 The powerful feature of Himmelweit's design was that the introduction of television in some parts of Britain but not others meant that comparisons between those with and without, or before and after, television were unconfounded by those factors which lead some households to acquire a new medium before others.

27 In this, she was probably mistaken, for at the same time Abrams (1959) was beginning to chart 'the teenage consumer' as a distinctive social category.

2

THE DIFFUSION AND
APPROPRIATION OF NEW MEDIA

FRAMING THE QUESTIONS

Young people's lives are increasingly mediated by information and communication technologies, yet their use of these technologies depends in turn on the social and cultural contexts of their daily lives. Before exploring this interdependency of the shaping, uses and consequences of media technologies, one must know the basic facts and figures about which media children and young people have access to at home and how much time they spend with them.

Although surveys of the adult population are increasingly abundant as issues relating to ICT rise on the policy agenda, these tend to exclude children and young people (although they may include adults speaking 'for' children) and to focus on media access rather than use. Yet the critical realisation in research terms is that of the imperative to 'go beyond questions of access', centring on use as a key concern. Policy domains appear slower to accept this imperative, perhaps because of the undoubtedly greater difficulties in researching, formulating and implementing policy regarding ICT use. An expressed concern with ICT access is often a proxy for a concern with use, even though the two are quite different and, in policy terms, provision that is not used or misused is surely as problematic as the absence of provision. In other words, if one cannot presume use from a knowledge of access, use will not be guaranteed by a policy designed to ensure access, and those social and cultural circumstances that determine the desirability of media, as opposed to their availability, must be considered. Consequently, detailed data on children's media access and, especially, media use (or 'exposure') are of particular value across a variety of academic and policy domains.

A contextualised focus on media use, as argued for in the last chapter, makes it clear that knowing the percentage of children with a television in their bedroom or a computer at home, or even the length of time that children spend with a particular medium each day, is not intrinsically meaningful. Rather, these figures become meaningful only when we relate them to some prior expectation or compare them with other figures of interest, thus explicitly or, all too often, implicitly contextualising them within everyday life. We may compare the media in young people's homes at the turn of the twenty-first century to the media available, say, during the 1950s or 1970s, or even during our own childhood. We may compare domestic media in Britain with those in America or elsewhere. Such comparisons are often prompted by the anxieties of popular discourse – 'Is Britain falling behind America?', 'Why are children's lives more media-saturated than when we were children?', 'Is the computer taking the place of television?' Yet the specific facts and figures available can only represent particular slices in time and place through a broader, cross-national – even globalising – process of the adoption of technological innovation.

Hence, in order to interpret the 'facts and figures' presented here, the chapter contextualises them by relating them to comparable access and use data from other times and places, while the next chapter relates them to the daily conditions of young people's lives. As we shall see, adopting a perspective that charts the adoption of media over recent decades and across other Western countries makes it clear that the inclusion of new media in UK homes today is part of a broader process of social change. This cross-national and within-nation process is strongly inflected by cultural factors, so that in different countries, and in different households, new media acquisition varies systematically. These cultural factors, which make for intriguing differences in the media environments of children and young people, are perhaps of most pressing importance in so far as they are a source of inequalities – of social class, of gender, and so forth – although their less obvious role in shaping the process of technological innovation, marketing and adoption is also crucial.

THE DIFFUSION OF ICT INTO THE HOME

This chapter begins to address the question of change by mapping and interrelating patterns of access and use. Theoretically, questions of access have traditionally been understood in terms of diffusion theory, a theory which offers a model of the typical acquisition path for a new medium from introduction to mass ownership (Rogers, 1995). As historians of once-new technologies have identified, there are strong parallels across

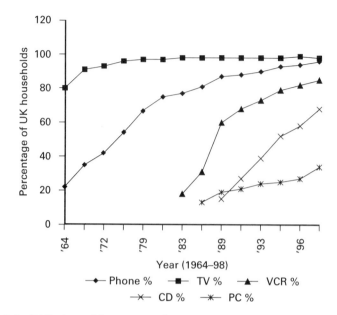

Figure 2.1 *Diffusion of domestic media*

Source: General Household Survey (1964–1998) and Family Expenditure Survey (1999–2000). Both London: The Stationery Office.

the diffusion of different technologies at different times (e.g. Flichy, 1995; Marvin, 1988; Winston, 1998). On this basis, in his now-classic theory of the diffusion of innovation, Rogers (1995) constructed a standard S-shaped diffusion curve by which to classify individuals into five categories:

*   Innovators (2.5% of the population)
*   Early adopters (14%)
*   Early majority (34%)
*   Late majority (34%)
*   Laggards (16%)

Each of these groups is defined according to the point in the diffusion curve at which individuals acquire a particular new technology. These diffusion curves can be clearly seen for the UK in Figure 2.1, making it immediately apparent that the pace of change varies by medium, with television reaching a critical mass much faster than the telephone, for example.[1] Indeed, acquired initially by the middle classes, television ownership rapidly spread 'down' the social grades so that from 40% of the population with a television in 1955 in Britain (most of whom could only receive BBC1), just a few years later in 1963 more than four in five had a set, and near saturation (93%) was reached by 1969 (by which time half could receive two channels and a little under half, three channels) (Mackay, 1995a). Diffusion of the Internet is proving the fastest in the history of ICT. In the USA, the 1990s began with few people even having heard of the Internet; by 1997, 19 million Americans were using the Internet, by 1999 that number passed 100 million and, having taken only seven years to reach 30% of American households (Cole), it is still growing reaching 72% of Americans during 2001 (Cole, 2001).

Rogers' approach draws on Simmel's (1990) so-called 'trickle down' hypothesis in explaining inequalities across households in media acquisition, for those who fall into the early adopter category are far from random. Rather, the highest socio-economic group in society is generally motivated and able to acquire a new medium first, for reasons of social distinction underpinned by symbolic and financial resources. Meanwhile, those lower down the social scale only gradually catch up, and the poorest group may never reach the point of acquiring the medium.[2] As Thomas (1995) argues, the pace of ICT change is so fast that those with money will always lead those without. Hence there will always be inequalities between those with faster, more efficient, more powerful machines. Moreover, as ICT developments build on existing technology and skills, the 'haves' will always be better placed to take advantage of new developments than the 'have-nots'. A typical diffusion finding is that of Lin (1988), in which early adopters of the computer were found to be younger, more affluent and already owners of other communication technologies.[3] Similarly, while *The UCLA Internet Report* finds that two in three Americans are online, these remain predominantly educated, affluent and young (Cole, 2000).

Problematically, these diffusion data mask the transformation in some of these media. Particularly, the 'computer' is a far more powerful and multifunctional machine than it was even a decade ago. And with the advent of first cable and satellite and now, more significantly, digital television, television too has been transformed during the 1990s, moving from a period of channel austerity to channel abundance (Curran and Gurevitch, 1991a), expanding from a few to many channels, from national to global channels, from mass market to niche channels (including children's channels). Similarly, the capability of the Internet to carry information, as well as the variety of services offered online, has increased dramatically over the past decade, transforming the meaning of the technology in the process. At present, these technologies are themselves converging to form Internet or web TV, video on demand, interactive television, and so forth, complicating the charting of straightforward diffusion data. Perhaps, as Rogers' diffusion of innovation theory originally intended, research should now be charting the diffusion of specific innovations (e.g. web TV) rather than specific media (e.g. television set).

This account of young people's access to and use of ICT has begun with diffusion theory because of its strengths, although later I shall draw out a number of significant limitations. Its strengths, to start with these, are that:

- it counteracts the 'presentism' in much discussion of new media by locating contemporary figures for media access within a historical perspective, for example interpreting the number of households with a computer today within the longer story of the arrival and adoption of the computer into UK homes over recent decades;
- it counters 'media-centrism' in its tendency to construe each medium as unique, by instead identifying the parallels across diverse media, so that the story of the diffusion of the computer can be seen as similar in key respects to that of television or the radio before it;
- it highlights the policy-relevant question of inequalities in media access, identifying how certain categories of user or household are, in a predictable manner, relatively privileged or disadvantaged during the diffusion process. Thus, current anxieties about the extent to which the apparently inevitable spread of ICT through Western societies is accompanied, apparently equally inevitably, by a so-called 'digital divide' between the ICT 'haves' and 'have-nots' can themselves be seen as part of a longer history of inequalities in access to the latest medium, whatever it is;
- at a point in the research culture in which the new truism of 'going beyond access' becomes, rightly, widely accepted, it seems that questions of access (as theorised by the diffusion process) may drop out of focus, yet these remain important to the overall picture;
- an account of access complements that of use: for individuals, access precedes and hence, in both direct and indirect ways, constrains the possibilities of use; yet as we explore below, the YPNM project shows that the inter- and intra-household factors operate in different ways in accounting for access and use.

However, the relation of access to use is not so straightforward. Problematically, diffusion theory tends to pose an overly linear process – from the market to the home, from the elite to the mass – which does not always fit the specific conditions under which different media are becoming available to specific groups. Indeed, at its simplest, it can be read as adopting the technologically determinist assumption that social change results from technological innovation, an assumption which many have challenged (MacKenzie and Wajcman, 1999). On this determinist view, an analysis of use becomes a search for impacts or effects of the introduction of a technology (Livingstone, 1996).

While not wishing to counter with the equally simple alternative of cultural or social determinism (W. R. Neuman, 1991), the argument here is for an in-depth and bottom-up analysis of use-in-context to identify more complex, subtle, and not necessarily linear processes by which ICT is rendered meaningful and so incorporated into pre-existing and novel domestic routines and practices. Perhaps surprisingly, it is only relatively recently that such questions of use have gained serious attention, stimulated by reference to the literature on mass consumption, or cultural appropriation, of domestic goods more generally (Miller, 1987), local practices of use which develop around a new object (or medium) once in the home, anchoring it within particular temporal, spatial and social relations and thereby rendering it meaningful. For example, Silverstone and Hirsch (1992) (see also Caron et al., 1989; Livingstone, 1992) traced the 'biographies' of media goods within the home for eighteen families, demonstrating the importance of spatial location in the home. They showed how the public meanings of media goods are transformed when they enter the 'moral economy' of the household according to the operation of four linked processes – appropriation, objectification, incorporation and conversion – arguing that, for example, the aesthetic display of objects within the home reveals the 'classificatory principles that inform a household's sense of itself and its place in the world' (Silverstone and Hirsch, 1992: 22).

In the research literature, it remains the case that media adoption – conceived first as a social and cultural process as well as an economic one, and secondly, as a process which encompasses both diffusion and appropriation – has still been little studied in relation to media goods specifically.[4] The YPNM project represents a step in this direction. As will be argued below, through comparisons across households and across national contexts, the cultures of both the household and the society shape access and use in complex but significant ways.

Media in the Homes of Children and Young People

The prevalence and importance of media in young people's homes is readily illustrated by the account which 10-year-old Kevin's parents give of his home. Kevin's mother works in a betting shop, his father is a taxi cab controller. We asked them: 'Look at this list of different pieces of equipment which people might have in their homes, and I'm interested in what you've got, and in which room you have things in.' Their answers show clearly the increasingly commonplace mixture of different media throughout the home, including what they have and use, what they have but no longer use, and what they may or may not plan to get next:

Father:	TV-kids' bedroom and our front room. No satellite (laughter directed at wife), she won't let me have it because we'd be watching football all the time. Teletext, yes.
Mother:	(Interrupts) No, it's broken!
Father:	Yeah I know, but we've still got one and we'll be getting it fixed. Errm, video recorder up here and in the kids' bedroom. Hi-fi stereo up here and in the kids' bedroom. Radio up here and in the kids' bedroom. Telephone, our bedroom and in the front room. Mobile phone in the back, we don't use it anymore. Fax machine, never. Camcorder downstairs. Gameboy downstairs in the kids' bedroom. Games Console in the kids' bedroom. Computer, kids' bedroom. Printer, haven't got one, getting one. Errm, multimedia computer, not yet but we're going to get a CD link-up when Gus [oldest child] improves. Modem, no way! Books, my bedroom, kids' bedroom.
Mother:	(Interrupts with laughter) Shelves! What about a bookcase?
Father:	Yeah.
Mother:	It's like a library.
Father:	Magazines, your department (to wife).
Mother:	They're underneath there [i.e. in living room].
Father:	Comics, Gus's got drawers full of them. Newspaper, yes. And that's it.
Interviewer:	So why did you say 'No way!' to Modem?
Father:	Modem? Have you got any idea how much the 'net costs?
Mother:	What's a modem?
Father:	It's the phone link to the Internet. When you go onto the Internet, it costs you the price of a call, depending on where-abouts it is, and what you link up to. The children could run up a bill astronomically.

Notwithstanding the theoretical and methodological issues involved in surveying the private, domestic, and taken-for-granted aspects of people's lives (Livingstone and Lemish, 2001), these questions of access and use will be addressed initially in a straightforward fashion. Central to the YPNM survey was a series of questions to children and young people (and, to confirm their accounts, their parents) regarding which media are available to them at home.[5] Further, to distinguish between household access and personal ownership of media, we asked them to tell us also which goods they have in their bedroom. Of course, media goods are moved around the home, typically, from communal spaces to bedrooms as newer goods are acquired to replace them, and some may be moved on a more frequent basis. However, mapping the relation between media in the home and media in the child's bedroom is sugges-tive of the ways in which parents and children view the role of media within the home and, in particular, the balance between locating goods

Table 2.1 *Percentage aged 6–17 with media in the home, by gender, age and social grade (N = 1287)*

		Gender		Age				Social grade	
	All	Boy	Girl	6–8	9–11	12–14	15–17	ABC1	C2DE
TV set	100	99	100	100	99	100	100	100	100
Hi-fi	96	95	96	93	93	98	98*	96	96
Video recorder	96	96	96	95	96	97	95	98	94*
Radio	95	94	95	94	95	95	95	97	93*
Telephone	93	92	94	96	92	92	91	98	89*
Shelf of books	87	86	89	92	88	87	83*	94	82*
Personal stereo	83	81	84	66	80	90	92*	86	80*
Teletext	71	73	69	65	71	72	75	76	67*
TV-games machine	67	78	56*	65	70	72	61*	61	72*
PC	53	50	56*	53	51	53	54	68	40*
PC with CD-ROM	31	29	33	35	30	31	28	46	19*
Gameboy	42	44	40	35	45	48	38*	47	39*
Cable/satellite	42	44	39	45	40	40	42	39	44
Mobile phone	30	30	30	26	31	31	33	44	20*
Camcorder	25	24	27	34	28	21	21*	32	21*
Internet/modem	7	8	7	7	7	8	7	14	2*

*Statistically significant difference.

Source: Livingstone and Bovill, 1999.

in communal or personal spaces is indicative of the expected patterns of use (placing a computer in the living room suggests shared family uses more than does the computer in the child's bedroom; see Chapter 4).

High levels of ownership of screen entertainment media particularly – television, VCR, games machines, etc. – point to the dominance within the UK of a screen entertainment culture. Table 2.1 shows the distribution of media across households with children, according to the gender and age of the child and the social grade of the household.[6] Nearly all households with children have a television and a video recorder, two-thirds have a TV-linked games machine (e.g. Sega, Nintendo, Play-station), and nearly half have cable or satellite television. Together with the screen media, some 'old' media are also near ubiquitous, particularly music media. However, one in fourteen has no telephone, and one in eight has few or no books, so even in terms of traditional media these young people may be considered information-poor. Of the newer media, over half have a personal computer at home, four in ten have multiple television channels, and a rapidly growing minority has Internet access.

The figures in Table 2.1 confirm that households with children 'lead' in the process of media diffusion. Comparing Table 2.1 with data for all households from the 1998 General Household Survey,[7] we see that more households with children have a video recorder (96% compared with 85% of all households) and, most strikingly, a personal computer (53%

compared with 34%). Such bald figures for domestic access to media are, of course, changing year on year. Figures available from National Opinion Poll's *Kids.net Wave 4* (Wigley and Clarke, 2000) show no change on the older media but significant increases in the latest ICT. Hence by June 2000, access in UK households with children to the computer had reached 70%, the mobile phone had grown to 77%, access to the Internet had multiplied considerably to 36% (with 75% of 7–16 year-olds having used the Internet in one location or another by 2001). And digital television, only introduced in 1998, had already reached 31% of households.

While the television and telephone have reached near-saturation point, the computer, compact disc player and video recorder continue to make significant gains. Looking back to the long-term trends in Figure 2.1, it appears that the computer is well past the transition from early adopter to majority status, particularly for households with children, while the Internet is just making this transition now. By the last quarter of 1998, the UK Government's *Family Expenditure Survey* found that only 9 per cent of UK households had home access to the Internet. A figure which rose to 20 per cent by 1999, 33 per cent by 2000 and to 35 per cent by the second quarter of 2001.[8] Some estimate that Internet penetration into homes will approach three-quarters of all homes within the decade.[9]

Social class strongly affects media in the home. As Table 2.1 shows, only for the most commonly-owned media – television, including cable and satellite television, and the hi-fi – are there no significant differences between higher (ABC1) and lower (C2DE) socio-economic grade households. Social inequalities in access to ICT are very evident. Children from middle-class families are much more likely than those from working-class backgrounds to have access at home to a computer (seven in ten compared with only four in ten), twice as likely to have a multimedia computer at home, and seven times as likely to have the Internet at home. While household income is crucial, some patterns of distribution of media in the home suggest a difference in middle-class and workingclass media preferences: working-class families are as or more likely to own screen entertainment media, particularly the TV-linked games machine, while middle-class families are more likely to own most other media, particularly books.

Children's age or gender makes much less difference than does household socio-economic status to media provision. However, families where there is a child in the middle age-range (9–14) are more likely to have a Gameboy and/or a TV-linked games machine in the home, while those with an older child are more likely to have a hi-fi, personal stereo or a computer. It is in the families of younger children that books are most in evidence. Interestingly, the personal computer and the TV-linked games machine are the only media which show a significant gender skew in distribution:

Table 2.2 *Percentage of 6–17 year olds with media in his/her own bedroom, by gender, social grade and age (N = 1303)*

	All	Gender		Age				Social grade	
		Boy	Girl	6–8	9–11	12–14	15–17	ABC1	C2DE
Personal stereo	68	65	71*	44	62	80	85*	71	65*
Shelf of books	64	62	66	69	66	64	59	73	58*
TV set	63	69	57*	46	60	71	77*	54	71*
Hi-fi	61	59	62	31	50	73	87*	57	63*
Radio	59	59	60	47	57	66	66*	64	56*
TV-games machine	34	48	19*	23	35	43	34*	27	39*
Gameboy	27	31	22*	17	32	34	23*	27	26
Video recorder	21	23	19	11	18	22	32*	14	26*
PC	12	16	8*	9	11	14	16*	12	13
With CD-ROM	4	5	2*	3	2	6	3	4	3
Teletext	8	9	7	3	5	8	14*	8	8
Cable/satellite	5	5	5	4	4	5	7	4	5
Telephone	5	5	6	4	2	6	10*	5	6
Internet link	1	1	0	1	1	1	1	1	1
Mobile phone	1	2	1	0	0	1	4*	1	2
Camcorder	1	1	1	0	0	2	0	0	1

*Statistically significant difference.

Source: Livingstone and Bovill, 1999.

almost three-quarters of boys compared with around half of girls have a games machine at home. That girls are slightly more likely to have a computer at home is explained by the greater tendency of parents with boys to put the computer in their son's bedroom (i.e. girls may have access to a computer at home somewhere – including in a living room or brother's bedroom, but are less likely to have personal access; see Chapter 4).

Traditional images of media use, especially television, centre on the family living room. But today's media are more personalised and are increasingly dispersed throughout the home (see Table 2.2). Children's bedrooms are well equipped with media. Music, books and television are all widely available for personal use, being present in two-thirds of bedrooms. Other media follow: games machines and Gameboys are owned by around one-third, and one in five have their own video recorder. Much less common at present, 12% have a computer in their own room, 5% have multichannel television or a telephone, and almost none (1%) have the Internet. Again, these figures, though not so much the demographic trends, are changing all the time. NOP's *Kids.net* survey in spring 2000 (Wigley and Clarke, 2000) shows a minor increase for television (72%), video recorder (35%) and computer (16%), and more substantial increases for the mobile phone (17%) and the Internet (3%).

Not all share equally in the well-equipped, media-rich bedroom. By contrast to media in the home in general, the age and gender of the child are primary factors in determining personal media ownership. On the whole, older children are more likely to own everything with the exception of books. Boys are more likely to own screen media, while girls have few advantages in access. As we shall see below, even though girls are more likely than boys to read, use the phone or listen to music, they are not more likely than boys to have their own books or telephone or hi-fi. Such gender inequalities are illustrated by one family we visited. Here, the 16-year-old daughter, Rose, and her 11-year-old brother, Sam, are being brought up by a single mother in a large suburban council estate. Sam has recently moved into the biggest bedroom, where he also houses books, games, television, a hi-fi, cassette player, radio, Gameboy, TV-linked games machine, as well as two computers, one broken, one lacking necessary software. Rose's bedroom is smaller, though it does have a television and hi-fi system. Notwithstanding this apparent inequality, Sam tells us that 'football is my life, like Rose's bedroom is her life ... I don't really like being in my room ... really I only think of it for going to bed in.' Rose elaborates:

> Boys I know don't like to spend their life in their bedroom. And I don't even know a boy that does. ... I'm very into musicals, like West End things and er I've got all the posters and leaflets all over my wall, you can hardly see the wallpaper. And my CD player – I've always got music on. That's what I usually do – I just sit in there and listen to music. Or I sometimes watch telly if Mum's watching something I don't want to watch. ... Whenever my friends come over we just usually go round and listen to music and talk and watch television. ... I spend most of my time in my bedroom or going out.

It seems that family constructions of gender are of greater importance here than are pragmatic considerations of the use of space.

While social class also makes a difference to media available in the bedroom, the middle class is not so consistently favoured as it is for the home in general, although middle-class children have more books and music media. However, the greater availability of screen entertainment media in working-class families, presumably not a matter of income but of preference, is very evident if we look at what children have in their own rooms. Working-class children are significantly more likely to have their own screen entertainment media – television, TV-linked games machine and video recorder – and such generosity may well be interpreted, by some children, as the mark of a fond parent. As this middle-class 12 year old explained, 'I could not get a better mum and dad because they ... actually buy us stuff that we don't deserve, and we know that, and we actually tell them that. But they just think it's, they just want to because it's their children. So we're like, fine, if you want to.'

Varieties of Domestic Media Environment

Households do not simply decide to acquire one medium or another, but rather they make broader decisions about the type of home they want, drawing perhaps on their more general orientation to technology or to home entertainment or on the priorities they have for their children's education or use of time. Moreover, most are financially constrained in the goods they can acquire. Further, while thus far we have characterised 'the average home' in terms of its combination of media, and this is also the most readily available output of the many surveys conducted, the multiplicity of factors which affect purchase of different goods by different households complicates such an average. Not only do different households differ in media goods, but they do so in systematic ways. For example, it may make a difference to the meaning and use of the computer in a household if it is acquired by a home which is already screen entertainment-rich, or a home which is instead bookish and screen-poor.

In the YPNM project we characterised households by type of media provision, looking first at provision in the house other than in the child's bedroom, and secondly, by examining provision in the bedroom (see Chapter 4). For the first typology, bearing in mind that this excluded consideration of children's bedrooms, three broad types of household emerged:

- Media-rich
- Traditional
- Media-poor

Media-rich homes, a label which encompasses nearly half of all households with children and young people, contain a wider range of old and new media than the 'average' household and so provide the children or, more typically, the teenagers who live there with a wide variety of media choices. They have a greater than average likelihood of owning books, a personal computer, Internet, telephone, VCR, teletext, cable or satellite television, a TV-linked games machine, hi-fi system, camcorder, mobile phone, Gameboy, walkman, and so forth. Predictably, these are most likely to be middle-class households with parents who claim to feel the most comfortable using computers themselves. Thus, the computer (other than those specifically acquired for children and placed in their bedrooms; see Chapter 4) is being incorporated into homes which are already media-rich. Consequently, it represents one of several types of screen available to the members of these households.

Around a quarter of households are best described as *traditional*, for their ownership of media is average for all media except the 'newest', of which they have comparatively few (namely, the computer, Internet, TV-linked games machines, walkman, camcorder, mobile phone and Gameboy). In short, these households combine television, music and books, providing a familiar media mix, and one that has long been available to children in recent decades. On the other hand, as they are as likely as the average household to contain such relatively new screen media as the VCR and cable or satellite television, they might perhaps be alternately described as 'IT-poor'. These households tend to contain younger children rather than teenagers, suggesting, unsurprisingly, that the presence of teenagers pushes a household into acquiring the latest media. Less obviously, these households span the range of income levels and so may be either middle or working class. The construction of a traditional household, then, appears to reflect less the financial resources of the parents and more their attitudes towards the media. In other words, for those with sufficient financial resources, the construction of a media-rich or a traditional home is a matter of choice. The parents in traditional homes generally feel that television provides children with good programmes, providing viewing is appropriately controlled, but they are least likely to describe themselves as comfortable using computers. Perhaps in consequence, although the comparative youth of these children is also a factor, these households are the least likely to provide media-rich bedrooms for their children (see Chapter 4).

Lastly, in *media-poor homes*, the last quarter of the sample in the YPNM project, every medium we asked about turned out to be less common than in the average home. Such a comparative lack of media is not confined to new media, for these homes are notably less likely to contain books, radios and a telephone as well as newer or more expensive media such as a computer, games machine, hi-fi, etc. Only for television and the VCR does their media ownership approach the average, while the time spent viewing by both parents and children is the highest. As may be anticipated, these are likely to be poorer, working-class households, containing children and young people of all ages. Clearly, financial restrictions dictate the provision in these homes. That maintaining a media-poor home is rarely a matter of preference is supported by the finding that while these parents tend to be unable to provide access to a computer for their children, they are particularly keen for their children to know about computers.

The Life Cycle of Domestic Technologies

Diffusion theory tends to treat media as separate if parallel in their adoption. Yet young people are, as shown above, combining media in different ways to create a personalised media environment which suits their circumstances, interests and values. Any new medium acquired by the individual or household is thus introduced into a pre-existing environment, gaining its meaning in part from the already-established orientation towards domestic media within that household. Moreover, each new arrival in turn also has consequences – anticipated or otherwise – for these previously 'new' media. In his account of the diffusion process, W.R. Neuman (1991) focuses instead on the sequencing in the uses of one medium over time, rather than following Rogers' segmentation of the population. He identifies three phases in the history of a new medium thus:

- Early adopter
- Mass market
- Specialisation

For Neuman, early adopter uses of a medium may vary significantly from its subsequent uses by the mass market. Further, once a medium has diffused from the elite (or early adopter) stage to the stage of mass adoption, as a now-old medium it must specialise to survive when challenged by yet newer media. This third phase, of specialisation, is defined by the other (older) media which contextualise it. For example, radio was a mass medium before television but changed after television from a generic to a specialist medium which broadcast primarily music and news: as television took the place of radio in the living room, radio became more portable, finding new uses in the car or kitchen. Today, we see a similar effect but this time on television, stimulated by the arrival of the computer in the living room. Thus there is a growth of specialist or narrowcast channels on cable and satellite television, and a multiplication of television sets in the home which facilitates more diverse uses, including the same casual viewing to accompany getting dressed in the morning or to go to sleep at night that radio has long been used for. This specialisation is proving successful thus far, with little consistent evidence for a dip in the popularity of, or time spent with, television. Doubtless the computer – currently a salient but generic or fairly standardised household acquisition – will undergo a similar process of specialisation in due course.

In short, the process by which innovations are transformed from elite to mass phenomena is not the end of the story. The third stage, specialisation, becomes most interesting because few innovations drop out of circulation altogether and consequently the dominant trend is towards the accumulation of available media. How these become specialised depends on a set of contingent cultural factors in the lives of children and their families (see Chapter 3). It is worth noting that some media appeal to specialised segments of the audience from the start, countering the assumption in diffusion theory that everyone is a potential adopter for a medium. The TV-linked games machine, for example, has probably saturated the market among boys aged 9–14, though it is not as popular overall as the video recorder or even books, both being media with mass appeal. With the multiplication of niche broadcast channels, this initial specialisation is likely to increase, competing then in a market in which a variety of older media (books, radio, television) have reached a high degree of specialisation already in their form, genres and content.

There are two key advantages to Neuman's approach. First, rather than treating each medium in isolation, the adoption of a new medium is put in the context of already widespread and established media. Secondly, access and use are integrated, rather than treated as discrete stages in a linear process, so that use of previous media both contextualises and, more importantly, is transformed by the acquisition and use of new media. Both are particularly valuable as we try to understand the significance of new forms of information and communication technologies for children and young people's lifeworld. However, the implicit linearity of the metaphors (e.g. career, trajectory, biography) often used to theorise the adoption of new media remains problematic. This is the case because all too often the home is construed as a 'black box' at the end of the process, rather than being opened up for investigation as part of a broader analysis which integrates domestic uses with a cultural and symbolic account of the construction of ICT meanings and practices across a variety of domains. The linearity of these metaphors is also problematic for, as historians of once-new media have noted, there are many complex and far from linear processes by which technologies are shaped socially and culturally before, during, and following their conception, design, packaging, marketing, purchase and use (Flichy, 1995; Marvin, 1988).

The case of the games computer illustrates this complexity admirably. LaFrance (1996) traces the huge economic success of the computer and video game industry thus. What LaFrance calls the first period, one of early, if narrowly based, success in the 1970s, centred on the Atari home computer combined with the early video arcade games developed for leisure sites outside the home. The second period began with considerable success following the adaptation of the game Space Invaders for the microcomputer in 1979 (in the USA), the invention of Pac-man and the introduction of the PC. This then turned into financial disaster as too rapid growth in a situation of incompatible and unreliable software led to a plummeting in turnover from one billion dollars in 1982 to one hundred million in 1985 (LaFrance, 1996: 303).[10] As Haddon (1993) notes, the 'fad' was not really over, but instead the games market moved to toy departments and continued to sell steadily although in smaller quantities. With the further technological innovation in the development of microcomputers, ambitious companies such as Texas Instruments 'envisaged micros which would not only run a variety of software, but which could eventually be connected to telecommunications systems and even have home control facilities' (Haddon, 1993: 129). This parallel trajectory was spawned not by commercial entertainment developers but by those developing computers and software for the workplace, accompanied by, if not driven by, the somewhat futuristic fantasies of the designers and developers.

The next period in the history of games machines was dominated by Nintendo (with Mario and SuperMario games) and Sega (with the Sonic character) from the mid to late 1980s, adapting for the home market their twin successes in other domains – card games and arcade video games – using a strategy of mass production, low prices and setting standards for their much improved software. While this period saw the near saturation of the domestic market (at least for households with boys under 15 years old), new developments in 32-bit and CD-ROM technology ushered in the next period in the mid-1990s, with the Sega Saturn, Sony's Playstation, and Nintendo's Ultra 64 and Virtual Boy. Speed, realism, sound effects, and complex scenarios characterise today's games and are being dramatically enhanced with each new market product. These games increasingly support an integration of video game technology, digital television and the Internet, making classification of game technologies ever more elusive.

At the same time, of course, the personal computer – for both work and home – has developed apace, providing a more or less popular platform for games-playing as well as for the other uses for which it was developed. Far from linear, this is a story of successes and failures over time and of multiple trajectories knitted together – from card games to the work computer, from the video arcade to the domestic Playstation. The PC is perhaps even more of a puzzle, being in its present incarnation a box designed for the workplace with its functional typist's keyboard and its dull grey design, yet being most often bought by parents in response to a considerable amount of marketing hype regarding children's education and the vague but compelling need to 'get ahead' and not get 'left behind'. By the time the PC reaches the home, it is already layered with multiple meanings both factored into its design and framed by its marketing. Yet uses are wholly dictated by neither design nor marketing. This is most evident in the common observation that these machines are more often used for games-playing, competing not so much with the typewriter or books, but with the games machine and television (Haddon, 1988; Miles et al., 1992).

The obvious disjunction evident in relation to the personal computer between innovation, marketing and use should warn us of the dangers of underestimating the extent to which contexts of use may shape future contexts of innovation and production. In the case of the 'PC', it seems that this object itself may undergo reinvention in the next few years, stimulated in different ways by developments in the Internet, digital television and mobile telephony. This reinvention will surely incorporate increased entertainment possibilities as well as further blurring the boundaries between work and fun, learning and entertainment, etc.

Mackay (1995b) proposes an integration of the 'social shaping of technology' approach, with its stress on the social conditions which give rise to particular technologies (MacKenzie and Wajcman, 1999), and the body of work on the consumption of technologies, with its stress on the appropriation (or domestication) of technologies within particular consumption contexts according to the notion of technology as text, that is as semiotically complex and open to decoding by users (e.g. Silverstone and Hirsch, 1992). Using the metaphor of the life cycle of a technology (a concept which is less linear than that of career or biography, although potentially just as normative), Mackay argues for the analysis of a technology in terms of three conceptually distinct spheres, which we can describe with some modification as:

- conception, shaping, innovation, development and design
- marketing, diffusion and access
- appropriation, use and embedding in daily practices

While the career or life cycle of a technological artefact – encompassing its shaping and design, its marketing and diffusion, and its appropriation and use – are indeed all part of one story, the focus in these approaches is technology. Such a media-centric story takes us away from the conditions of childhood and family life, inviting us always to begin the story with the experts involved in the process of technological innovation. Unsurprisingly then, most empirical investigation has focused on the first two spheres: innovation and development, diffusion and access. This study concentrates on the third, appropriation, while recognising the connections with the former two. The concern with the incorporation of technologies in everyday life can be justified in two ways. First, the opportunity to identify those sociocultural conditions which, by giving rise to particular priorities or preferences on the part of users, inform the social shaping of technology through the identification of the supposed needs of a future market (see, for example, Ceruzzi, 1999, on the social shaping of the personal computer). Secondly, the opportunity to identify those social conditions which mediate the uptake of technological innovations, resulting in the appropriation of technologies in particular ways. That daily life represents both the start and the end of this process serves to underline its cyclic nature; technologies both arise from, and find their place within, the conditions, practices and meanings of ordinary people's lives.

There are strong parallels here with the study of more traditional media forms. In research on film, the press and especially broadcasting, production, text/channels and audiences are the three mainstays of media research. Yet a parallel argument has taken place here also, stressing that what was once conceived as a linear process – from production/sender via message to receiver – is instead a cyclical process. Thus in Hall's (1980) classic paper on encoding/decoding, mass communication is reconceived as centred on two mutually articulated spheres – one of encoding by media producers and one of decoding by media audiences, each dependent on an overlapping set of cultural knowledge, conventions and resources, each sufficiently underdetermining of the other as to loosen the dependence of cultural meanings on economic conditions, each potentially both impacting on and impacted on by the other, and with the text – the cultural product at the centre of the process – not fixed in its meaning but open to diverse interpretations depending in part at least on the cultural conditions of its reception.[11]

Particularly, it is important to counteract the popular impression, conjured up by the popular discourses surrounding ICT or 'new media', of an innovative and fully formed technology entering and possibly disrupting, certainly transforming, an already-established set of norms and practices surrounding those familiar media now redefined as 'old'. Even the children we interviewed rejected this opposition as too simple a view of the diverse media mix available to them in their everyday lives. However, children are much clearer than the academic literature to date that there are many intra-household issues of selection and negotiation regarding both media acquisition and use, all of which gain in complexity as media goods in the home themselves multiply. We can only trace the links between access and use, as well as the consequences of new for older media, if we consider both the specific social contexts of use and the general cultural assumptions that shape the appropriation of new media into the home. An account of children's media use must therefore incorporate the murky area of cultural constructions of media, parental permission and values, physical and symbolic location of goods, lifestyle expectations, and personal preferences. While parental and cultural expectations and practices are crucial, it is also in the relation between access and use that we can discern the enactment of children's own agency, as well as the social meanings, practices and contexts that make up their lifeworld.

THE CULTURAL MEDIATION OF ACCESS

The construction of a particular domestic media environment draws on the combined influence of multiple factors. The above discussion has already encompassed financial, educational, experiential, and attitudinal factors in order to account for the different types of media environment identified among households with children. These support the view that meaningful use of media does not simply 'take over' the process of ICT adoption at the point where access, ensured according to the diffusion model, leaves off. Rather, useful though diffusion theory is in incorporating the spread of all innovations through society within a single framework, some significant qualifications are required to the assumption that all technologies diffuse according to a straightforward path from adoption by innovators through to the mass market. Before focusing on the question of use, this section explores two kinds of evidence – first, at the level of the household and, second, at the level of a nation or culture – for the argument that cultural factors systematically mediate access to new media.

Household Mediators of ICT Access

While some media are prime examples of the trickle-down hypothesis – as with the telephone, first acquired by the wealthy in society and, as we saw above, still absent from the homes of one in fourteen children – others are not. The degree to which the diffusion process differs for different media provides a clue to the cultural mediators at work. For instance, the different time scales for diffusion, with the proportion of homes still lacking a telephone, for example, exceeding that of households without such newer media as the television or video recorder, point up the importance of a screen entertainment culture both in UK households in general and for certain social strata in particular. Thus as Tables 2.1 and 2.2 show, screen entertainment media such as the TV-linked games machine and multichannel television are most acquired by those in the middle-to-lower socio-economic groups, as are television sets and video recorders in their children's bedrooms (which, notably, are already overtaking books in children's bedrooms). In contrast, these same screen entertainment media are not taken up to the same extent by the more educated, primarily for cultural reasons, or by the poor, primarily for financial reasons. If one looks back over the recent history of screen media in the UK, a similar story emerges. Ownership of multiple television sets has spread evenly across all social grades except the lowest, again not supporting the trickle-down theory, while both the video recorder and cable/satellite television followed an inverted U-curve rather than a spread from higher down to lower social grades, being initially adopted *en masse* by blue-collar workers and only then spreading both up and down the social grades (Mackay, 1995a).

Such diversity in diffusion paths makes generalising from one medium to another hazardous. Particularly, television provides a poor indication of the likely diffusion of newer media. While, initially, television followed the classic trickle-down pattern of the telephone, albeit very much faster, multichannel television has instead followed the very different pattern of other screen entertainment media such as the games machines and video recorder. While at the turn of the twenty-first century the domestic personal computer has undoubtedly 'taken off', social class inequalities in acquisition are persisting significantly longer than was the case for television, particularly in Britain (d'Haenens, 2001).[12] As the entertainment potential of the computer increases, with or without convergence with the television, there is a genuine uncertainty in the market as to how acquisition and use will relate to the socio-economic position of the household. One might wonder if the computer will be bought and used differently by those who appropriate it into a context of education, books and work than by those who appropriate it into a context of computer games, television and entertainment. But this is to beg the question of the relation between income and education, for socio-economic classification is itself becoming more complex and less predictive of household behaviour.

Indeed, if one teases apart the effects of household income and parental education, as we did in the YPNM project, one finds that the relative importance of these two imperfectly correlated factors can be discerned (see Livingstone and Bovill, 1999). In the main, household income is crucial for determining availability of media in the home, while parental education determines media in the bedroom. Income strongly influences the acquisition of domestic media, with better-off parents buying more media goods, and this is as true for the possession of books or music media as it is for the computer or Internet. However, there are occasions when income may have the opposite effect to parental education, and this is particularly the case for screen entertainment media. In short, domestic acquisition of cable or satellite television, the TV-linked games machine and the camcorder, are all associated with higher income but lower parental education – in Bourdieu's terms (1984), these are households with more economic than cultural capital. By contrast, acquisition of books and the Internet are associated with both higher income and higher educational levels for parents. For the computer, income is the main factor, suggesting that whatever their education, parents are now purchasing computers, provided they have the financial resources.[13] This variability in levels of education or symbolic resources may have some interesting consequences for competence and expertise in computer use.[14]

Income is less often a predictor of children's personal ownership of media in their bedroom, for, in the main, personal media are acquired according to the age or gender of the child. As we have seen, older children, and boys, have more goods, in general, particularly screen entertainment media. While parental education and income both have a part to play, their effects may be opposed, and it is certainly not simply the more affluent who have more. Rather, those in lower income households are more likely to have a television or TV-linked games machine in their bedroom. Meanwhile, more highly educated parents are less likely to put a television or video recorder in their children's bedrooms, but are more likely to provide them with books or, in the household if not in their bedrooms, a computer. These very different adoption strategies for computers and games machines make clear that the term 'computer' – widely used by children to refer to both these technologies – insufficiently defines the potential uses of different machines. Murdock et al. (1995) foresee a continued, even a growing stratification or information divide in which the middle classes acquire more expensive, multifunctional computers which support computational, word processing and, increasingly, communication facilities, while the working classes adopt comparatively cheap games machines ('interactivity without power').

Beyond the importance of household income and education, it turns out that family circumstances are associated with differences in domestic media provision (Table 2.3). Particularly, while two-parent households (and households with working mothers) are much more likely to provide a media-rich home, reflecting their considerably higher incomes, single parents are just as likely to provide media-rich bedrooms for their children. Further, the presence of siblings makes a media-rich home more likely, but a media-rich bedroom less likely; in other words, parents with several children tend to provide for the household rather than for individual media use.

Table 2.3 *Media environment in child's bedroom and elsewhere in the home, by family composition*

	Family type (N = 1275)		Siblings (N = 1302)		Mother in paid work (N = 939)	
	One parent (%)	Two parent (%)	Yes (%)	No (%)	Yes (any) (%)	N o (%)
Media-rich home	27	50	47	36	52	39
Media-poor home	43	25	29	33	23	31
Traditional home	30	25	24	32	25	29
Media-rich bedroom	24	24	23	32	22	28
Media-poor bedroom	28	23	25	20	20	28
Other bedroom	49	54	53	48	59	44

Note that home and bedroom types are defined in Chapters 2 and 4 respectively.
Source: Livingstone and Bovill, 1999.

Indeed, interviews with single parents suggest that they make special efforts to prioritise the needs of their children, possibly over their own.

She has got the video in her room. ... She drives me mad with it, that's why. I chose to let her have it up there. That's the TV, the video recorder, the stereo CD player, radio, telephone. She's got a Gameboy. Books, magazines, comics and daily newspapers. Most of these.

(Divorced working-class mother of 16-year-old girl)

Well, look at the videos! I mean you've only got to go in there and see the toys (laughs). Yes, I do over-compensate and I always have. I very often do with material things. I know that I am over-compensating and I know why. But I still can't compensate for what other people can do. My children haven't got a proper computer. All their friends have.

(Widowed middle-class mother of girl, 12 and boy, 10)

In sum, the history of media diffusion across UK households raises some key uncertainties in predicting future ICT diffusion. Can a trickle-down model be assumed, given its application to many media in the past, or will the screen entertainment bias of middle – low income groups prevail in determining acquisition? Will inequalities persist, as for the telephone, or rapidly disappear, as for television? Will education work in tandem with income, sustaining inequalities in access, or will its effects oppose those of income, opening up a media- and technology-rich but not necessarily knowledge-rich segment of society? How will the diversification of family structures mediate – and so complicate – the diffusion process? While this survey of media history provides a number of lessons for the future, one of these, surely, is that diverse cultural factors must be taken into account. These are also evident in the current ambivalence – visible among both the public and the policy community – over whether new information and communication technologies should be regarded primarily as information resources (part of the worlds of work and education) or as entertainment media (part of the world of leisure and commerce). This is, at least in part, a national or cross-national level, as much as a household-level, debate.

Cross-cultural Mediators of ICT Access

If one analyses the diffusion and appropriation of ICT on the level of national or cross-national comparisons, once again the mediating role of cultural context becomes apparent. The comparison explored here is with the present findings for UK access to ICT compared with parallel data for Europe and America. Such a comparison is practical in so far as directly comparable data are available, and is worth pursuing in that these countries comprise not only a common research culture but more importantly a common policy context, resting on broad similarities in both media environments and conditions of childhood (Livingstone et al., 2001).

Perhaps not surprisingly, available data from America and from other European countries show that many broad patterns of media access and use are similar across the developed countries compared here.[15] If we consider screen media generally available in the home, it is evident that children and young people at the turn of the century have access to high levels of screen media (Table 2.4). And as Johnsson-Smaragdi (2001) shows, the typology of media-rich, traditional and media-poor households is also replicated across a diversity of European countries, suggesting that this offers a common characterisation of household types in these comparatively wealthy countries.

There are, however, some cross-national differences of note.

- Clearly, the USA 'leads' in terms of access to most media, the one exception being that of cable/satellite television where national histories of broadcasting make for very different contexts for the expansion of multiple channels, for reasons of policy, geography and cost (no data on cable/satellite penetration are presented here for the Netherlands, for example, where cabled households are near universal; van der Voort et al., 1998). This applies to both new and older forms of media: significantly, the USA is 'ahead' for diffusion of the computer, CD-ROM and, especially, the Internet, although figures for the EU countries are steadily increasing.

Table 2.4 *Comparative data on children and young people with access to screen media (%)*

	UK	USA	DE	FR	ES	NL	CH	FI	DK	SE
AT HOME										
Television	100	99	96	99	97	99	90	95	98	97
VCR	96	98	87	92	74	92	72	91	92	92
TV-linked games machine	67	82	31	57	54	48	42	43	24	62
Cable/satellite TV	42	74	83	24	21	n/a	50	35	22	64
PC	53	73	50	n/a	54	84	60	70	n/a	66
PC with CD-ROM	31	63	39	19	39	46	43	46	53	47
Internet/modem	7	48	9	8	9	18	17	26	25	31
CHILD'S BEDROOM										
Television	63	65	40	28	31	30	19	38	60	49
VCR	21	36	14	9	9	5	9	15	30	21
TV-linked games machine	34	45	19	25	33	17	19	20	24	34
Cable/satellite TV	5	30	28	3	4	n/a	9	9	22	21
PC	12	21	18	n/a	19	11	19	24	n/a	22
PC with CD-ROM	4	15	13	3	13	3	11	14	16	15
Internet/modem	1	10	2	2	2	1	3	7	5	8

Note: Abbreviations are as follows: Germany (DE), France (FR), Spain (ES), Netherlands (NL), Switzerland (CH), Finland (FI), Denmark (DK), Sweden (SE).

Sources: UK data for 6–17 year olds collected during 1997 (Livingstone and Bovill, 1999); USA data for 8–18 year olds reported in Roberts et al. (1999); other European countries' data approximated by collapsing across data reported for boys and girls, and collected for 6–7, 9–10, 12–13 and 15–16 year olds during 1997–98 (d'Haenens, 2001).

- There are grounds for concluding that the USA and the UK have particularly favoured a 'screen entertainment culture' (Livingstone, 2000). While the USA is strong on information technologies also, the comparisons for the UK are particularly stark. Here we see high levels of screen entertainment media – multi-set homes, VCRs, TV-linked games machines and so forth – yet rather lower levels of take up for the more 'serious' information technologies than is evident in Nordic (Denmark, Sweden and Finland) and smaller European countries (Netherlands, Switzerland).

- By comparison with other European countries, Britain leads in personal provision of screen entertainment media, and Denmark comes very close. The picture is particularly striking for the numbers of 6–7 year olds with a TV set in their bedroom, although figures for other screen entertainment media (e.g. VCR and TV-linked games machine) show a similar pattern. In the UK, 50% have their own set. This may be compared with 25% in Sweden, 21% in Spain, 17% in Germany, 16% in Switzerland and France, and only 12% in the Netherlands (d'Haenens, 2001).[16] In such personal media access, however, the UK appears to be following trends set by the USA, where personal provision for children and young people is, and has been for some time, notably higher than in Europe.

- Very broadly speaking, usage trends go hand in hand with access. This is shown by the greater amounts of time spent by British and American children and young people with screen media – most notably, television and computer games – than by children in other European countries, again endorsing the notion of a strong screen entertainment culture in the USA and UK.[17] For example, British children watch up to half an hour more television per day than in the Netherlands, Sweden and Spain, and as much as an hour per day more than in Germany, France and Switzerland (Beentjes et al., 2001). Again, in this respect UK children are closer to those in the USA, where viewing figures are similar or higher (Roberts et al., 1999).

Clearly, provisioning children's bedrooms reveals the importance of cultural factors as well as those of cost. In the finding that fewer UK homes have books than have television sets and that no more children own books (two-thirds in all) than have their own television set (Tables 2.1 and 2.2), we see the outcome of a longstanding cultural struggle between print and screen media in which these are typically construed as if in competition for people's time and attention. In both the low proportion owning books and the high proportion owning a television, the UK stands out within Europe (d'Haenens, 2001). To put it another way, as screen entertainment media are more expensive than all other media with the exception of computers, yet as television sets are found in the majority, and TV-linked games machines and videos in sizeable minorities, of children's bedrooms – in the UK and elsewhere – this is presumably the result of judgements on the part of both children and parents regarding appropriate uses of leisure time. This screen entertainment culture may be seen to have its roots in adult attitudes to both media (where screen media are seen to challenge the traditional values of an elite print culture) and childhood (where the various threats to innocence are sufficient for entertainment at home to be seen as preferable to leisure outside the home) (see Chapters 3 and 4).

Meanwhile, households in the Nordic countries and the Netherlands may fairly be termed 'pioneers of new technologies', not only because of their greater domestic provision of computers, but also in terms of time spent with interactive media, reflecting a more established culture of domestic and educational ICT (Livingstone and Bovill, 2001a). In the British context, it must be of concern that while across Europe, access to ICT at home varies greatly, the UK figures are among the poorest. To take a specific cross-national comparison, in the UK only 27% of 15–16 year olds had access to a personal computer with CD-ROM at home in

1997–8. Similar figures were found in France (21%) and Italy (34%). But in many other countries, figures were much higher. In Denmark, 63% of 15–16 year olds had a multimedia computer at home, as did 55% in Sweden, 52% in Switzerland, 51% in Spain, 50% in Germany, 48% in the Netherlands and 47% in Finland. Similarly, at the time of the survey 7% of UK 15–16 year olds had Internet connections at home, and similarly small percentages were found in Italy (12%), Spain (11%), Germany (9%) and France (5%). However, access is much more common in Scandinavian countries: Sweden (38%), Finland (30%) and Denmark (26%).

On the other hand, young people's interest in and desire for computer-based media in the UK is strong. For example, when the YPNM survey asked UK children which media they most want to get for their next birthday, a personal computer was top of the list among those who do not already have one at home – 35% want this, and this was the same for boys and girls, middle- and working-class children. Indeed, one in seven children (more boys than girls this time) who have a computer at home but not in their bedroom would still like to get one of their own for their birthday. It is worth noting here that, while a computer is wanted by more than twice as many as want anything else on our list, next most frequently chosen as a desirable birthday present by those who don't have such a medium at home is a mobile phone (by 11%), a TV-linked games machine and a hi-fi (by 10% in both cases); only 7% chose a television. As one group of middle-class 12-year-old boys chorused enthusiastically, when we asked them, 'a multimedia computer with CD-ROM: what you think when you see that?'

- – I want that.
- – I want that.
- – I want it.

Thus, television's continued role at the top of the hierarchy of leisure activities would seem to be threatened by the growth of such new leisure media as computer and video games and the Internet. When we asked children in our research which one medium they would choose if they wanted excitement or to stop feeling bored, they were as likely to choose a computer game as they were television; a choice they explained in interviews in terms of the feelings of mastery and control that game-playing provides (see Chapter 6).

The national policy contexts which give rise to such differences in patterns of ICT adoption are multidimensional, and cannot be simply reduced to such factors as national wealth, being peripheral/central to

Europe, size of the language community, etc., although each of these plays its part (Livingstone et al., 2001). The scale of these differences, however, notwithstanding the broad Western trend towards increasingly media-rich homes and leisure, is sufficient to lead Krotz and Hasebrink (2001) to critique the view of diffusion as a neutral or mechanistic and passive process, belying the complacent hope that all groups and societies will 'catch up' eventually, as if there were a single endpoint to the process. Instead, they identify distinct pathways in the diffusion of new media technologies, leading them to view diffusion as a fundamentally cultural and constructive process. While we have here dwelt on ICT in the home, it emerges that in some countries but not in others, this goes hand in hand with ICT diffusion elsewhere in the society and particularly, for children and young people, in schools. For example, our comparative project on young people's media environments suggests that while the Nordic countries and the Netherlands 'lead' in both ICT adoption at home and school, and while Germany lags in both, in other countries, however, there is a discrepancy between provision at home and school. The United Kingdom, for example, appears to be 'ahead' in terms of computer use at school, while lagging behind for access to a computer at home, reflecting the screen entertainment focus of families which contrasts with the apparently advanced policies of business and education. This 'public/institutional' path to ICT diffusion contrasts with the more private path common in other European countries, and exemplified most clearly in Spain, where about half of all Spanish children have access to a computer at home but only one-third have access at school, suggesting that here it may be parents who are the more advanced (Krotz and Hasebrink, 2001).

Cross-national data such as these illustrate a persistent dilemma in national debates over new media, namely whether changes are specific to the society one knows best or whether they are more widespread, even global. While most of the data presented in this volume relate, strictly speaking, only to the time and place where they were collected, in this case the UK in 1997, the interpretation of these data is always and inevitably comparative. Rather than leaving implicit such comparisons with 'then' or 'somewhere else', this chapter has incorporated cross-national comparisons for media diffusion and appropriation in order to reveal something about the relative priority accorded to the domestic ICT environment in different countries. Not only does such a comparison improve our understanding of our own country, by putting its features into a broader perspective and providing a better knowledge of other countries (Øyen, 1990; Teune, 1990), more importantly it also allows a recognition of how, despite the many different processes and trends operating in different cultural contexts, there are also common, transnational processes facilitating (or hindering) the spread of new media technologies across the globe.

FROM ACCESS TO USE

In key, but not all, respects today's new media are following a similar path through society as did previous media, although the cultural factors operating at both national and household levels significantly impact on this process. Thus, broadly speaking, diffusion theory provides a fairly satisfactory theoretical framework for accounting for the patterning of media access across times and places. However, it suffers two significant limitations. First, to the extent that it attempts to fit all new media into the same mould, it oversimplifies, omitting significant cultural consider-ations. Secondly, and more important to our developing account of the place of media in young people's lives, the diffusion of media through the market tells only part of the story. In pursuing what we might term the 'career' or trajectory of particular media within the home, rather than simply as far as the front door, we need to consider the context, nature and extent of media use, here theorised in terms of appropriation. As media use is thoroughly embedded in the lifeworld, this will require us to honour the commitment of the preceding chapter by listening to children's voices when talking about the importance of media in their lives. In so doing, we will begin to understand how children, young people and their parents actively appropriate, and so render meaningful, specific media within specific domestic and cultural contexts. In the remainder of this chapter, I turn to the nature and extent of time spent with media, while in subsequent chapters I consider the meanings of spatial and familial contexts of media use.

Time with Media

Surveys may readily track diffusion of new media into the home but the conditions of actual use of a medium within a household are far from transparent, there being many a slip between access in the home and actual use by children. As one mother commented, 'We've got radios all over the place. We don't listen to them much, do we?' In short, the task of interrelating access and use opens up an empirical exploration of the complex, messy and far from obvious relations among ownership, access and use. These are particularly important for children, because while it may be fairly assumed that goods in the home are available to the adults who live there, children and young people often lack power in determining household purchases and use practices. Indeed, a fair starting assumption would be that households are likely to contain goods that the children are not able or not allowed to use, even assuming they want to.[18]

The mismatch between access and use works both ways. Some children do not use a medium that is available in the household for reasons that concern parental permission or personal preference. Both these factors may in turn be shaped by cultural capital (Bourdieu, 1984) or expectations regarding appropriate interests and behaviour. On the other hand, some children may be regular users of media which the household does not in fact possess, drawing on networks of friends which both provide and are, in turn, constituted through such shared media use. Such highly desirable goods, motivating children to seek access outside their homes, are often ICT goods; interestingly, by contrast with new media, books tend to fall into the category of available but undesirable, being present in most homes but not always read (Johnsson-Smaragdi, 2001). And during the course of our household interviews we also came across broken, unreliable or out-of-date computers, or computers without the necessary software or printers, which could still find themselves listed as possessions, again creating a disjunction between 'access' and use.

In the YPNM survey we asked 6–17 year olds to estimate the amount of time spent with each medium in their daily lives.[19] In what follows I consider use within leisure time (i.e. excluding any classroom use of ICT), noting that most but not all of this use is at home. The tables below report, first, the percentage of 6–17 year olds who use a medium at all, and secondly, how much time in spent, on an average day, by those who use the medium.[20]

Table 2.5 shows the balance between use and non-use for each medium. While many media appear ubiquitous in children's lives, the media actually used by children represent a subset of media at home. For example, while the majority of children and young people listen to music, one-fifth of children – particularly younger boys – never listen to music. Similarly, one-fifth never watch videos and one-third – particularly older girls – never play computer games. The computer and Internet stand out in being used by only a minority of households, though this is changing rapidly: two-thirds of children do not use a computer for non-games uses in their leisure time, particularly children from lower socio-economic status homes. And the print media appear rather specialised; as expected for relatively old media (W. R. Neuman, 1991), nearly half

Table 2.5 *Percentage of 6–17 year olds who use the medium*
at all during their leisure time

	All	Gender		Age				Social grade	
		Boys	Girls	6–8	9–11	12–14	15–17	ABC1	C2DE
Aged 6–17 (N = 1303)									
Television	99	99	99	99	98	100	99	99	99
Music media	86	81	90*	71	83	91	97*	85	86
Video	81	83	79	89	79	79	77*	84	79*
Computer games	64	79	48*	63	70	73	49*	62	65
Book – not school	57	49	64*	67	62	52	45*	64	51*
PC – not games	36	38	34	30	36	39	39	48	26*
Comics	28	33	23*	42	38	21	12*	29	28
Internet	19	23	15*	5	14	25	34*	24	16*
Aged 9–17 (N = 980)									
Magazine	66	56	77*	n/a	56	71	71*	67	66
Newspaper	36	38	33	n/a	21	29	56*	33	38

*Statistically significant difference.

Source: Livingstone and Bovill, 1999.

of all children never read books, particularly boys, teenagers and children from lower socio-economic status homes. Comics appeal particularly to young boys, magazines to girls and teenagers, newspapers to teenagers. Apart from the computer and Internet, these patterns of use/non-use are unlikely to reflect patterns of access or cost. Rather they tell us something about how different media appeal to different children, or how children and young people select from the set of media available to construct their own 'media menus'. And even for the computer and Internet, Johnsson-Smaragdi (2001) shows that it is particularly for new media that access underdetermines use, with these being both the media relatively underused when available and also those most sought out at friends' or relatives' houses when desired but unavailable at home.

To understand these patterns of choices, we must also examine time spent with media. Table 2.6 reports average number of minutes per day spent by users only. The alternative calculation, averaging time use figures across the whole population and so including those who neither have nor use a medium, was felt to be confusing. However, when such overall averages are calculated (as in Beentjes et al., 2001), we see that UK figures are broadly comparable with those from other countries, particularly in the demographic patterning of media exposure, just as the figures for media access in the home were comparable.

While in the UK we see in Table 2.6 that children and young people watch television for an average 147 minutes per day, in the USA, Roberts et al. (1999) report a slightly higher figure of 166 minutes per day. On the other hand, consistent with the greater stress on screen entertainment

Table 2.6 *Average number of minutes per day spent by users only, by medium*

	All	Gender		Age				Social grade	
		Boys	Girls	6–8	9–11	12–14	15–17	ABC1	C2DE
Users aged 6–17									
Television (1135)	147	148	145	101	142	165	167*	133	158*
Music (1024)	76	68	84*	36	46	72	127*	72	80
Computer Games (754)	45	57	24*	35	47	47	50	39	50*
Video (965)	39	41	36	37	42	40	34	32	44*
PC – not games (409)	29	32	26	14	22	28	44*	27	34
Book – not school (671)	26	24	27	25	27	24	27	27	25
Comics (302)	7	7	6	8	7	7	3	5	8
Users aged 9–17									
Magazine (639)	13	11	13	n/a	10	13	12	11	12
Newspaper (337)	13	14	11*	n/a	8	10	16*	12	13
Internet (226)	8	6	5	n/a	3	6	7	6	6

*Statistically significant difference.

Source: Livingstone and Bovill, 1999.

culture in these countries, both the UK and USA figures are high by comparison with other European countries (Beentjes et al., 2001), being half an hour per day more than in Germany or Spain, and three-quarters of an hour more than in the Netherlands or Switzerland, these latter being countries described earlier as comparatively high in domestic access to new media technologies.

Let us now summarise what we have learned about children and young people's use of media, old and new.

Television Despite all the hype about new media displacing old media, for most children television remains far and away the most popular medium in terms of time spent with it, followed by music, video and computer games. Television is watched by 99% of children and young people aged 6–17 years. It is watched every or nearly every day, for an average of two and a half hours per day. As Table 2.6 also shows, in the UK (as elsewhere), older children watch for longer, with teenagers spending an hour a day more than the youngest age group watching television. Similarly, children from lower social grade households watch for longer – nearly half an hour more than those from middle-class households. Boys and girls spend similar amounts of time with television. Its importance in their lives is also underlined by answers to the YPNM survey, which showed that television is the medium they would miss most, it is what they most often talk about with friends and, for parents, it is the activity they most often share with their children.[21]

Music　Nearly all (99%) have access to either a hi-fi or radio, and almost all (86%) listen to it. On average, children and young people listen to music five days per week, and those who listen to it do so for around one and a quarter hours per day. Unlike for television, however, there are strong gender and age differences. Twice as many boys as girls do not listen to music at all, and among the majority who do listen, girls spend around an hour and a half a day compared with just over one hour for boys. Age-related differences are especially noticeable: the proportions listening to music in their leisure time, and the amount of time spent by listeners, increase steadily through childhood and adolescence to encompass nearly all 15–17 year olds, each spending some two hours per day listening to music.

Video　While few lack a VCR at home, one-fifth of children aged 6–17 say they do not use it. Moreover, unlike both television and music, videos are watched sporadically, on average for 2.4 days per week, and for around 109 minutes on each occasion (making the average daily time spent, at 39 minutes, somewhat misleading). Videos are especially popular among the youngest children.

Books　While 87% of children have books at home, they are read by a little over half (57%) of 6–17 year olds. The style of use resembles computer games rather than television, for most children read occasionally (perhaps every other day) and for a comparatively short length of time (average of 51 minutes on each occasion). Thus the average time spent per day by readers is around half an hour. While reading books decreases markedly in popularity with age, younger children tend to read for relatively short stretches at a time, while a minority of teenagers read for much longer periods on the days they do read. Interestingly, while more girls than boys and more children from middle-class compared with working-class families read, there are no gender- or social grade-related differences in the time spent by readers.

Other Reading Materials　Comics are read by only half as many as read books, and more often by boys than girls and by children than teenagers. Because they are read only occasionally, and for relatively brief amounts of time, the average time spent per day by users is only seven minutes. The opposite picture is evident for magazines, for the numbers reading magazines increase markedly after the age of 11 and many more girls than boys read them. Like comics, however, magazines are read occasionally rather than daily. Around one-third of children over the age of 8 read a newspaper. Young people aged 15–17 are twice as likely to read a newspaper, also spending longer reading them, and boys spend a little longer reading than girls.

Computer Games Computer games (whether on a TV-linked games machine, a computer or a Gameboy) are played by two-thirds of children and young people aged 6–17. Use is occasional – around three days per week, for around 79 minutes on each occasion (making for an overall average of three-quarters of an hour per day). Few children and young people (6% of boys and 14% of girls) have no means of playing computer games at home (i.e. most have one, or several, of a Gameboy, TV-linked games machine or computer). However, nearly one in five boys and two in five girls have access to such equipment but say they do not play computer or video games in their leisure time. Computer game-playing peaks between the ages of 9 and 14. Among game-players, most play occasionally for a short time, although one in five – especially boys, especially working-class children – plays regularly for substantial amounts of time.

Personal Computer Overall, the YPNM survey found that one-third of children and young people use a computer for purposes other than games during their leisure time, a figure which is likely to be rising. While overall they spend around half an hour per day using it, this represents an average of one hour's use per day on 2–3 days per week. Predictably, having a computer at home makes a notable difference, with the result that working-class children spend far less time using a computer in their leisure time. Having a computer at home does not, however, wholly determine use. Of those who have a computer at home, 33% of middle-class and 45% of working-class children (and 34% of boys and 42% of girls) say they do not use a computer for non-games purposes in their leisure time. This may be because they only use it to play games, or because they lack interest in computers, or even because their parents forbid their use. Furthermore, of those who do not have a computer at home, 9% say they do use one at least sometimes in their leisure time: overall, around a quarter of boys and one-fifth of girls sometimes visit a friend's house to use a computer. Most significantly, while older teenagers make the most use of the computer for non-games purposes, there are no such differences in time spent or style of use between boys and girls or among the different social grades.

In the survey, we asked computer users to estimate what proportion of their time was spent on games and homework. Perhaps predictably, game-playing emerges as a much more common use of the computer for boys, while girls are more likely to use it for homework. A parallel pattern exists for age, with game-playing decreasing and homework increasing as children get older. Interestingly, given popular prejudices about computer use in the home, for those who have access and use a computer at home, there are no significant differences in the balance between game-playing and homework by social class.

Internet   While most children still do not have access to the Internet at home, those who use the Internet in their leisure time, whether at home or at a friend's or relative's house, are more likely to be boys, older, and middle class – the classic pattern of early adopters of a new medium (Rogers, 1995). The 'average minutes per day' figure is misleading in so far as Internet use tends to be very occasional, but when they do use it, users claim to spend around 50 minutes per session. The figures available for June 2000 from *Kids.net Wave 4* (Wigley and Clarke, 2000) show greater numbers gaining access to the Internet but only slightly increased amounts of time being spent with the Internet. This reflects the balance that adults and children are striking between what is still seen, on the one hand, as a comparatively expensive service and, on the other, as an ever more rich and comprehensive service.

Appropriating New Media

Having surveyed access to and time spent with media by young people, let us look a little further into the 'black box' of the home. Immediately, we are invited to assess the significance of the new media on a human or generational time scale rather than a technological one. After all, that which is already familiar from one's youth is generally incorporated into daily routines more readily than that which becomes familiar only with parenthood or in middle age, for such a process of incorporation or appropriation draws on the cultural meanings and frameworks available at the time. Having interviewed people from earlier generations, O'Sullivan suggests that those recollecting the early days of television can be divided into those born before the Second World War, for whom television was seen in comparison with pre-television domestic life, and those 'born into domestic circumstances where television had less and less novelty as an apparatus or spectacle, as it rapidly became part of the accepted, everyday, familiar landscape of "home"' (O'Sullivan, 1991: 163). Thinking forward to the 'new' media of today, a similar division separates the parent generation, brought up without computers (and with just one television in the living room) from the child generation for which computers (and multiple other media) are indeed part of the familiar landscape of the home.

While for children the multiplication and diversification of media goods in the home is largely taken for granted, for their parents the acquisition and subsequent location and use in the home of a computer, multiple television sets, or cable or satellite equipment involve decisions which distinguish their children's childhood from their own. In making these decisions, and in negotiating with their children, today's parents are fashioning a vision of modern childhood and family life with perhaps as much effort as that which the ICT industry puts into marketing the 'latest innovations'. Both efforts are constructive: families no more succumb to the image of the family 'imposed' on them by a powerful industry than the industry simply provides goods which families 'need'.

A generational perspective on the appropriation of media goods, just like a diffusion perspective on their market availability, leads us to take a longer-term perspective than would follow if one simply responded to the urgency implicit in popular talk of 'the new media'. For example, it seems that people's perceptions of new media today, especially the computer, are remarkably similar to those of television in its early days, offering benefits of education, entertainment and a marker of social status, yet representing a technological unknown until incorporated into familiar routines in the household. Like the computer today, 'purchasing the hardware [the TV set] for the majority of families was a considerable investment, and one that was not achieved without fairly explicit discussion of the likely benefits to be gained' (O'Sullivan, 1991: 164). These explicit discourses regarding the acquisition of new media tend to centre on their educational benefits, for part of the role of the contemporary family is to support and promote the learning and advancement of its members. This must be thought through and accepted by parents and so, while many families have already bought a computer, others are still 'coming round' to the idea, as this working-class father of a 10-year-old boy tells us:

> *Father:* The way of life, aye, so I mean I feel it's really important for everybody to be able to master a computer now.
> *Interviewer:* So have you any plans for yourself or –
> *Father:* Well I think we all have in the future when they get sort of older ... worthwhile then it would be, I think it would be a good asset for the family.

Children are well aware of this argument, as this working-class 15-year-old girl told us: 'I do my homework and that on it. ... My Dad thought it [multimedia computer] would be good to have, like educational.' However, these discourses are not necessarily the motivating factor in acquiring a computer. When we compared the views of parents in households with and without a computer, in relation to values such as concern about their child's future job prospects or educational standards at schools, there were no differences. In other words, while those who acquire a computer often give an educational justification, those who have not or cannot acquire a computer are no less concerned about their children's education and employment prospects.

Interestingly, the perception of television offering educational benefits has not been superseded by the computer. Many parents (57% in the YPNM survey) think that their child has learned a lot from television, and this again may contrast with their own childhood:

Father: Well, I mean when we got television we only knew [home town], that's it.
Mother: Well yes, I mean TV makes your world get bigger.
Father: Yeah, it's an educational thing. And it lets you see what the rest of the world is like.
Mother: We could never do that. ... I mean even now I am amazed when I see things like animals in their natural environment and all that.
Father: Well yeah, he knows that, he knows all about that, doesn't he?
Mother: But we didn't.

(Working-class parents with son aged 13)

The fascination of these parents with television instead seems to hold the clue, for while concern for their children's education provides the justification for providing new domestic technologies, the interest that these hold for parents appears the more motivating of their initial acquisition. Hence, in the case of the computer, parents who have acquired a computer differ from those who have not in being more positive in their attitudes towards computers (even after taking into account their household income and demographic variables). As one couple explained to us:

Father: Well I find it exciting, this is why we are going to have a look at computers tomorrow. I think that it is a thing of the future and I think that in the future everyone is going to have one so I think that now is the right time to go and get one, it's no good us leaving it until Karen leaves school because we'd never get one. I think that it is exciting.
Mother: I think that if we get the use out of it then we might even buy one for ourselves if Karen takes that one to university.
Father: Yes, that's right, and there are those laptops that we could get. Yes, I think that we are in an exciting age.

(Middle-class parents of a 15-year-old girl)

In sum, certain factors have been shown to contribute to both acquisition and use. The cultural and economic capital of parents, most notably, affects both media goods acquired for the home and also the patterns of use through which they are accommodated into family life. However, these factors also differ in crucial ways. It will be apparent from a comparison of the tables presented here on media access and use that while socio-economic status is crucial in accounting for differences in media access in the home, age and gender are much more important in accounting for patterns of use. In this context, the observation that socio-economic status accounts for considerable differences in access to a computer at home, but for no differences whatsoever in time spent with the computer by users, is particularly telling. Indeed, this might lead one to some optimism regarding national policies to improve access to ICT across the population. But, while this is encouraging as regards children's motivation, it remains noteworthy that both working-class children and girls are less likely to use a computer when available. Moreover, it would be naïve to neglect other cultural factors operating within the home that serve to differentiate the quality or value of different types of use.

Akin to the use of Bourdieu's (1984) concepts of economic and cultural capital, as used above, Murdock et al. (1995) identify three categories of resources – the material, social and symbolic – which contextualise media use within the home. Each is differentially available within society, making for different possibilities for social distinction or exclusion. While household income has already been shown to be crucial to young people's access to ICT at home, Murdock et al. (1995) suggest that social resources – 'the role of social networks in fostering and sustaining new practices' (1995: 273) – are important in maintaining use. Certainly, in their interviews with users and non-users, Murdock et al. identify many whose disillusion with the home computer reflects limitations of social resources which go beyond simple questions of access. Knowing how to buy the appropriate machine, to update software, to mould initially inflated expectations regarding the computer to realistic aims, these all depend on both social capital (through concrete networks of support) and symbolic or cultural capital (particularly, educational and professional expertise). And the absence of these may account for those who confound the diffusion hypothesis by acquiring and then dropping out as users (Murdock et al., 1995). These are, of course, related to economic capital: it is the better-off children who not only are more likely to have the latest ICT at home, but are also more likely to have friends or relatives able to demonstrate or help with such technologies (Livingstone and Bovill, 1999) and are more likely to have parents with the knowledge or expertise to guide and support.

But while finances matter in terms of access for socio-economic groupings, other distinctions become important in relation to use which depend rather on social and symbolic resources. Gender is a primary concern here, for while girls and boys share a common media environment at home, in many respects they make consistently different use of key media. Consequently, boys' preference for screen media and girls' preference for music and print media primarily reflects differences in social and symbolic resources. Over and over again interviews suggest the importance for both parents and children of actively reproducing and sustaining, rather than undermining, gender distinctions through everyday practices. As shown by Lemish et al. (2001) for European countries, and by Kubey and Larson (1990) for the USA, these gender differences in media use are widespread, being as much defining of gender identity as they are of media use. In short, although there are some gender differences in domestic access, differences in gender – which in key ways may also become inequalities – arise predominantly, though not entirely, from differences in content preferences, and these are in turn dependent on differences in leisure interests deriving from an equally gendered peer culture which families are more often concerned to sustain than to challenge.

MEDIA AS DOMESTIC INFRASTRUCTURE

This exploration of young people's access and use of media has revealed a variety of ways in which access underdetermines use, taking us beyond simple, causal questions of whether technological change brings about social change, towards a more complex charting of the social and cultural conditions which both shape and are shaped by new media, as pursued in the chapters which follow. Since the last decade or two of the twentieth century, 'old' or long-familiar media have been incorporated into new arrangements of space and time in Western societies as households increasingly come to possess multiple televisions, telephones, video recorders, radios, etc. In the chapters that follow we shall explore the implications of the multiplication, diversification and personalisation of media goods for the social contexts within which these media are used, including those of family, friends, community and school.

I will end this chapter, however, by proposing that the diffusion and appropriation of media into the practices of everyday life plays such a key role in defining the home, in spatial terms, and daily life, in temporal ones, that domestic media have become part of the infrastructure of family life. In other words, just as the family is supported by, or regulated in accordance with, a legal infrastructure specifying marital and parental duties and responsibilities (see Chapter 5), an economic infrastructure which facilitates certain kinds of family structure and undermines others, an educational infrastructure which is placing increasing responsibility on the family, and a spatial infrastructure by which certain kinds of living arrangements are supported through an implicit conception of family membership and family life, so too we might see the penetration of media throughout the home as establishing a certain set of expectations, practices and uses and hindering others.

Star and Ruhleder (1996) define the concept of infrastructure in terms of the following characteristics:

- Embeddedness in other social structures of everyday life
- Transparency in use, invisibly supporting daily tasks or practices
- Reach or scope beyond a single event or practice
- Learned as part of membership of a community of practice
- Linked with the conventions of a community of practice
- Embodiment of standards, expectations or values
- Built on an installed base rather than established from scratch
- Becomes visible on breakdown

If we compare the television and personal computer with each of these characteristics, it is clearly the domestic television set that has acquired the status of infrastructure. It is embedded in the sociality of daily life, invisibly supporting a variety of daily activities, including homework, family time, meal times and bedtime, and with a scope which extends to an increasing variety of daily practices. Familiarity with television content and habits is indeed expected by most people and especially perhaps by children and teenagers. This familiarity arises because an engagement with television is integral to the other conventions of those communities, being part of the expectations regarding shared knowledge and humour, and contributing to the construction of social identities, fandom, world views and future ambitions. Further, television, in both its status as a consumer durable and as a source of mediated content, embodies certain standards or expectations regarding what it means to be a young person today. It has also been argued that the introduction of television, while popularly discussed as a dramatic innovation in daily life, in practice established both its contents and its habits of use on the foundation previously established by radio, film and, to a lesser extent, the press. Visibility on breakdown shows itself on those occasions, always discussed with much fascination by the media themselves, when for whatever reason one has to spend some time without access to television; suddenly its status as part of the infrastructure of daily life is thrown into sharp relief. One group of 13–14-year-old girls reacted with horror when asked, 'what would happen if the TV broke down?', ready to leave their homes entirely:

Emma: I cried, my TV broke down last week and I cried.
Sharon: Oh golly.
Anne: I would go and live with my Grandma.
Sharon: I'd go to my dad's.

At the same time, we are witnessing a shift in this domestic infra-structure (and, of course, work-related and educational infrastructure also). The newly arriving forms of ICT, currently centred on the computer, have not yet attained this status of domestic infrastructure. On the contrary, the presence in households of computers and the Internet is highly salient, not yet fully 'domesticated' (Silverstone, 1994), not yet rendered a transparent part of the temporal and spatial routines of daily life (Scannell, 1988). The computer is, instead, very visible, not only because its breakdowns are more frequent than its successful usage, but more importantly because it has not yet become embedded in the social structures of family life. Where to put it, how to update it, how to regulate its use and to realise its potential, all these and other issues are still unresolved. Indeed, the process of learning to use the computer is a significant and somewhat difficult part of domestic life, one with which parents and children are still struggling, such that the conventions of practice which doubtless will, in the near future, serve to embed the computer into daily life are as yet still unclear and problematic. Yet the signs are already there that the computer will become part of the domestic infrastructure, changing the home in the process.

Thus, a key moment in the cycle of innovation, diffusion and appropriation is reached when the technology is established as part of the infrastructure of daily life. Diffusion curves (Rogers, 1995) suggest that when a medium first enters the home, a greater amount of time is spent with that medium than will be the case subsequently. People are attracted by the very unfamiliarity of the new medium, and so they must try out various possibilities for where, when and how it might become part of their lives. While longitudinal data would be required to chart trends in use over time, our interviews with families certainly suggested that early heavy use of a new medium does not necessarily last. Here a working-class mother with young children describes the early days after they first obtained multiple satellite television channels:

Ooh, God, the kids, as soon as they got up at 7 o'clock in the morning they were watching it, straight up, 'cause that's on from, like, 7 o'clock to 7 o'clock. … And they would just sit there glued to it and not get ready for school or anything so I had to turn it off.

Another mother describes first getting the computer in similar terms, when asked if her son spends a lot of time on his Amstrad computer?

> At first he did, but now he seems to be bored with the games because they are all too easy. But he's had that for over 2 years now.

However, while the immediate conditions under which a technology arrives in the home both shape and are shaped by the new arrival, it is only when the technology is sufficiently incorporated as to become part of the infrastructure that its longer-term significance becomes apparent. Arguably, too, it is only once the domestic infrastructure is altered – where this generally means adjustment more in accordance with the contingencies of daily life than with the specific features of the technology – that we can see the role media play in setting the conditions for the arrival, and potential appropriation, of yet further media. Rather, then, than oppose 'old' and 'new' media, let us instead consider technological innovations as traversing a path from the unfamiliar to the infrastructural, from goods understood primarily as rather indigestible technological artefacts to goods understood primarily as transparent mediating devices.

The metaphor of 'transparency' emerges strongly from interviews with media users (Livingstone, 1992). Some technologies are seen as somehow opaque, forcing a focus on their physical characteristics, their technological features, the challenges involved in positioning and using them within the home. Others are seen as somehow transparent, even invisible, primarily seen as providing opportunities to engage with certain kinds of content rather than interesting as objects. Silverstone (1994) writes of the dual nature of domestic technologies, being both part of our discourse of objects and consumption and part of our discourse of texts, meanings and reception. This duality is evident in relation to both popular and academic discourses surrounding domestic technologies. But it is important to recognise the dynamic process that links the two.

New media generally start out as opaque. A new medium is initially a difficult object in the household. It has unfamiliar physical characteristics – its size and appearance, its wiring, knobs and manual. It poses new problems: Can it be afforded? Where should it be placed in the home? Why does its use turn out to be so complicated or other than anticipated? How can it be regulated? What does it say about you to your neighbours? Only gradually do new media become transparent as we learn to master them, at which point their potential as mediators of content becomes more salient than their status as objects (Livingstone, 1999b). Everyone knows how many computers they have at home, but we must stop and think how many radios we possess. The Internet may be highly desirable, but for most, life without television is unthinkable.

Children in our interviews often confused familiar media, tending to treat the television and video, or the radio and hi-fi, under the same, content-defined, umbrella terms – they would talk instead of cartoons, soaps or music, seeing 'through' the hardware to their contents and paying little attention to the means of delivery. By contrast, more recent media (Internet, email) are often exciting and glamorous *qua* technologies but they may lack a content to which many children and young people can relate. A number of children we interviewed were keen to have a fax machine in their bedrooms, but they had little thought of to whom they might send a fax or why. Terminology is often unclear: listen to the difficulty of one boy, in the group of 9–10 year olds, in conveying to us that he has a personal computer:

> *Ben:*   Yes I've got a TV, a video machine and a Sega.
> *David:*   I've got Sega.
> *Darren:*   I've got a Nintendo, Super Nintendo.
> *Neil:*   Well I've got a computer, like it's a big computer, a real computer like Apple Mac but it's not got an Apple on it.

While a fascination with technology for technology's sake – on the part of parents as well as children – may at times lead to purchase, it is only the association of such goods with desirable contents or uses which can make them an integral part of the leisure environment. The hardware soon becomes uninteresting, however, once the uses of a medium are established. For early adopters, this process of transparency is already evident among new media users. As one 17-year-old middle-class boy told us:

> It's kind of transparent really. I don't think of email being email, it's just another method of communication. There is the guy I knew from my old school … he can never remember how he got this piece of information because if he was to confront me with a piece of information and I said where did you hear that, and he would say on the grapevine. He wouldn't know because he's got email, he's got fax, he's got phone, he's chatting face-to-face at school and he's got all other methods of communication, letters whatever and it's difficult to pin it down to where it came from.

What is gained by labelling the arrival of new media in the home a matter of infrastructure, rather than, say, describing media as part of the changing context, the environment or the ecology of everyday life? While these concepts each have their value, thinking of the media as increasingly crucial to the infrastructure of the home is illuminating. Most obviously, it sensitises us to the easily taken-for-granted ways in which the media – like electricity or town planning – subtly structure the practices of daily life. More significantly, each of the characteristics of infrastructure identified earlier can be seen as mapping out the 'tasks' faced by ICTs if they are to become part of the domestic infrastructure. They must become embedded, transparent, diverse in scope, and so forth. Also important, the infrastructure metaphor invites us to consider how things could have been otherwise. As Star and Bowker (2002: 153–4) note, 'a given infra-structure may have become transparent, but a number of significant political, ethical and social choices have without doubt been folded into its development' (see also Winner, 1999). This can be seen partly in the design and marketing of television over recent decades and of computer-based media today, instantiating as they do certain idealised conceptions of family life, childhood, pleasure, value, and so forth, any and all of which can and have been critiqued for their normative, conservative assumptions and their tendency to marginalise alternative lifestyles and lifeworlds. Some of these conceptions remain controversial for television also, in so far as television is itself changing as a medium, with contro-versy (or in Star and Ruhleder's (1996) terms, with a lack of acceptance into the community of practices and standards) centred on its growing commercialism (especially in countries with a strong public service tra-dition), its globalisation (especially in relation to national identities and cultures) and its facilitation of individualisation through the multiplica-tion of niche channels. For computer-based media, as we shall see in the following chapters, the struggle – both cultural and domestic – is more obvious as people seek to appropriate various ICT forms and services into their lives.

Although ICT is not yet part of the infrastructure of the home, it is rapidly becoming so. Yet, the 'struggle', in which state, commercial, and consumer interests are all variously at odds with each other, is still evident. Indeed, although public discussion of ICT has widely voiced the expectation that 'information' will become the new infrastructure, controversy remains. This can be seen to centre on each of the aspects identified earlier as characteristic of infrastructure:

- *Embedding and transparency*. How will ICTs become embedded in the domestic, educational, community and employment structures of everyday life? And what are the educational and training challenges in making ICT so familiar as to become transparent in use, invisibly supporting daily tasks or practices? This raises questions of literacy, or of multiple literacies, which need to become as invisible as are reading and writing on paper.

- *Scope.* Given the reach of ICT beyond any single event or practice, how will the hitherto rather distinct domains of our lives become ever more interconnected – work and home, education and home, etc.? ICT is hardly the only infrastructural development affecting this integration, but increasingly it mediates – and mediation is rarely neutral – the political, economic and social moves to blur the boundaries between diverse domains of practice.
- *A community of practice.* If use of ICT becomes a condition for community membership, what about those who are left out, without access to the technology or the competence required to use it? Infrastructures embody certain expectations regarding use (the dependence on the screen assumes a sighted, literate user, the keyboard assumes a trained and dextrous user, etc.). They also embody particular social relations: the Internet links English-speaking populations more readily than those speaking other languages, its services are more accessible to the wealthy than the poor, etc. The degree to which ICT interfaces draw on conventions developed for games software, or based on the analogy of the academic library, may favour boys and men, and middle-class users respectively.
- *Standards.* ICTs, like other infrastructures, embody standards, expectations or values, and although currently much controversy surrounds the harmonisation of such standards, these debates are fundamentally political, centring on dilemmas concerning intellectual property and copyright, universal access and the public right to know, civil liberties and potentially harmful or illegal information, and so forth.
- *An installed base.* To what extent is it problematic that ICT is far from established from scratch, but rather rests significantly on a basis in computer science, and hence is seen as technical, masculine, educated, faddy? Would its use become wider and more open (or, conversely, more managed and commercialised) if the installed base were shifted to that of either television or web TV (through various forms of multimedia convergence)?
- *Visibility on breakdown.* Infrastructure not only becomes visible on breakdown but also highly problematic. While a breakdown in an information-based infrastructure at work is often already highly problematic, this is not yet generally the case in the home; in any case, domestic ICT is still far from invisible (though of course its all too frequent breakdown is certainly experienced as problematic).

It is hoped that a contextual approach will avoid any simple technologically determinist ascription of change to the introduction of new media *per se* (MacKenzie and Wajcman, 1999), for as Star and Bowker (2002: 153) point out, 'historical changes frequently ascribed to some spectacular product of an age are frequently more a feature of an infrastructure permitting the development of that product'. These may themselves be technological – nothing since the initial introduction of the telephone has made salient the nature of telecommunications networks like the growth of the Internet. But more often they are economic (the expansion in global products and brands, for example, has stimulated a market not only for those products but also for the global television channels or web sites which depend on them for content), political-economic (the conditions which give rise to social exclusion have a far longer history than current concerns regarding inequalities in ICT use), socio-economic (it is the changing nature of work which has stimulated interest in domestic ICT which bring work and education into the home), and cultural (it is primarily the diversification in family composition and lifestyles, rather than the diversification in media contents and forms, which is supporting the individualisation of lifestyles).

Recognising the diverse domains within which ICT remains controversial has opened up a broader agenda than I shall attempt to take on in the chapters to come. But the thrust of such an infrastructure-focused analysis, which stresses the thorough contextualisation of media innovations in the contingencies of everyday life, as well as a number of the specific questions raised above, will indeed guide the following account of children and young people's changing media environment. Because we are talking here of a human infrastructure, one consisting of temporal schedules and spatial arrangements (though it also encompasses an arrangement of wires or hardware), the stress is also on gradual change rather than any dramatic effects of technology, for people and, especially, routinised social relations are slow to change, whatever the technological innovation available. Moreover, such change is not simply a quantitative matter, there being more commercialised, globalised or personalised media, but also a qualitative shift from one kind of cultural context for childhood and youth to another. This should be understood in terms of qualitative changes in the infrastructural arrangements by which relations between public and private, home and community, education and leisure, family and friends are managed. The discussion thus far has conceived of media in the home as part of the structure of the home, part of the domestic infrastructure. However, in extending the notion of a 'communication infrastructure' for communities as well as households, Ball-Rokeach (2000: 2) broadens the discussion to propose that 'the vast landscape of communication flows produced by people talking with one another, media producing stories, and local organisations bringing people together, are the milieu of daily life'.

NOTES

1 These figures parallel those available for the USA among other countries (Lievrouw, 2000).

2 See Murdock et al. (1995) and Schoenbach and Becker (1989) for the application of this approach to ICT in particular. See Compaine (2001) for a counter–argument, namely that the so-called 'digital divide' is closing.

3 This nicely relativises the concept of 'new media', for media new to the majority of the population are already familiar to the early adopters, and of course they are 'old' technology for the developers (Livingstone, 1999a).

4 Although see Lull (1990), Moores (1993), Silverstone and Hirsch (1992).

5 These data were derived from surveying children and young people aged 6–17. Parents were also surveyed, and where discrepancies arose, parents' responses were used to correct their children's answers just for information about media in the home elsewhere than in the child's bedroom.

6 Note that data on the diffusion of new media date rapidly, making it advisable here to stress sizeable differences or trends rather than absolute values. Sociodemographic differences (age, gender, social grade) are likely to prove more resistant to change.

7 See Bridgewood et al. (1999). The faster diffusion of ICTs to households with children is further confirmed by figures from 1999–2000 (Down, 2000).

8 see http:www.statistics.gov.uk

9 Global Expert Panel of the Future Media Research Programme, London Business School (June/July 1999).

10 At the same time, the first British home computers launched by Sinclair in 1980 and 1981 strengthened the hobbyist rather than the games-playing conception of the computer, for these were sold 'as products able to explore the world of computing' (Haddon, 1993: 129).

11 See Woolgar (1996) for the development of such ideas in relation to technologies more generally.

12 European comparative research shows that in the UK the differentials between lower and higher social grade households in access to both

multimedia computers and the Internet are much more marked than in the Nordic countries especially (d'Haenens, 2001).

13 See also Lin (1988), whose American data also suggest that economic rather than cultural capital is increasingly the significant predictor of new media ownership.

14 On the other hand, IT expertise, often gained at work, is itself proving a stimulus to acquiring access. Turow (1999) found that once a computer has been acquired at home, it is not education and income so much as parental experience with the Internet that determines whether an online connection is acquired at home.

15 Here I draw particularly on the twelve national comparative projects of which the YPNM project comprises the UK component (see Livingstone and Bovill, 2001a). For parallel American survey findings, see Annenberg Public Policy Center (1999), Cole (2000) and Roberts et al. (1999).

16 A parallel survey shows also that multi-set households are most common in Britain – almost four in ten British teenagers live in homes with four or more sets (compared with 8% in Germany) – whereas in Germany almost three in ten live in single-set homes (compared with 7% in Britain); Italy and France fall somewhere in between (see Livingstone, Bovill and Gaskell, 1999).

17 For comparative time use data across European countries, see Beentjes et al. (2001). For American data, see Roberts et al. (1999).

18 Empirically, these are matters on which not only parents but also children must be asked, for just asking parents about their children's use of media – though it is certainly easier, and seen by some as more 'reliable' – is perhaps akin to surveying husbands on how their wives spend their time at home.

19 One should not underestimate the methodological difficulties in measuring time spent with media, especially for young children. In the YPNM survey, 9–17 year olds estimated their media time use by estimating both days per week spent with the medium and hours/minutes spent with a medium on a day when they used it. For 6–8 year olds, we asked them more simply to estimate days but not hours, the hours/minutes data being provided by their parents. These two figures (days and hours) were then combined to estimate a figure for average minutes per day spent with each medium. Discussion of the methodology used and the issues raised is pursued in the appendix to the published report (Livingstone and Bovill, 1999).

20 Thus, average figures for any category of children overall – including users and non-users – can be calculated by combining data from the two tables.

21 Livingstone and Bovill (1999).

3

MEDIA, LEISURE AND LIFESTYLE

Two-thirds of UK children and teenagers have a television in their bedroom. Over half of UK homes with children have at least one personal computer, with Internet access growing rapidly. Overall, 6–17 year olds are spending some five hours per day with the media (Livingstone and Bovill, 1999). Roberts et al. (1999) obtain similar findings – of five and a half hours – in the USA. This is a considerable investment of time, revealing children and young people's priorities and preferences, as well as the constraints which structure the leisure options available to them. Of this five hours, around half is spent with television (46% on average), a further fifth on music, around 10% on each of videos, computer games and reading, leaving currently some 4% on the computer for non-games uses. Doubtless, this latter proportion is growing rapidly, but whether it is significantly displacing any of other media, or rather adding to the overall amount of media time, remains to be seen. What does all this mean for daily family life? How is this changing the nature of childhood? Have we reached the point of saturation with media? These and similar questions arise as soon as the undeniable quantitative increases, and the rather more contentious qualitative changes, in access to and use of media become apparent.

It is easy to frame questions that focus attention on the media alone. But doing so runs the risk of transforming objects of undoubted fascination and desire into scapegoats for the supposed ills of childhood and of social change (Barker and Petley, 1996). Certainly we cannot understand children and young people's engagement with media without accounting for that fascination. Equally, though, it is important not to be tempted into a discourse of moral panic. First and foremost, an explanation for the central place which media occupy in children's lives should be sought not in the nature of media themselves – their inherent features, attractiveness or contents – but in the contexts of daily life into which they have been introduced, and specifically in relation to the alternative leisure opportunities available to them. In short, rather than adopting a media-centric position, there is merit in standing back and asking what alternatives are available to children and young people and, crucially, whether these have also been changing over recent decades in ways that can account for the growth in mass-mediated leisure. To place media use in this broader context, then, this chapter will review the alternative leisure activities engaged in by children and young people. This invites attention to the ways in which these activities are popularly conceptualised, and here we see some tension between adults' and children's views, a tension that reflects a wider sociocultural shift in the meaning of leisure, the home and the family (Rojek, 1995).

In addition to putting the five hours per day of media use into a broader leisure context, this chapter will explore the variation in patterning of media use that this bald figure masks. In an age of media abundance, charting access and use of each medium in turn is insufficient to characterise its place in people's lives. Rather, it is the relations among media that matter. The use of any one medium is itself part of the context which makes the use of another meaningful. Moreover, these relations among media differ for different people, raising questions about the appropriate way to subdivide the audience. Thus, given a diversifying media environment, one may ask about the mix of media available to young people, the match between different young people and particular combinations of media, and the meanings and patterns of use associated with different media 'styles'. Given the enhanced potential for choice and specialisation, I then consider how these choices reflect value judgements regarding time management. The chapter concludes by arguing that leisure activities, media use and the experience of time are all interlinked through the construction of leisure lifestyles, a process which is itself framed by the broader historical trend towards individualisation. Through the construction of more or less individualised lifestyles, young people combine media and non-media leisure activities in particular ways, making use of the time they have at their disposal to pursue themes or interests which become, in turn, constitutive of their identities.

CONTEXTUALISING LEISURE WITHIN EVERYDAY LIFE

Media have undoubtedly become central to children's lives. Yet, in key respects it is adult conceptions of childhood, and adult provision for childhood – or lack thereof – which have made them so. We can see how these conceptions frame young people's leisure when we consider their impact on both time and space for leisure. Thus we may ask how media use fits into leisure more generally by identifying how children find time for media given competing options for disposable leisure time, and we can focus on where media are used, given a particular arrangement of public and private leisure spaces. We will also see that, much as children and young people enjoy media, their first inclination is often towards activities with friends. It is the social and economic conditions of childhood rather than children's preferences that so often make the media their most convenient leisure choice. While an overview of non-media leisure may seem to distract attention from the main subject of this book, one cannot understand the importance of media for children and young people today without first understanding the opportunities and constraints which structure their leisure time, and the discursive or social construction placed on children's leisure by both adults and children. As Allan (1985: 63) puts it, while 'the essence of leisure is freedom ... [this] underemphasizes the extent to which the leisure "choices" open to people are themselves structured by social factors over which they have relatively little control'. In short, a key context for media use is non-media leisure. And while changes in the media environment are widely recognised, changes in the broader leisure environment may be less readily apparent.

Let us begin with how children and young people themselves regard the attractions, and the problems, of their disposable leisure time. When we interviewed children and young people for the YPNM project, we would begin by explaining how we were generally interested in young people's lives, and how we were visiting different families or schools to talk to lots of children – older and younger, girls and boys, living in the countryside or the town, etc. Then we would ask, what's it like to live round here? Or, what's it like being 9 years old (or 11 or 15)? We would follow up such questions with a request for them to take us through a typical weekday, starting with getting up in the morning. This series of questions would generally put children at their ease, whether they were being interviewed in focus groups or on their own, and they would cheerfully tell us – or, sometimes complain to us – about their daily lives. But for us as researchers, listening to children's answers very effectively opened up a number of frameworks for contextualising media within the structures of their everyday lives, as well as throwing up further issues for exploration.

Children's answers are crucial to an understanding of their lifeworld (Graue and Walsh, 1998). Particularly, we were interested to see at which point in this very general conversation they would spontaneously

Table 3.1 *What three things would you do 'on a really good day' and 'on a really boring day'? (%)*

	On a really good day	On a really boring day
Go to the cinema	41	2
See friends	39	6
Play sport	35	7
Homework on PC	23	12
Play tapes/CDs	19	22
Go out to a club	18	4
Play computer games	15	19
Look round shops	14	14
Go to a concert/theatre	14	10
Watch TV	14	41
Phone a friend	14	7
Make something/hobby	9	14
Go to a the park/country	5	12
Practise music	5	21
Read a book	5	28
Read comic/magazine	5	13
Watch a video	4	22
Talk with mum/dad	4	12
Listen to radio	3	15

Source: Livingstone and Bovill, 1999; data from the YoungView panel, 10–16 year olds.

introduce the media as a topic. At this point we would often home in on the media, this indeed being our main research focus, but it was always informative to see where and why the media would enter, given this very open questioning. Most often, the media were spontaneously mentioned in relation to 'boredom', when describing their home or, especially, their bedroom and as markers of structure in their daily timetable. For example, when we asked one 7-year-old girl, living in a rural area, 'what's a really boring day at home? What would you do?' she told us: 'I would play with the computer if I had to – *Chips Challenge* and *Peter Pan*'.

These observations from open-ended interviews regarding the close links between media and boredom, domestic activities and regularity in leisure practices were confirmed by the survey findings. In the preparatory phase of the YPNM project, we asked some 700 children aged 10–17 which three things they would do on a really good day and which three they would probably end up doing on a really boring day (see Table 3.1). Their replies made it quite clear that a good day is when you go out, a boring day is when you stay home with the media, thereby contradicting the popular myth that children are natural 'couch potatoes'.

On a really good day, only one in seven would turn to television. Instead, the rare pleasure – actually managed on average less than once a month – of 'going to the cinema' comes top of the list, while the more everyday activities of 'seeing friends outside school time' and 'playing sport' are almost as popular. When asked to imagine what they would be likely to end up doing on a really boring day, watching television was by far the most common response, with reading, videos and music next in line. Clearly, as children and young people see it, using the media at home tops the list of things you do on a boring day (though this does not make them necessarily boring activities) while activities outside the home are the least often named; the reverse is true for a really good day. In this, their views match those of their parents: as one working-class father told us, 'I like them to be involved in things like activities, I mean I would just die if they wanted to sit in front of that box all day, I would really.'

Indeed, this desire to go out with friends, away from the family, was a recurring theme, and children repeatedly implied that time spent with media at home comes a poor second place. In effect, the main division in the way children think about their leisure distinguishes between time spent inside and outside their home, an apparently simple distinction that is strongly invested with a variety of meanings important to children and their parents. Going out is seen as offering independence, sociability and opportunities for exploration, with exciting potential for the unexpected. By contrast, staying home is boring and safe, albeit also comfortable and familiar. We pursue the significance of this spatial distinction in leisure opportunities in the next chapter.

Two exceptions are apparent in this mapping of good day/boring day onto outside/inside. First, of course, going to the cinema is an engagement with media, the important point being that as the medium used outside the home it is simultaneously as desirable but as constrained in availability as are other activities pursued outside the home. Secondly, it is significant that 26% of boys and 19% of girls name 'spending time with a computer (PC) doing homework, surfing the Internet, etc.' as something they would do on a really good day, twice as much as on a boring day. This confirms that new media especially hold a considerable amount of glamour for young people.

The media do not simply occupy time and space, they also structure it and give it meaning.[1] In the previous chapter it was suggested that familiar media, typically but not only mass broadcast media, have become part of the infrastructure of the home. Certainly, when we listen carefully to how children discuss the opportunities and restrictions which frame their leisure, we find that in many ways, the media play an implicit or explicit structuring role in children's lives in relation to:

- the structuring of time and the timetabling of everyday life (discussed in this chapter)
- the structuring of space and the relation between staying at home and going out (see Chapter 4)

Each kind of structuring is associated with significant opportunities and restrictions, as perceived by children. In rather different ways, parents also express both ambitions for and concerns regarding the structuring of their children's daily lives. This focus on the structure of everyday life allows us to see first how media fit into and contribute to these structures and, secondly, how new media have begun the process of adapting, or more often of being adapted to, these contextualising domestic structures. In Chapter 5, we then pursue the ways in which, through these issues of time and space, the media play a more-or-less implicit role in the family home in relation to the construction of age and the management of relations between childhood, adolescence and adulthood.

Going Out: Alternatives to the Media

> One night a week Sam goes to Scouts, one night a week he goes to football training. Until now he did another night at football. ... Probably one night he'll go swimming after school. ... My whole life seems to revolve around dropping them off and picking them up from somewhere.
>
> (Working-class mother of an 11-year-old boy)

> Well, I have two jobs. My mum works in an optician's so I clean there to get some money and I also work at a Mill bakery which I do three nights a week after school and Saturdays. Erm ... Ventures and a heck of a lot of homework. On Friday nights I would usually go down the pub or, I'm going skating tomorrow, or go to the cinema depending on what's on really. ... I am in the hockey team so we might practise or have a match after school. I am also on school council where we have several meetings, most of them are after school and I am on the sub-committee as well where we are trying to formulate a policy to prevent bullying. ... I do housework for my granddad at weekends.
>
> (15-year-old girl living in a middle-class family)

When one listens to children and their parents talking about the family's daily routine, one might suppose there is little time available for the media. Engaging in a variety of after-school and weekend activities occupies a significant chunk of leisure time, and much of this is spent in activities outside the home, most of which are highly social, adult organised, generally of an educational or 'improving' nature, and provided at some cost to parents by either public or commercial organisations.

Table 3.2 *Average number of clubs attended at least once a week (Parents' survey, N = 972)*

		Age			
Social grade	All	6–8	9–11	12–14	15–17
AB	1.6	2.1	1.8	1.5	0.7
C1	1.2	1.3	1.7	0.9	0.7
C2	1.0	1.2	1.3	1.0	0.5
DE	0.9	1.1	1.1	0.8	0.5

Note: Average number of clubs attended varies significantly by social grade for all but 15–17 year olds.

Source: Livingstone and Bovill, 1999.

Table 3.3 *Percentage of children who attend activity at least once per week (Parents' survey, N = 978)*

		Gender		Age				Social grade	
	All	Boy	Girl	6–8	9–11	12–14	15–17	ABC1	C2DE
Sports club	28	37	19*	26	37	30	19*	36	21*
Swimming lesson	22	22	23	40	33	11	5*	26	19*
Scouts, Guides, etc.	18	17	20	28	24	14	7*	23	14*
Music lesson	16	13	19*	14	21	18	9*	21	11*
Youth club	13	12	14	8	16	17	11*	11	15
Dancing class	9	2	16*	15	9	7	4*	11	7*
Computer club	3	2	3	2	2	3	3	3	3
Other	4	4	4	4	4	4	2	4	3
No clubs, etc.	21	21	22	18	13	22	34*	15	27*

*Statistically significant difference.

Source: Livingstone and Bovill, 1999.

In the YPNM survey we asked parents about the different activities their children engaged in (Table 3.2). Overall, children attend between one and two clubs after school or at the weekend each week, with attendance being almost twice as common for children of higher social grade households and twice as common also for the youngest age group compared with older teenagers. Middle-class 6–8 year olds stand out particularly in terms of their participation in such activities, while financial constraints make it more difficult for working-class parents to structure their children's leisure in the same way as their middle-class counterparts. When we asked parents what regularly leads to arguments with their child, working-class parents were much more likely to name 'going out', 'how much money they can have' and media with open-ended costs such as 'using the phone'.

Table 3.3 shows that only one-fifth participate in no organised leisure activities outside the home, these being twice as likely to be working- than middle-class children (27% of working-class versus 15% of middle-class

Table 3.4 *Percentage of 6–17 year olds who engage in a variety of leisure activities*

	All	Gender		Age				Social grade	
		Boys	Girls	6–8	9–11	12–14	15–17	ABC1	C2DE
All aged 6–17 (1303)									
Spend time with friends	86	85	87	82	80	89	92*	88	84
Play/mess about outdoors	66	69	63*	80	77	66	42*	69	64
Paint/draw/make things	54	50	59*	81	69	42	27*	54	55
Go out to a club	50	55	46*	47	52	52	49	58	44*
All aged 9–17 (980)									
Do homework	72	71	74	–	70	79	68*	78	68*
Go to the cinema	62	61	63	–	54	64	67*	68	57*
Write a letter	33	20	48*	–	30	31	38	36	31
Play a musical instrument	27	22	33*	–	36	27	19*	35	21*

*Statistically significant difference.

Source: Livingstone and Bovill, 1999.

children). The majority divide their time among a variety of organised activities, with sports, swimming and youth organisations being the most common. With the exception of youth clubs, middle-class children are more likely to occupy their time in this way – learning swimming, dancing, music, sports and participating in scouting organisations – than are working-class children.

Few of these after-school activities are gendered – both boys and girls learn to swim, attend youth clubs and such organisations as Scouts and Guides. However, while there are few differences overall in the average number of clubs attended per week, dancing and music lessons are more popular with girls, and nearly twice as many boys as girls attend a sports club. While participation is generally higher for younger children, this is especially the case for swimming, dancing and scouting organisations. Membership of sports clubs peaks at 9–11, while music lessons and belonging to a youth club are most popular between the ages of 9 and 14. In general, attendance at clubs drops off after the age of 14: one-third (34%) of 15–17 year olds do not attend any.

In the last chapter, we saw that younger children spend less time with media in general than do older children and, especially, teenagers, for whom television, music and computing are all more time-consuming. We also saw differences in the time spent with screen media especially between middle- and working-class children. As the above tables show that younger children, and middle-class children, have considerably less

Table 3.5 *Frequency (in days per week) with which 6–17 year olds engage in leisure activities (for those who do at all)*

	All	Gender		Age				Social grade	
		Boys	Girls	6–8	9–11	12–14	15–17	ABC1	C2DE
All aged 6–17 (1303)									
Spend time with friends	4.7	4.8	4.6	4.4	4.8	4.6	4.9*	4.3	5.0*
Play/mess about outdoors	4.6	4.8	4.3*	4.9	4.9	4.3	3.9*	4.3	4.9*
Paint/draw/make things	2.6	2.6	2.6	3.0	2.7	2.0	1.9*	2.5	2.7
Go out to a club	1.7	1.7	1.7	1.5	1.9	1.8	1.7	1.7	1.7
All aged 9–17 (980)									
Do homework	4.1	4.0	4.3*	–	3.1	4.7	4.5*	4.5	3.9*
Play a musical instrument	2.8	3.1	2.6	–	2.9	2.9	2.7	2.9	2.7
Write a letter	0.7	0.6	0.8	–	0.6	0.6	1.0*	0.6	0.9
Go to the cinema	0.3	0.3	0.3	–	0.3	0.3	0.3	0.26	0.31*

Note: 6.5 = 6–7 days a week; 4.5 = 4–5 days a week; 2.5 = 2–3 days a week; 1 = once a week; 0.25 = once a month; 0.1 = less than once a month.
*Statistically significant difference.

Source: Livingstone and Bovill, 1999.

time available for leisure at home in general, this may help explain the relatively lower amounts of time they spend with media.

Not all leisure activities are formally organised. Tables 3.4 and 3.5 show the percentage of 6–17 year olds who engage at all in a variety of informal leisure activities and the average number of days they do so in a typical week. Taken together, these tables show that spending time with friends is both a near universal and a near daily leisure activity, and this is especially true for older teenagers and for working-class children.

Unstructured outdoor activities – such as 'playing or messing about outdoors' – show a predictable pattern by gender and social class, with girls and middle-class children being more restricted in this respect. Older teenagers are less likely to do this also, or at least less likely to recognise this as a description of their leisure activities. Organised outdoor activities (clubs, etc.) are also more common for middle-class children, and also for boys. Going to the cinema, despite being very popular, is a relatively marginal part of children and young people's lives, at least in terms of its frequency (though most, especially older and more middle-class young people, do go on occasion).

Table 3.5 shows that middle-class children claim to do more homework, as do girls. And middle-class, younger children, as well as girls, are more likely to play a musical instrument (though for those who do play, there are no demographic differences in frequency of playing). These too represent competition with the media, helping to account for the relatively lower amounts of time with screen media spent by middle-class children. Letter writing, in so far as it occupies any time at all in the average week, is relatively more common among older girls.

Some activities show strong age trends – painting, drawing or making something being a good example, and this is also more commonly done by girls. In addition, then, to younger children's greater participation in formal activities outside the home, these informal and traditional ways of passing time at home may also compete with time with media and so explain why younger children spend less time with media overall.

It is important to note that the activities which compete with media for children's time vary by age, gender and class, and these demographic variations themselves reflect differences in the priorities – or restrictions – which both children and their parents place on leisure time. Thus, for younger children the choices are between media and friends, playing outside, indoor hobbies or formally organised clubs or lessons. For teenagers, friends and homework are the main rivals for media use. For middle-class children, formally organised activities and homework play a greater role than for working-class children, where unstructured time outside and/or with friends is of greater importance. For girls, rival activities are more likely to be located at home, while for boys they are more likely to be outside the home. For each of these groups, then, time spent with media, being generally unstructured, home-based and not particularly 'improving' in character, takes on a somewhat different meaning in so far as it functions as the alternative to structured or formal or educational or outside activities.

Staying in: Arranging the Media Mix

Displacement   Such historical evidence as exists supports the argument that the introduction of media does not displace but rather supplements the diversity of leisure activities available. What shapes the media and leisure mix available to young people is not simply the range of available media technologies but more importantly the broader sociocultural shifts in the balance between leisure and work, home and community. It is arguable that, as a result of these shifts, young people have more spare time overall than hitherto (Furnham and Gunter, 1989: 172). While part or even most of this may account for the growth in time spent with media, when reviewing trends in leisure in America over the twentieth century, Fischer (1994) found evidence both for increased private leisure at home and for increased public, participatory leisure. At the same time, over the past century there is consistent evidence of a rise in commercialised leisure, although no evidence for the commensurate loss of informal leisure (Fischer, 1994). One should note, however, that good historical data on informal leisure are sparse: people tend not to fill in a time-use diary with 'doing nothing', and doing nothing leaves little record in admission figures or participation rates.

Other scholars suggest that some displacement among leisure activities may have occurred. Putnam (2000) blames the apparent erosion of participation in civic organisations in post-war America on the rise of mass-mediated leisure. O'Sullivan's (1991: 169) interviewees recall television 'as having had a much lower priority on an agenda that encompassed more outgoing social and leisure pursuits and more demands associated with household maintenance and family work'. At the time, Himmelweit et al. (1958) had expressed concern that the arrival of television was displacing 'doing nothing', a way of spending time which they saw as valuable. Even this comment in itself indicates a cultural shift over the past four decades, for now many would see time with television as itself a way of doing nothing. A straightforward displacement framework tends to ignore historical shifts in the meanings of leisure activities. Using a framework of transformation rather than of displacement, Brake (1985) interprets as central to the growth of youth culture in Britain the way in which informal activities have become increasingly incorporated into the commercial sphere, through consumption-oriented leisure, rather than maintaining their distinctiveness from it. Overall, the picture appears to be that young people are spending growing amounts of time with commercial leisure both at home and outside the home. Evidence for changes in participation in formal organisations, and in informal leisure outside the home, however, remains equivocal. Less equivocal is the evidence that young people are spending increasing amounts of time at home with media. It has been clear ever since the introduction of television that, as each new screen medium is introduced into the home, these immediately attract noteworthy proportions of children's leisure time, and overall the amount of time that young people spend with the media is considerable.[2]

The possibility that time spent with television in particular directly displaces other leisure activities has long been a concern among the public, policy-makers and academics alike. One wonders how room is found for new media within the context of already full lives and, adding a nostalgic gloss, at what cost? Broadly speaking, the many studies of displacement[3] indicate little effect of the introduction of television on bedtime or homework time, although there is some evidence of the displacement of radio listening, cinema attendance and comic reading. For example, Murray and Kippax (1979) compared children in communities with either no television, with only one public channel, or with one public and one commercial channel, examining the impact on use of other media among 8–12-year-old children. They found that those without television spent longer with radio, records and comic books than those with television, although interestingly, those with television also spent more time reading books but less time reading comics. Himmelweit et al. (1958) proposed that it is those media which are used for similar purposes that constitute the key candidates for displacement: hence, it seems that television and comics, but not television and books, fulfil similar entertainment functions. Ever since the work of Schramm et al. (1961) in the USA, and Himmelweit et al. (1958) in the UK, it has been confirmed that reading books – the activity whose possible displacement has aroused the most public anxiety – shows the fewest clear displacement effects, and there is some evidence even that television has stimulated book reading. This lack of displacement is partly because, as Neuman (1988) points out, children have never spent much time reading books – a figure of 15 minutes per day, on average, holds in both the USA and the UK, both in the 1950s and today (Livingstone and Bovill, 1999).[4]

With each new decade, potentially displacing new media are introduced, giving rise to the same questions yet again. Today, one may ask whether cable and satellite television are displacing viewing of terrestrial channels, particularly public service channels, whether computer games displace viewing altogether, or whether the widening range of media options detracts from time for reading? Schoenbach and Becker (1989) surveyed the impact on households (i.e. adults and children) of media introduced in the 1980s (particularly VCR and cable/satellite television) across a variety of Western countries. They found little evidence of a reduction in time spent on non-media leisure, nor did they find much evidence of a reduction in time or money spent on print and auditory media. Instead, there was consistent evidence for increasing specialisation in uses of all media, not just the new ones: integrating transformation of media uses with the functional similarity hypothesis, they therefore concluded that while there is little evidence that new media create new audience interests, they may provide new means of satisfying existing interests. Ten years later, again looking across Europe, it still appears that there is no simple relation between number of available channels and time spent viewing by children, and a variety of factors would appear to determine the audiovisual culture of different countries. The Netherlands, for example, has one of greatest number of channels available and yet the lowest viewing figures by children, while in Finland, a country with a considerable concentration on national, public service channels, viewing figures are relatively high (d'Haenens, 2001).[5]

The issue of displacement cannot be satisfactorily answered in any project without a longitudinal design enabling the comparison of time use before and after the acquisition of a new medium, for it remains possible – plausible even – that children already reluctant to read are precisely those most likely to acquire and use new media. Moreover, longitudinal designs are no longer practical in a complex media environment in which different media are acquired at different rates, resulting in different combinations of media possessions in homes. However, the account of the use of each medium in Chapter 2 confirms that today new media are adding to the media mix rather than simply displacing older media. In general, time spent with different media is positively rather than negatively correlated (Livingstone and Bovill, 1999). In other words, the more time children spend with one medium, the more (rather than the less) they tend to spend with others – with only one, telling, exception, namely that, for boys especially, the more they watch television, the less they read books. This may suggest that any rise in overall time spent with the media is likely to have been bought at the expense of non-media rather than media time. Furthermore, despite the considerable hype regarding new forms of media, television and music remain the media widely used by children and young people on a daily basis. While television appears most successful at timetabling the lives of its viewers, as we see below, music is listened to regularly because it provides the backdrop to a range of other activities, although this is also becoming a feature of television use. Most other media are used occasionally rather than routinely, fitting into, or even facilitating, more individualised patterns of leisure use. The amounts of time devoted to newer media (computer games, video, PC, Internet) are still relatively small compared to overall media use, suggesting that while they add to the repertoire of leisure activities available to young people, they are only beginning to find a slot in the regular daily timetable.[6] As Newhagen and Rafaeli (1996: 10) note: 'the evolution of mediated communication rarely leads to extinction. We have had conversation, lecture, letter writing, storytelling, playing, acting, exhorting, defaming, creating – and we still have them. The Net will no doubt become one more place where these occur.'

The Media Mix It appears that new media rarely replace or even, *displace*, older media. Rather, new media add to the available options, to some extent prompting new, more *specialised*, uses for books, television, radio, etc. How this occurs depends on how readily new media may be incorporated into young people's pre-existing practices and priorities.

Thus, although the evidence for displacement of older media by new media is weak, the evidence for ever more complex and individuated media menus is compelling. This is strengthened by the observation that within the five hours per day spent with the media, there is huge variation among children, with the top 20% spending as much as nine-and-a-half hours a day with media while the bottom 20% spend only one-and-three-quarter hours per day.[7] Traditionally, media researchers have drawn on the theory of uses and gratifications to account for media or genre choices.[8] Rubin (1984) summarises these choices as of two kinds – instrumental (seeking knowledge, reality orientation, social utility, etc.) and ritual (especially habitual, mindless viewing) – while Katz et al. (1973) show these to vary systematically across media. Although criticised for tending to reify audience 'needs' without considering social contexts of use (Elliott, 1974), such a reification was not intended by the early uses and gratifications theorists (Blumler et al., 1985). Indeed, given the swing in audience research away from individual psychology towards the social context, one might reinterpret the expressed 'needs' or 'preferences' of audiences in terms of discursive justifications for media uses, these in turn reflecting both material constraints on media choices and normative representations of the 'gratifications' media can provide.

However we interpret these 'choices' or 'needs', children undoubtedly employ such a language of choice themselves (see later discussion of 'boredom'). Notably, when the YPNM survey invited children to name media best suited for excitement, relaxation, and so forth, their preferences were consonant with the emerging patterns of media time use which characterise children's leisure. Specifically, the top choices for 'excitement' were playing computer games (20%), watching television (24%) or a video (19%). For relaxation, children chose listening to music (30%) or watching television (23%). To relieve boredom, watching television (25%) and playing computer games (23%) were again the most popular, while reading a book (35%) or using the PC (30%) matter primarily when children want to learn about something. Television is even the top choice (22%) when children don't want to feel left out (followed by phoning someone, at 20%). Clearly, television retains its enormous popularity because it is seen to satisfy all moods or desires for the majority of children and young people. All other media are chosen for particular reasons, and are favoured by particular demographic subgroups, indicating a more specialised mode of engagement, though the observation that computer games are popular for both reasons of positive choice ('excitement') and because of the perceived absence of other activities ('to relieve boredom') must account for their dramatic success as a contribution to children's – or at least boys' – leisure.

But all 'children and young people' cannot be lumped together in their use of media. In the YPNM report we used cluster analysis to identify four broad combinations of media among 6–17 year olds, arguing that, depending on access, children and young people generate their own styles of media use.

First, *traditionalists* spend the bulk of their time with 'traditional' media, very little with computers and relatively little on computer games. They are a heterogeneous group with no strong affiliation to any particular medium but a readiness to enjoy television, books, magazines and music. They tend to lack a media-rich bedroom. The majority of traditionalists are aged 12–14, for after this young people have usually developed more specialised media tastes. Traditionalists are a little more likely to be girls, with no differentiation by social grade.

Secondly, *low media users* spend below average amounts of time with all media. Given the widespread interest in young people's media use, it is worth noting that one in five stand out for making relatively little use of media across the board, when compared with the majority. Low media users are particularly likely to be young: two-thirds are under 12 years old and one-third are between 15 and 17 years old, while in the middle age range (12–14 years) we found no such users. They are not especially associated with either gender or social grade groupings, though they do appear to have relatively more educated parents (though not higher income households). Predictably, they have relatively fewer media in their bedrooms. Yet even for these children, television is important. Although they make rather little use of most media, television occupies a larger proportion of their 'media time' and they turn to it for both excitement and relaxation.

Thirdly, *screen entertainment fans* spend considerably more than average amounts of time watching television and videos and playing computer games and very little time with books. This style of media use is particularly popular among working-class boys and is most common in the 12–14 age group. Sport is the main interest of screen entertainment fans – as an outdoor activity, a favourite computer game and television programme, and as a much valued skill when judging, for example, what 'makes you popular with people your own age'. This suggests that it is interest in content that is shaping their choice of media style, not an interest in the technologies *per se*. Interestingly, despite having often comparatively media-rich bedrooms, this group are among the least likely to spend a great deal of time in their own rooms; thus it would be a mistake to regard this as a group of isolated children – their interests in sport, and in screen entertainment generally, are typically shared with both friends and family.

Fourthly, *specialists* spend more than average amounts of time with one particular medium. We identified three kinds of specialist: *book lovers, PC fans* and *music lovers*.

- More often from middle-class homes, though equally boys and girls, *book lovers* spend a considerable amount of their leisure reading books. They are more common among both younger children and 15–17 year olds. While their home environment tends to be 'media-rich', they spend comparatively little time watching television, but make considerable use of the PC. These young people buy books with their own money, swap them with friends, talk to friends about books, happily turn to a book if they want to learn about something, and have a generally positive attitude to both school and parents, suggesting that there is less conflict in this group between their values and those of the adults around them.
- *PC fans*, at least before mass-market saturation of the PC, are girls and boys from media-rich middle-class homes. They appear to share in a screen-based rather than a print-based media culture, reading comparatively little and preferring television and computer games. The computer provides them with a source of excitement, a reason for spending their pocket money (on games), and a favourite topic to discuss with friends.
- *Music lovers* emerge as a special interest group among 15–17 year olds. More often girls and from working-class homes, these young people spend considerable amounts of time with both music and television, making them the heaviest media users of all. Although not book readers, they are among the most avid readers of magazines, comics and newspapers. However, they do not play computer games and are the least comfortable with computers. They are also generally the least satisfied with their school, community, and family. Music plays a significant role in their social interactions: they often swap and buy magazines, music tapes or CDs and videos, and they discuss music with friends.

The overall trend is for media 'menus' to become more specialised as young people grow older, and for the new computer-based media to play an increasing role in leisure lifestyles. Those who are overall low media users are particularly common among the youngest age group, traditionalists (who use a variety of 'old' media in combination) are common in middle childhood, especially for girls. Screen entertainment users tended to be more working class, and more boys, again in the middle of our age range. And the specialists are interestingly unrelated to gender (i.e. being a book or a PC specialist is not more typical of boys than girls) except for girls tending to be music lovers, but they do increase with age and they are more middle class.

There is clearly a social developmental account of media and non-media leisure to be drawn out of the findings overviewed in this chapter. Looking mainly at non-media leisure, Hendry et al. (1993) proposed a three-stage model to account for the age trajectory in time spent in different kinds of leisure activity. In their model, young children engage in a number of formally organised, but often non-commercial activities through to the age of about 14. This is followed by a period of more casual activities in the middle teenage years. And third, from around 16 years old (or when they begin to earn some money through part-time work) they increasingly engage in commercial leisure activities. While these stages describe young people's leisure outside the home, we can put this together with the picture obtained in this and the previous chapter regarding leisure and media use within the home to produce a more complete picture of young people's leisure. Notably, the data invite a subdivision in childhood, as the formally organised, non-commercial activities which Hendry et al. observed to continue to 14 appear now to be declining somewhat earlier, while the characteristics of adolescence (greater media use at home, greater unstructured leisure outside the home) are, similarly, evident at an earlier age than hitherto. While in no way offering a rigid sequential stage model, the different leisure patterns observed as characteristic of different age groups may be described as follows:

- *Activity-focus*. Early to middle childhood (in the YPNM survey, 6–8 years) sees children engaged in a diversity of play activities at home, resulting in low media use, combined with relatively formally organised activities outside the home. Thus, not only does this group spend modest amounts of time with television and other screen media, but they are not yet spending a lot of time listening to music, although they do read more than those older than them. And of course, they spend more time in non-media activities at home – playing, painting, making things, etc. On the other hand, they take part in far more organised clubs, sports and extracurricular activities. While most of these, as Hendry et al. note, are not heavily commercialised, they can be expensive, as reflected in the differential take-up by middle-class and working-class children.
- *Structured entertainment*. The stress here is on screen entertainment at home and formal participation in clubs outside the home; hence, 'structured' here refers to the way in which, whether at a club or in front of the screen, leisure contents are structured – scheduled, arranged, formatted – for the child by others. Late childhood (approximately 9–11) is already notable for the early signs of two trends which define adolescence – considerable media use at home,

participation in often unstructured and increasingly commercial clubs outside the home. Thus, while in some respects late childhood retains much of the character of middle childhood, this period also sees the peak in screen entertainment media use at home, with a marked increase in time spent with television especially which continues through to the late teens. Participation in sports clubs peaks at this age and youth clubs begin to be important, while other formally organised activities outside the home now decline, as does non-media leisure at home (hobbies, making things, etc). What ties together screen entertainment at home with participation in clubs outside the home, whether organised or casual, is that both provide structured environments focused on entertainment which guide and frame children's leisure.

- *Media-rich, casual leisure.* Early to middle teens (12–14): time spent at home with media is much greater than in childhood, with music becoming a significant activity and time watching television increasing yet further. While homework occupies more time, going out to clubs remains important, although extracurricular lessons of various kinds have come to occupy less time. As a result, this period combines high media use at home with casual leisure activities outside the home. While leisure activities are not heavily centred in commercial locations outside the home, this period of leisure is heavily commercial in two senses: first, the provision of a personalised, media-rich environment is costly, and secondly, the content of these media-centred leisure interests is commercialised, particularly through fandom for pop music, actors, football teams, and so forth.

- *Diversification and specialisation.* Late teens onwards (15–17): at home, the media mix shifts once again although the overall level of media use remains high. Thus, although television remains a dominant activity, both music and computer use become increasingly important. At the same time, playing computer games drops significantly for many though not all after the middle teens, as does the number reading books for pleasure. As teens become more selective in their media mix, it becomes harder to characterise the age group as a whole. Outside, participation in extracurricular activities or clubs organised specifically for young people is further reduced, while time spent with friends, including at commercial leisure locations such as the cinema, increases.

Overall, there are two trends evident as children grow older: within the home, an increased media use together with a changing media mix; and outside the home, a shift from formal to informal, and public to commercialised leisure. These combine to generate a particular leisure context for any particular age, and it is within this context that one should locate particular media and media uses, for example asking how the Internet may be fitted into children and young people's lives. The developmental trend towards specialisation parallels the historical evidence regarding the diffusion of media through society (Chapter 2), so that both for the story of media 'careers' and young people's leisure 'careers', the trajectory is one of increasing specialisation. These come together, as the last section of this chapter discusses, to make youth culture in the present day the furthest yet witnessed along the road towards the individualisation of leisure.

But before developing this argument, let us first consider, drawing on more qualitative research, the meaning for children and their parents of the contrast between free and structured time, seeking to identify the role of the media in both occupying free time, but also, simultaneously, structuring it to generate the taken-for-granted routines of everyday life. Following this, in Chapter 4, we explore further the role of media in structuring the relations between home and outside, turning from the temporal to the spatial dimension of leisure.

THE VALUE AND EXPERIENCE OF TIME

Look, if it's a Monday we go football training.

(10-year-old boy living in a working-class family)

On Mondays I've got drama and then I've got Guides after, then Wednesdays I've got another drama, and Fridays I've got horse riding straight after school, so I do quite a few activities.

(12-year-old girl living in a middle-class family)

It is a common observation that, in post-war Western society, the pace of life is speeding up, so that pauses for thought or contemplation become lost in the imperative to use time productively. Certainly we have seen that in Britain, children and young people's lives can be heavily timetabled, not only with school but also with organised after-school activities. Crucially, this sense of the demanding pace of life – which arises both as a result of the economic or workplace demands on parents and the felt need to provide stimulating and educational extracurricular activities for their children – is experienced by parents as problematic for family life. Specifically, the parental lament is that of lack of time. This is of concern in adult relationships also. In an earlier study, one woman described to me her life with her husband as 'like ships in the night' (Livingstone, 1992: 127); but certainly many parents express the wish for more time to spend with their children.[9]

One working-class mother told us about home life with her 7-year-old son as follows: 'I mean in the evenings we are all together, but our minds are always busy. I feel bad because I'd like to do more with the children but we have the shop and my mind is always on it and my husband is in there all the time. We've even got a mini television in the shop now for him to watch and the children as well when they are in there.' Another mother, a middle-class woman who has recently returned to study, describes the life of her 12 year old thus: 'He's had to have a very structured life while I was at university, mainly because I had to be structured to be able to run the home and do a full-time degree, and there was no room for manoeuvre.'

In consequence, while one might describe those who attend many clubs as rich in activities, the corollary is that they are time-poor. By contrast, it is those without so many clubs and after-school activities who have much more free time. This kind of flexible and plentiful or 'non-curricularised' free time still describes the lives of many children. For example, one working-class mother says of her young children:

> They have quite a lot of free time, you know, after school, so it's only Mondays and Fridays that they specifically do things, one of them might have a friend round for tea one day, or, you know, one of them might be going somewhere another day, but they do what they want really. I try not to sort of drag them shopping and things.

On the other hand, in response to a perception of excessive time pressure, one middle-class mother described a deliberate policy of relaxing the demanding timetable her 10-year-old son had been following: 'He opted to drop cubs and things like that, 'cause he couldn't have friends round and that. We've relaxed it a little bit more and tried to fit in, 'cause we have a couple of free days.' This deliberate strategy of subsequently undoing some of the structures put in place when children are young is not uncommon, and by the time young people have reached their middle teens, many seem to have moved on from this kind of timetable, just as they also claim to have moved on from other kinds of parental regulation. Thus the middle-class mother of a 16-year-old boy told us, 'there is less structure at the moment, because they've given up sort of all the activities they did'.

While clearly such time pressure can be felt by children as well as adults, James et al. (1998) suggest that in general 'time' means something different to children and adults, thus making the easy assumption that the adult experience of time applies also to children inappropriate. Instead, they suggest that children tend to live more in the present, experiencing themselves in the here and now, rather than as tokens of the adults they will become. On the other hand, as adults tend to regard the time their children have available as an opportunity to invest for the future, they implicitly endorse the economic metaphor 'time is money' (Lakoff, 1980). For adults, then, time must be spent wisely, not wasted or thrown away. One factor behind this may be levels of parental fear of the future competition their children face, such that the time of childhood itself becomes a time for preparation. As James et al. (1998: 74) put it, 'whether in relation to education, work and employment, or in respect of their spiritual, physical and mental well-being, children are judged, nurtured and protected with the future adult in mind'. Ennew (1994) is more critical, noting that children's time has become ever more specialised, commercialised and regulated.

Many applications of what O'Sullivan (1991) terms the 'time economy of domestic life' are evident in everyday discourse; we say giving your time to others is an act of kindness, spare time is to be cherished, the thrifty will plan their time effectively. The timetabled lives of, especially, middle-class children appear to reflect this parental concern about 'wasted' time. The ways in which the media fail to teach children to use their time effectively is also sometimes a source of complaint:

> Modern children could be shown how to put a model together and how to paint it up, and show them what to do with their leisure time. And with programmes then, yes, you get cartoons and peculiar things where they are sort of jumping in custard on a Saturday morning. ... I know that ours sit down and make models and things. Children have to be educated on how to play all these things, don't they?
>
> (Middle-class mother of a 13-year-old boy)

This economic metaphor is evident in parents' talk about the media, particularly among the middle classes. One middle-class parent describes getting cable television as 'a waste of time. ... I mean sometimes the cartoons that were on weren't very educational or anything like that.' Another complains about how television is an ineffective use of time: 'I don't agree with having it on all day, every day. There are other things that they can do.' A 9-year-old, working-class girl uses the same metaphor when she says: 'My mum wouldn't want me to spend too much on my hi-fi because I put it up too loud, and I'm not allowed to spend too much time on my computer in the morning because I'm always late for school.' Intrinsic to the economic metaphor is the value placed on a product: where children enjoy an activity for its own sake, parents are more likely to value it – or not – depending on its outcome. One mother of a teenage daughter complained to us that 'she's at the age where she can spend endless hours just laying around chatting with her friends and not doing much at all'. Children and parents clearly diverge in their estimation of what is wasted time and what is time well spent. Yet for the most part, developmental psychologists are generally on the children's side here, placing considerable importance on free play, on self-structured rather than adult-structured time, and on the self-reflection and informal social interaction that occurs as part of such play. Countering many parents' concerns with valuable outcomes, Opie (cited in Hill and Tisdall, 1997: 101) suggests that for children the very charm of play is that it is simultaneously wholly absorbing and yet inconsequential: 'A game is … more powerful and important than any individual player; yet when it is finished, it is finished, and nothing depends on the outcome.'

Related to the 'money' metaphor for time, a second metaphor often used in relation to the media – and equally moralistic in its specification of good and bad uses of time – is the 'diet' metaphor. One middle-class 10-year-old girl we interviewed had picked up from her mother the notion of trying to 'cut down' on media use. Generally, parents would like children to watch what is good for them, not to over-indulge, to watch (or eat) 'rubbish', but rather to favour a good balanced diet of 'suitable' media and leisure activities. Just as even fruit and vegetables can be 'bad for you' if eaten to excess, children know that their parents will disapprove of any activity if not balanced 'sensibly' with others. Thus, in the following interaction, these 12–13-year-old middle-class boys show that not only are they well aware that their parents have moral opinions regarding appropriate media use, but that it is the balance across activities which is regarded as crucial.

Frank:	My parents disapprove and approve of me [pointing to books]
Interviewer:	They disapprove and approve of books.
Frank:	Yes, because they think it's good that I do read books and spend time reading them, but they also disapprove that I read them all the time.
Interviewer:	So it's a question of anything you spend too much time at parents disapprove of.
Frank:	Yes.
Peter:	Yes.
Interviewer:	What do they want you to be – why?
Peter:	Because they want you to spend time doing lots of different interesting activities.
Frank:	Yes. That's exactly what they say.

Through the diet metaphor, with its stress on 'balance', parents ward against the supposed evils of media addiction, this being the excessive use of one medium to the exclusion of all others.

Mother: I mean even the little 'un, he's addicted, he loves it. I mean every time that he's bored he wants the computer on.
Father: Yeah, he really loves it, they all do.
Mother: Yes, as soon as they come home from school they sit down and watch what they want to watch and then they say 'Oh mum can we have the computer on?'

(Working-class parents of a girl, 9, and boy, 6)

Children may not see things the same way: as one 10-year-old boy told us regarding computer games, 'some people just spend ages on them and people think that they are addicted to them but then the next day you could be out playing football or something, or listening to the radio'. In fact, as we have seen above, rather few children spend time with one medium exclusively, though of those who come close, books are as likely as television, and more likely than other media, to be thus focused upon, challenging the values of those who warn against such 'addiction'. Yet undoubtedly, as parents and other adults see it, time can be spent well or wasted, and it can be used to improve or undermine one's mental health. Interestingly, these metaphors for media use, centring on money and diet, share the ambivalence of an advanced industrialised society towards its own wealth: the culture values a media-rich, information-rich, nutritionally-rich, financially-rich society, but not one which is over-indulgent, lacking in challenge or 'fibre', and not one which creates the poverty – information-poor, media-poor, nutritionally-poor, etc. – against which such riches are distinguished.

Boredom

While parents may look back to a childhood in which the media played an occasional, contingent, rather than a more or less ubiquitous and necessary, role in their leisure time (see Chapter 4), children and young people are clear that the media are central both now and to their future conceptions of leisure and home. In thinking about the present, it also appears that by contrast with their parents, children do not generally draw upon these metaphors of time or diet to describe their media use (although they are often familiar with adult discourses relating to media use and can reproduce these on request). Rather, then, than sharing that very adult anxiety of worrying about wasting time, they express their greatest fear, implicitly, as that of boredom.

If you're in and you're bored you can just watch TV.

(9-year-old girl living in a working-class family)

When you get bored you watch videos.

(12-year-old girl living in a middle-class family)

Over and again we heard children and young people complain of the boredom in their lives – the unstructured gaps between activities which, while not always long enough, face them with the awful prospect of 'having nothing to do'. While adults strive to fill their children's time constructively, and so to reduce the time their children can spend with the media, children may collude in this not because they too value the future-orientation of time spent 'well', but because their greater tendency to live in the present makes boredom an unpleasant experience rather than a waste of time. In the main, children overwhelmingly regard the media as a means to fill up the gaps in a parent-determined timetable. For if faced with a choice between friends and media, children choose friends, leaving media to fill the moments of boredom or loneliness. The media – especially television – thus represent a lifeline or safety net, a guarantee of pleasurable activity, however unpromising their surroundings. Since its introduction in the 1950s, it seems that very rapidly, two kinds of television viewing became established (O'Sullivan, 1991): the valued activity of watching a favourite programme and the 'filling in' of otherwise unstructured time. These two kinds of viewing remain central to young people's experience of television today, making sense of the otherwise paradoxical observation from our interviews that television is strongly associated with boredom (the time-filling aspect), and yet certain programmes are discussed with great enthusiasm as vital pleasures in the day (soaps or sport, for example) (Livingstone and Bovill, 1999).

As a middle-class 15 year old explains, 'if you're with your friends you probably wouldn't bother with TV, you'd want to go out and do something because, just TV's something you watch if you're, well unless it's like a cliff hanger and you want to know what happens, when you're bored and you've nothing else to do'. In other words, although there are times when children positively choose to use the media, there are at least as many times when the media are of primary importance in filling the gaps: as one 9-year-old boy said, television 'just makes the time go faster'. However, if time with friends can include time with media, children often favour the combination, although the freedom children have to visit friends, the portability of media, and the peer-group valuation of media all make a difference.

Children's complaint of boredom is so widespread that one should consider its meaning seriously. Perhaps, in a culture where adults both structure children's time and judge the worth of children's activities according to adult criteria of educational value and future investment, the refrain 'it's boring' does indeed represent the resistance to adult values and decisions that parents often experience it to be. 'Boring' is also used for activities valued by adults which children perceive as difficult, in other words where the effort demanded of the child does not match the value they themselves perceive it to be worth: reading a book is an obvious case, but a variety of IT-related skills are similarly rejected by children as 'boring'. As we saw earlier in relation to the activities engaged in 'on a boring day', the media are simultaneously 'boring' (i.e. used on a boring day) and 'essential' (in order to allay boredom). This is not to say that media are really seen as boring but that they are the most readily available resource to combat boredom, and so are firmly associated with the risk of boredom in children's minds, as illustrated by this quotation:

> I really, really like watching my television and if I didn't have my television, especially in the mornings and at the weekends before I got up I would be really bored ... it wakes me up.
>
> (11-year-old girl living in a middle-class family)

Computers are rarely talked of with this kind of ambivalence, as both boring and yet essential, thus indicating that they are far from taken for granted. Rather they are at present both highly desirable and yet rather dispensable.

Daily Routines and Media Schedules

Established media are inextricably part of our everyday routines, but new media have to find a place in our everyday lives: the notion of routine – explored in Chapter 2 – discriminates 'old' and 'new' media, for the latter are precisely outside existing routines and need to be, somehow, fitted in – or not. A contextualist position stresses that disposable leisure time – and within that, media time – for young people consists of whatever is left over once school, sleep, homework and organised activities with or arranged by parents have all taken their bite out of the day. Although the explicit account of their leisure time offered by children is that these activities structure their day and the media fill up the gaps, this underestimates the structuring role that the media actually play in their everyday lives. For not only are these activities regular, but so too is media use. Indeed, perhaps the most significant aspect of the modern media is their taken-for-granted, and hence often invisible, role in constructing the daily routines of family life. Too often the media are thought of within a discourse of choice, and it is indeed the case that, in principle, families face many choices for their media and leisure time. But these choices are rarely remade anew every day in practice. Rather, they are allowed to fall into a pattern that offers familiarity as well as practicability, obviating the need for continual decision-making. Given the legitimacy of past practice within the household and often shared across a community of peers, these practices rapidly become not only habitual but also 'normal', at which point the 'lifestyle choices' (or the constraints) which led to them are themselves no longer particularly visible. Bryce (1987) has argued that these 'choices' reflect the implicit structure of family time more generally. From her ethnographic research she contrasts the Andrews family, who adopt a 'clock' orientation for both media and family time, to the 'polychronic time' of the Brady family, for whom activities flowed one into another. Hence, 'rather than activities forming the frame and television the filler, as in the Andrews family, [for the Bradys'] television was itself the frame and other activities were temporally oriented around it' (1987: 126).

Certainly, in children's accounts of their leisure time, the external constraints (the school day, bedtime, etc.) and the media choices (favourite programmes and preferences) are inextricably tied together.

> Well, after school we've got like a routine in our house. We watch *California Dreams* then.
>
> (12-year-old boy living in a working-class family)
>
> Or music – when I'm getting dressed in the morning I put it on and then I go to school.
>
> (12-year-old girl living in a middle-class family)

This construction of routines is negotiated between children and parents, and the stories from parents (of control) and from children (of evasion) may not always coincide:

> Of a morning I always allow them to watch half an hour of TV when they sit in the living room and eat their breakfast. But if they are going to start messing me around and I feel that they are watching too much telly and not eating breakfast then off goes the telly until they are washed and dressed and everything is in place. Then they can have the TV back on.
>
> (Middle-class mother of a 7-year-old boy)
>
> It's because it's [computer] got games on it and everything, so I can play them without my dad having to sneak in and tell me not to play it. Like, it is in my downstairs hall, so I play it when they're not in, or sometimes when they're in bed or something in the morning.
>
> (12-year-old boy living in a middle-class family)

Nowhere are these routines, and their difficulties, more evident than in discussions of bedtime, a notion that our European study suggests is a very British preoccupation (Bovill and Livingstone, 2001). Most simply, the day ends at bedtime. Yet as parents and children are well aware, bedtime is a socially constructed and hence negotiable convention, established perhaps in accordance with how the parents were governed as children, or a lay conception of medical advice regarding sleep, or after some trial-and-error learning of what suits individual children. Also influential are the often implicit norms and conventions which specify that staying up late is morally disapproved of, that the obedient child goes early to bed, and so forth. Far from neutral in its values, bedtime is celebrated in nursery rhymes and in such rituals as the bedtime drink, the bedtime story, and the bedtime routine so beloved by child care experts.

Children report (and their parents generally agree) that their weekday bedtime is around 8 pm for the 6–8 year olds, rising to nearly 11 pm for the 15–17 year olds, and around an hour later when there is no school the next day. However, as one mother said to us, 'they officially have a bedtime, but it doesn't always work'.[10] In short, whether children actually go to bed at these times is less certain, but bedtime in Britain is taken to be a key marker of whether the parents are successful in imposing rules on their children, therefore representing a site of struggle between parent and child:

> [Bedtime] varies in the summer. He had three very late nights, well, not late nights in comparison to some of his friends. Last week he managed to stretch it to 10 o'clock. Well I say he managed, I didn't mind him staying up for 10 o'clock, I don't mind him staying up providing he doesn't get silly with it.
>
> (Middle-class mother of a 12-year-old boy)

Often, the television schedules are used to define bedtime:

> When *You've Been Framed* has finished we go to bed on Sunday.
>
> (6-year-old boy living in a working-class family)

> He is allowed to stay up until 8.30 on a Wednesday to watch Rolf Harris. That is the only extension on his bedtime that he has.
>
> (Middle-class mother of a 7-year-old boy)

Once the family routines are established, they are often experienced as inevitable, somehow transferring the automatic features of the technology to its place in children's lives:

> Well if it's a Thursday night I have to watch 999.
>
> (7-year-old boy living in a middle-class family)

I've got to watch or listen to my music. Even if I have dinner I wear my headphones.

(15-year-old boy living in a working-class family)

As soon as I wake up in the morning it [the radio] automatically turns itself on and whenever I am in my bedroom I sort of switch it on and listen to it.

(15-year-old boy living in a working-class family)

The children watch, you know, they have like, *Alvin and the Chipmunks* every morning, that is a must before they go to school.

(Working-class mother of a 10-year-old boy)

While all media play a role in filling gaps in the timetable or in alleviating boredom, television plays a particular role in structuring the day, as is apparent in the above quotations. This may partly explain why, when we asked children and young people in the YPNM survey which of a long list of media they would miss most, nearly half chose television (45%), followed a long way behind by music (13%), TV-linked games machine (8%) and telephone (7%).

In charting the history of the television schedules, Scannell (1988: 25) argued that 'the pattern of output is carefully arranged to match what is known of the daily working, domestic and leisure patterns of the population'. This itself represents a change from the early days of broadcasting, for as Scannell shows, broadcasters began by attempting to make viewing selective, occasional, and concentrated, but subsequently gave up this attempt in recognition of how quickly viewing became established as more or less continuous, casual and often inattentive. Thus broadcasters instead attempted to retain the audience through the use of continuity links rather than spaces between programmes, previews of programmes rather than the assumption that viewers refer systematically to the programme listings, and so forth. Yet one may suggest that television does not merely fill up our time but, like the clock, it structures the day's media use just as school or work structures other parts of the day. And in so doing, the television schedules have instigated a significant restructuring of family routines. For, as Scannell points out, television schedules play a key role in marking the difference between weekdays and weekends and between ordinary days and special occasions, while on a daily basis breakfast television defines breakfast time, daytime programming accompanies the daily tasks of 'the housewife', Children's Hour sets bounds on the period when children may reasonably dominate the living room, the 9 pm 'watershed' indicates the approved bedtime for small children, and so forth.[11]

It is not easy to determine whether the schedules are fitted to the rhythms of family life or, conversely, whether they dictate the nature of these daily rhythms. It is noteworthy, for example, that children rarely watched television before school in the days before breakfast television and morning cartoons, whereas since the advent of such broadcasting, breakfast viewing has become commonplace, often accompanying or even supplanting the meal after which it is named. This account of breakfast time, from a group of 13–14-year-old girls, holds few surprises:

Chloe:	And headphones while I'm eating my breakfast because my mum don't like it loud.
Rosanne:	I don't have breakfast, I don't eat breakfast. I don't have time.
Interviewer:	Right, does anyone watch TV in the morning?
Grace:	Yes, sometimes, the *Big Breakfast*.
Amy:	Yes, or sometimes MTV in the morning.

Doubtless the schedules are still co-evolving with contemporary lifestyles, and the diversification in the present and future audiovisual environment hints at yet further diversification in household routines. Notably, the new media offer a flexibility that undermines the structuring role of traditional terrestrial television. In response to the time shifting offered by the VCR and the cable or satellite channels which offer news, or cartoons, or music, at any hour, terrestrial television also has extended its broadcasting hours. One outcome is the spread of viewing across the day. For example, while the period after school has been defined as children's leisure time since broadcasting began, increasingly the period before school, and later into the evening, is becoming incorporated into children's television day, as morning television, multichannel options and, particularly, multi-set homes, become common. Thus, by contrast with the early days of television, the YPNM diary[12] suggests that about 20% of children and young people watch television or video in the morning and about 30–40% are watching at any one half-hour time period after school and into the evening. While viewing is greatest in the afternoon and evening (this extending later for older teens), there is an early peak in the mornings on school days and a slightly later morning peak at the weekend.

For many families, then, television is built into the structure of the day from early morning to late at night. This structure is generally established by parents rather than children. The YPNM survey shows that one-fifth of 6–17 year olds wake up to find television already on, for one-third it is on when they come home from school and nearly two-thirds say it is still on when they go to bed (see Table 3.6). This is particularly likely to be the case when children are younger and when they live in a working-class household. Having siblings, and having a

Table 3.6 *Percentage of children saying that television is usually on at different times of day (N = c. 1230)*

TV is 'usually on' when the child ...	All	Age				Social grade	
		6–8	9–11	12–14	15–17	ABC1	C2DE
Wakes up	21	21	24	19	18	16	24
Gets home from school	35	32	34	42	32	27	42
Goes to bed	62	67	70	63	50	58	66

Note: Both age and social grade differences are statistically significant for each row variable.

Source: Livingstone and Bovill, 1999.

mother not in paid work, is also associated with living in a television environment.[13]

Other than television, most media are, or are treated as if they are, free of scheduling or time-based rules of use; thus they may be inserted into routines with relatively few constraints. After all, nothing about the technology dictates that the radio should be so heavily used in the morning, but it is then that its portability and its provision of continual music, makes it fit in well with other, visually demanding, activities. Even the cinema shows the same film every day for weeks, allowing some flexibility. And print has always come with few time dictates beyond the daily or weekly incidence of newspapers and magazines. But books, computer games and, to a large degree, the Internet can be used at any time of day or night, as the user wishes. Only in relation to television – the medium that has constituted the heart of the home, family, nation even – do we see this struggle over scheduling versus user-flexibility.

This is not to say that other media are used randomly across the day, of course, but that their use patterns are fitted to the structures of everyday life, rather than vice versa. In this sense, the media support the individualisation of family timetables. Here two mothers comment on their family's daily routines:

> I've got a clock radio that comes on in the morning, and usually Rose's got something entirely different on, and then when I come downstairs there's something different on in the kitchen as well.

> I usually come in at about 3.30 and watch some television, and if they are not here in the afternoon I might watch a film sometimes. Jamie likes his tea fairly early but Harry doesn't come home until about 7, so most of the evening is spent cooking and washing up.

And here a 15-year-old girl concurs:

> We normally basically all just do our own thing in the mornings. We all get our own breakfast and we each go our own way, shower and off out.

The YPNM diary shows that on weekdays, computer games are hardly played in the morning or late evening, and the main peak is from 4–7 pm, although, as with television, the after-school peak is strongest for the youngest group, while playing is more spread out for the older groups. Unlike computer games, music is often a secondary activity, and this can be seen in the observation that it is listened to across the day, from early morning through to late in the evening. Reading is particularly concentrated at bedtime, with the peak around 9 pm being most marked for 9–10 year olds, and more spread across the evening for older children. That the weekends have no structure common to the population is shown by the sporadic occurrence of reading, computer game-playing, and other media uses across the whole day. Doubtless this depends on a myriad of individual circumstances, but it also demonstrates overall the ready availability of the media to fill gaps when they arise.

Perhaps in avoidance of this attempt to schedule everyday life, and perhaps merely because television is a gap-filler, television is often talked of as 'just' a medium rather than in relation to its particular contents. In contrast to the notion of scheduling as a kind of technology of control, as conceptualised in the audience measurement industry (Barwise and Ehrenberg, 1988), it is often 'telly' which is valued as appropriate to certain times, moods or normative conceptions of 'the day'. Listen to these descriptions of the after-school period:

I usually just come in, watch telly, tidy my bedroom some nights, get a bath, sit down and watch telly more.

(10-year-old boy living in a working-class family)

So what they do first is that they go to their room and make sure their room is tidy. Then they come downstairs and watch some telly, and then they have their tea and then they watch some more telly and then they either stay in or they go out.

(Working-class mother of a 9-year-old girl)

Given that everyday life is structured by a multiplicity of factors which are predominantly unrelated to the media – the requirements of school, of parents' work, of domestic tasks and non-media leisure – the impression given of television as a 'drop in' medium makes sense. Other media fill various time zones, playing a greater or lesser role in young people's leisure depending on the time of day. Music is for the morning, television is for after school, reading is for bedtime. Looking back over the twentieth century, then, we might see the flexible, time-free nature of most media as the norm and the attempt of television in the second half of the century to structure people's lives as an influential but only temporary experiment, characteristic of the relatively normative, national culture of that period (Coontz, 1997). Whether media-derived or freely chosen, the origins of daily routines are for most people near impossible to reconstruct. Nonetheless, such routines establish meaning in young people's lives, provisding a means of structuring leisure time and a context for conducting social relations with family and friends. Children are attached to 'their' routines: they retell them in great detail, knowing that they thereby tell us about themselves.

INDIVIDUALISED LIFESTYLES

This chapter has explored the meaning of leisure time for young people, locating time spent on media in the broader context of everyday routines. While parents are concerned with spending time 'well' and with arranging the leisure timetable so as not to 'waste' time, their children are concerned to find free, unstructured time for play, for friends and for media, employing various tactics of evasion to achieve this. At the same time, they are strongly motivated to avoid boredom; if bored, again they turn to the media. Far from neutral in their time-filling role, the media are both integral to daily routines of domestic life and they also play a role in structuring those routines. Thus children's culture 'emerges in and through the temporal, as well as spatial, interstices of adult social structures' (James et al., 1998: 75).

Much of this is not new, and one should not exaggerate claims for social change. Indeed, while many feel that we are witnessing an information revolution, others are rightly sceptical of the overblown and ill-specified claims about societal changes that may follow technological innovation. If we compare the childhood of today's children with that of their parents, the pace of change appears more equivocal. As we have seen in this chapter, a comparison between the present and past children's leisure in the 1950s shows considerable similarities. Children grow up, watch television, ride their bikes, play football, argue with their parents, go to the cinema, make and break friendships, follow the latest craze, read comics, study hard or become disaffected with school, just as they always did. And, then as now, they would still generally prefer to spend time with their friends than with the media, using the media to fill the boring gaps in their day, and so gaining something in common to discuss with friends or do with parents. While parents and teachers may wish children would read a good book instead, worrying about the content of electronic media and about children's educational prospects, these concerns also have changed little in half a century. But today more than ever before, the media cannot be contained in distinct times and places. Rather, time at home, chatting with friends, eating with the family, being alone in one's bedroom, all these and other ordinary activities involve a central engagement with the media.

This penetration of media into other domains of everyday life does not necessarily imply the homogenisation of ordinary culture. For, in parallel with the temporal and spatial spread of the media, we see the diversification of the media away from its once-dominant form shared across the nation. In several respects, we are now witnessing a diversification of lifestyles strongly facilitated by a diversification in the forms of media and media contents available. The media are less able to dictate the temporal structure of the day, they contribute in more varied ways to the leisure mix, and they provide the resources for diverse, perhaps even fragmented, forms of identification. This partly reflects changes in the media themselves, both quantitative (more media goods, more channels, etc.) and qualitative (a shift from national mass broadcasting to a diversity of more specialised, selective, global and interactive forms of media) (Becker and Schoenbach, 1989). Thus developments in new technology play an increasingly significant role, marking high status activities, mediating valued identities, and facilitating the integration or interpenetration of leisure and work, education and entertainment, community and home. But these are also broader historical shifts, reflecting the changing character of the leisure environment (as discussed in this chapter) and a wider cultural shift in the relations between public culture and private leisure (Chapter 4) and in the composition and life course of the family (Chapter 5).

The individualisation thesis proposes that traditional social distinctions, particularly social class, but also gender, ethnicity, region, etc., are declining as determinants of the life trajectory of young people, resulting in a concomitant fragmentation or undermining of those traditional norms and values which hitherto defined how people live their lives.[14] Thus 'traditional means of young people's socialisation, such as family, school and community, are seen as becoming much weaker and the influence of peers and media much stronger' (Hill and Tisdall, 1997: 114). 'Socialisation' is a term now little used in contemporary studies of childhood and youth, because of its heavily normative, functionalist tradition of use, implying a single, linear, path towards a socially approved conception of maturity.[15] But the importance of family, peers, community and, increasingly, the media in brokering the relation between social structure and identity formation remains firmly on the academic agenda (Hall, 1996; Shotter and Gergen, 1988). Given the changing structure of family life, the decline in religious and regional traditions, and the loss of an expected job or career for life (see Chapter 5), young people are engaged in a struggle to establish their own independent biography:

> Every child is increasingly expected to behave in an 'individualised way' ... children must somehow orient themselves to an *anticipated* life course. The more childhood in the family is eclipsed by influences and orientation patterns from outside the family ... the more independent the opportunity (and drive) to making up one's own mind, making one's own choice ... described here as the *biographization* of the life course. ... Examples of such areas of independence might include deciding individually what to buy, planning and managing space and time, the selection and shaping of 'leisure careers', determining media consumption patterns, displaying personal tastes, or choosing appropriate modes of communication and social activities. (Buchner, 1990: 77–8)

Whether, as Adorno and Horkheimer (1977: 383) witheringly pointed out half a century ago, these lifestyles are merely 'the freedom to choose what is always the same' remains a moot point. But undoubtedly, choice, specialisation, diversification and individuality are key to young people's own conception of their leisure and engagement with media, as well as to the forms of address which structure 'their' media.

One consequence is that researchers and policy-makers can no longer presume a knowledge of media use from a knowledge of socio-structural positioning (Reimer, 1995). Rather, the task becomes one of tracing the diversity of individualised patterns within which identities are constructed, practices are routinised and contexts of sociality sustained. In her study of the meaning of domestic possessions, Rochberg-Halton (1984: 349) concluded that, 'when the question of *having* is shifted to that of *meaning*, many class differences collapse'. Just as everyone values their old photos, their favourite records, and their childhood teddy bear, so too do demographic differences collapse when it comes to media contents. While socio-economic status in particular is becoming less important (though remaining far from unimportant), more individualised factors – such as lifestyle choices, parental experience with computers, attitudes towards education, etc. – are of increasing importance.

Individualisation refers to a continuing process rather than a radical break with tradition. In many ways, young people's lives remain heavily circumscribed by long-standing social inequalities – ICT adoption patterns reveal a perpetuation of unequal social stratification (see Chapter 2); their participation in formal activities depends on parental expectations, finances and ambitions, and these too, as we have seen in this chapter, vary systematically according to the age and gender of the child as well as the socio-economic status of the household. However, the language of individualisation, and its associated stress on 'lifestyle', allows recognition of the ways in which the meanings and practices of everyday life are underdetermined by traditional socio-structural determinants. In his characterisation of the key features of the concept of lifestyle, Chaney points to the space opened up through this underdetermination, within which the interpretative and reflexive resources of culture – and the people who enact the practices of culture – can act. As he elaborates (Chaney, 1996: 11–12):

- 'Lifestyles, as patterns of action and as a distinct type of social group-ing, are embedded in the social order of modernity.'
- 'They work as a set of expectations which act as a form of ordered control on the emerging social uncertainties of mass society.'
- '[They are] ... patterns of ways of living that flesh out the general contours of class structured distinction.'
- 'People use lifestyles in everyday life to identify and explain wider complexes of identity and affiliation.'
- 'They are part of the practical vocabularies of everyday life ... inter-pretative resources – forms of local knowledge that are necessarily approximate but nonetheless significant in the politics of mass society.'

His conception of lifestyle as both a means of social control and a resource for symbolic action captures the ambivalence of many com-mentators when analysing the role of the media in constructing lifestyles. For example, Kinder (1999: 19) argues that 'kids' media culture' is cru-cial to the politics of everyday life thus:

> Popular texts and the conflicting discourses around them contribute to children's growing understanding of themselves as gendered, raced, socially connected members of a network of linked communities, and to their emerg-ing perception of their own position and potential empowerment within a changing global public sphere.

Yet she also stresses that not all children respond in the same way to the media. Indeed, as many audience reception studies have shown, the dis-cursive and concrete contexts of reception crucially mediate the mean-ings derived from the media (Livingstone, 1998b). As people construct lifestyles – and media preferences and interpretations as a key compo-nent of these – to identify and explain their social relations and sense of self, this complicates and in some ways undermines or re-frames the 'forms of ordered control' attempted by the mass media.[16] Crucially, in so far as the effect of this complicating process is in the direction of diversification – of preferences, interpretations, identities – it is this effect which the media industry, in attempting to manage and exploit 'kids' culture', is now chasing.

In other words, to the extent that, traditionally, media preferences and tastes were successfully addressed by the media industry, this was precisely because they were significantly constructed by that industry as mass tastes stratified by social class in a predictable manner. However, as changes in family composition, workplace structures and social movements impinge on the cultural tastes and practices of the population, the economics of the mass market are giving way to that of multiple diversified markets, markets which in many ways appear to follow – as much as subsequently formalise and represent – the emerging patterns of ways of living. If once local reception contexts were the main source of diversification introduced into an otherwise monolithic media culture, increasingly that media culture is itself diversifying. However, to finance this shift from a mass to a diversified address for children's media culture, given that the child market has always been regarded as a minority market of doubtful, if growing, economic importance, the child and youth market has been in the vanguard of media globalisation. For ironically, while popular fears regarding 'kids' culture' have stressed the homogenising effect of commercialisation,[17] the strategy proving more commercially effective today is to capitalise upon the process of individualisation.[18] But only on a transnational scale can there be a viable commercial basis for the many distinctions which today characterise mass-mediated youth culture. This in turn further detaches young people from the traditions of their parents, their class, their locale. For example, Flichy notes how the development of music in the mid-1950s, with its specific appeal to young people everywhere, irrespective of social class, undermined the family listening situation of early popular music, thereby contributing to 'the emergence of adolescence as an autonomous age-group, in conflict with the adult world' (Flichy, 1995: 163).

Let us not overstate the case, however. As we have seen in this chapter, specialisation is central particularly to teenagers' media lifestyles, yet the particular specialisations observed are still related to traditional socio-economic distinctions – book lovers and PC fans are more often middle class, music fans are more often working class. Moreover, while young people say little about social class or, unless explicitly asked, ethnicity, they are explicit about the symbolic importance of age, gender and generation in defining their media tastes. The evidence for media tastes as both globalised and individualised is stronger in relation to content preferences within the range offered by particular media – whether music tastes, favourite television programmes, or styles of Internet use – rather than for the ways in which different media are themselves combined, this still depending significantly on differential cultures of access across households. Music appears most thoroughly globalised, while the struggle between national public service-oriented versus global commercial television channels, especially for children, continues (Blumler, 1992). These content offers, and preferences, should not be understood simply in terms of homogenisation or fragmentation, for while individualisation undermines traditional forms of cultural expression, it also opens up the possibility for alternative forms. Hence Ziehe (1994: 2) argues that lifestyles are not reducible to consumer styles or individual expression, but rather they are 'collective ways of life ... [which] point to common orientations of taste and interpretations; they demonstrate a certain group-specific succinctness of usage of signs'. In this way they constitute 'environments', 'representational worlds of symbols' within which social action takes place.

Comparing the 1950s with the 1980s, Ziehe sketches out the historical changes which are leading society towards 'an increasing orientation towards questions of life style' (1994: 2). The new consumer opportunities of post-war Western societies were conceived in terms of living standards. For the first time, new goods became available and affordable for the mass market, while the bourgeois middle class cultivated a culture of asceticism, disapproving of the extravagance of the new consumerism, itself often construed as Americanisation. He characterises this ambivalence thus:

> The power of the fascination with new consumerist opportunities is opposed by deeply rooted behavioural and judgmental values that immediately detract from uncensored enjoyment. The offers to the consumer do not yet have the character of freely moving signs but are, at first, sited within social hierarchies. (Ziehe, 1994: 4)

For Ziehe, this ambivalence between desire and fear, stemming in part from the recent conditions of war-time and post-war austerity and danger, crystallised in the emerging discourse surrounding youth, thereby encoding cultural change in terms of generational conflict: 'adolescents were subjected to a fresh-air semantic, which prescribed cold showers and a clean thinking mind ... one transgression and a daughter was in danger of "ending up in the gutter"' (Ziehe, 1994: 5). But from his discussion of the importance of rock and roll (and the record player) for youth culture it is clear that he also sees the media as crystallising these concerns. By the late 1960s to early 1970s, Ziehe sees youth culture as offering young people independence from their parents through a new semantic of naturalness, openness and informality. In Giddens' terms (1991), dramatic new opportunities and dangers were central to everyday lifestyles, offering new consumer goods, new aesthetics, American connections, popular pleasures, and so forth, and if the dangers were less clear in practice, moral disapproval and anxiety made up for that.[19]

Ziehe (1994: 11–12) characterises lifestyle in terms of three formal components:

- self-attention, a subjective disposition which 'raises the question – even outside privileged life situations – of a successful life as an everyday expectation';
- stylisation, in which 'objects, situations and actions are placed into a coherent sign arrangement and "presented"';
- reflexivity, whereby 'life styles are an expression of an orientation pressure which has turned inwards. The new questions are "what do I actually want?" and "what matters to me?" [resulting in] an everyday semantic of self-observation and self-assessment'.

All this and more is readily evident in young people's talk about the importance of media in their lives – witness their often unrealistic ambitions, their horror of boredom, their enthusiasm for buying, collecting, updating and arranging belongings, and their existential uncertainties and self-absorption. Listen, for example, to Sophie, a working-class 16 year old, discussing the individualising role of music for her peer group:

> I don't like the music in the charts or Indie music, I like the MCs and hardcore rappers and things like that. ... Most of the people I like don't like it at all, but we all have different tastes in music anyway. ... Well, Gerry is a kind of a classical person, but I think that he gets that off his parents. Julie is into *Oasis* and things like that and Emma likes people like *Manic Street Preachers* and other stuff I suppose (laughs). ... They try and listen to what I like and I try and listen to what they like but, erm, sometimes it just gets a bit too much (laughs).

Similarly, Kathy, a middle-class 15 year old, stresses the importance of a music collection which is not only repudiated by her mother, but which also differentiates her from her friends:

> Well, I suppose me and my friend really got into music when we were about 12 or 13 and most of my music now is unheard of and people say 'who?' and I think 'yes! It is someone that they haven't heard of!'. And I buy quite a lot of tapes and have got nearly 200, that has been collected over the last couple of years. ... Well we have a stereo at school, but it is usually a lot of stuff that I don't like. It is on all the time when I do my homework, my mum can't understand how I can listen to music when I am doing my homework. When my friends come around we usually have it on in the background somewhere and one of my friends is really into music with me says 'Oh wow, you have got to hear this band' and my other friends don't really appreciate them. And

> I go to quite a lot of gigs and stuff. I have been to a couple of the large festivals and stuff like that really. ... I like a band because their music is good and they can play their instruments, they are not there just because they are good looking.

Kathy goes on to make the explicit link between a preference for 'anything that is not ordinary' and music with which 'I suppose that I can really be myself, sort of thing'. This link between a media preference and both social and personal identity is made more commonly, and more readily, for music than it is for other media. Thus music, and perhaps also sport, appears especially effective in facilitating the process of individualisation, for both allow for the expression of many fine distinctions according to different lifestyles, subcultures and personal preferences.

Both Sophie and Kathy illustrate a key mode of engagement with media among young people, one which provides a rationale for the particular uses they make of the different media available to them, namely being a fan. For many young people, fandom is the 'glue' which connects personal identity, social and peer relations, and taste preferences within a media-rich environment (Jenkins, 1992). It also provides a familiar frame with which to approach new media. Notably, as young people gain access to the Internet, it is their fandom – for Manchester United, or Boyzone, or *The Little Mermaid* – which determines the favourite web sites, the successful search terms, the most common uses of this new resource (Livingstone, 2001a). Crucially, fandom is intertextual, operating through the cross-referencing of content themes according to a common interest, and transtextual, interrelating diverse media and non-media leisure activities (Drotner, 2000; Kinder, 1999). Sports fans play football, watch their team play, watch football on the television, buy the associated clothing and bedroom décor, and visit football web sites. Being a music fan often involves playing, attending and listening to popular music. Disney fans follow their chosen theme or character through cinema, television show, comic books and collectable toys. And so forth. To be sure, media producers promote fandom, in order to maximise profits, by widening the promotional mix – marketing across video games, television cartoons, competitions, films and videos, comics, the toy industry and children's goods from bedclothes to school bags. But this also:

> ... helps to surround the child with a coherent environment of signs. Surrounded by multimedia, children have no difficulty in shifting from one medium to another. While adults see the multimediatization of cultural firms such as Nintendo, Disney and other American majors as harmful (it enables these firms to market a wide range of products derived from a film or

videogame), children find the recurrence of signs reassuring in their attempts to organise their environment.[20]

In sum, it has been argued that childhood and youth is a key period for the construction of the self, as young people make the transition from their family of origin towards the wider peer culture. Notably, as traditional structures which confer identity, at all levels from the family to the nation state, are being undermined, others are actively sought by young people, and these are readily addressed by the market. The integration of individualisation and consumerism is also an increasingly globally structured process, transcending national boundaries. This makes for a heady context within which young people seek to construct a meaningful life project that is more or less shared with their peers, conceived locally and globally, enacted both face to face and electronically mediated. Against this context of new opportunities, a more critical analysis stresses the transformation of leisure culture into promotional culture. Thus, as modern marketing directs flows of popular culture, identity is refashioned through consumption and the citizen (or viewer) is transformed into the consumer. However, whether conceived optimistically or critically, the media provide much of the content that mediates children and young people's insertion into social networks, both traditional and new.

NOTES

1 See Adam (1995) for an insightful account of how, notwithstanding some interesting exceptions and evasions, the 'clock time' of modernity controls, commodifies and colonises everyday life.

2 Yet the trend in viewing figures ever since the introduction of television gives pause for thought. Viewing time for the television-owning population rose rapidly to one and a half hours in 1955 and nearly two hours by 1963. As Himmelweit et al. (1958) showed, figures for children were similar: in 1958 they found children (aged 10–11 and 13–14) watched 11–13 hours per week on average (i.e. just under 2 hours per day). As figures today average two and a half hours, any displacement of other activities would have occurred during the 1950s and 1960s, when television viewing first became both popular and familiar, with rather less additional time to be accounted for by the rise in viewing time in more recent years.

3   These have been usefully reviewed by S.B. Neuman (1991); see also Lin (1988) and van der Voort (1991).

4   Any longitudinal comparisons across studies must be interpreted with caution, as differences in methods, samples and analysis are not always apparent. Moreover, apparent displacement effects are often temporary: as Himmelweit et al. (1958) and others have shown, while the initial impact of introducing television was to reduce time spent on certain leisure activities, this returned to the previous level after the novelty wore off.

5   On the other hand, it was the case in the YPNM project that, particularly for 9–11-year-old girls, getting cable or satellite television was associated with a considerable increase in time spent watching television, suggesting that this group has not been well served by the standard terrestrial diet.

6   Contextualising new media use in relation to other media and leisure activities surely serves to diffuse public anxieties about addicted or isolated children. In the YPNM project we found only a tiny minority of children (1%) spending a worrying proportion of their leisure time with television and computer games.

7   See Johnsson-Smaragdi (2001), for a pan-European demonstration of these and related data, and Roberts et al. (1999) for similar American data.

8   For an account of the theory of uses and gratifications, and associated debates, see Blumler and Katz (1974), McQuail et al. (1972) and Rosengren et al. (1985).

9   This is especially the case for mothers who work full-time outside the home, these being twice as likely to be concerned about having enough time to spend with their children (Livingstone and Bovill, 1999).

10 In the new multi-set household the adherence to bedtime has some curious consequences, as evident in one interview with an 11-year-old girl, who shares her favourite programme with her mother but who watches it upstairs in her bedroom while her mother watches it in the living room, it being broadcast after her bedtime.

11 See Oswell (1998a, 1999), Buckingham et al. (1999).

12 Part of the YPNM project obtained completed weekly diaries from 358 children and young people aged 9–10, 12–13 and 15–17. In this diary they recorded the time they spent on each of ten activities at half-hour intervals through the day, thus providing a typical time profile for each medium, as well as a picture of how different groups of children and

young people use different media according to the day of the week and the time of day (Livingstone and Bovill, 1999).

13 Roberts et al. (1999) term these 'constant television households'.

14 See, for example, the writings of Beck (1992), Giddens (1993), Meyrowitz (1985), Reimer (1995) and Ziehe (1994). More critical positions regarding the individualisation of youth culture are developed in Lieberg (1995) and Pollock (1997).

15 See the discussion of the social meaning of age in Chapter 5.

16 For Reimer (1997) the concept of lifestyle – understood as multidimensional and as located in historically contingent cultural contexts – offers the theoretical link needed in audience studies between macro-level analyses of social structures and micro-level ethnographic analyses of reception contexts (see Livingstone, 1998c).

17 This homogenising effect may be problematic in its consequences. For example, Kinder argues that, as boys appear more reluctant to watch girls' programmes, and older children to watch younger children's programmes, than vice versa, global marketers favour broadcasting programmes designed for older boys – notwithstanding that these tend to be the most action-oriented and aggressive in content – so as to maximise audience size.

18 Of course, popular fears have since attached themselves also to an individualised media culture, linking the personalisation of 'me-TV' to the selfishness of the 'me-generation'.

19 Ziehe (1994: 6) quotes German rock musician Udo Lindenberg who said: 'Before Elvis we were told that we were too young for that. After Elvis we could retort: you are too old for that.'

20 Quoted in LaFrance (1996: 313); see also Kline (1993).

4

THE MEDIA-RICH HOME:
BALANCING PUBLIC AND
PRIVATE LIVES

PUBLIC AND PRIVATE LEISURE SPACES

Thus far I have discussed the domestic diffusion and appropriation of new media in the context of competing leisure alternatives. I now focus on how 'the home' is itself changing as a context for family life and media use. At the turn of the twenty-first century, 'the home is now commonly accepted as providing personal fulfilment and satisfaction as well as the means of recuperating from the pressures of the working day' (Allan, 1985: 57). However, it was not always thus. Segalen (1996) argues that the model of the single family home emerged first in the middle classes, especially in the early twentieth century, with a strict separation of public and private spheres: 'home sweet home ... is the household interior, an over-decorated and embellished space held in the highest value' (Segalen, 1996: 400). 'Home making' was of course the woman's realm and the focus of much of her energy as well as of much of the advice directed at her. As a refuge from the world, and a centre of proper values, home represents the source of love, morality, freedom and happiness for those who have also to go out into the world (Putnam, 1990).

In the second half of the twentieth century, with the growing significance of domestic mass media, two distinct trends regarding the home can be identified, both concerning the privatisation of leisure and, more recently, of learning also. These trends help us to understand the considerable differences between childhood in the 1950s, when television arrived, and childhood at the turn of the twenty-first century, when the computer made similar inroads into the home. The first may be characterised as the changing significance of 'the front door', i.e. the boundary between the home and outside. The second trend pursues this spatial focus by considering the growing significance of 'the bedroom door', i.e. the boundary between the living room and the bedroom. If the first raises questions of the relation between the public community and the privacy of the family, the second raises concerns of the balance being struck between communal family life and the private life of the child.

To take the first trend first, it appears that a continued shift from children's leisure time spent outside (in the streets, woods or countryside) to that spent primarily at home is contributing to changing cultural conceptions of childhood over the past half century. Certainly, when we interviewed parents about their own childhoods, the dominant image was neither that of a media-rich nor a media-poor home, but rather that of a carefree childhood spent out of doors. Idealised though this doubtless is, it is important to recognise that, as Hill and Tisdall (1997: 93) observe, 'adults seek to impose or negotiate rules and limits, adjusted over time, aimed at reconciling children's freedom and security. ... The nature of the local environment and the availability of formal recreational services, ranging from parks to clubs, crucially affect how children negotiate their relationships and use of space outside the home'. The point too easily overlooked is that these factors are just as significant in affecting how children negotiate their relationships and use of space inside the home also. From a historical perspective, Cunningham (1995: 179) sees the two as interconnected, noting that, especially for working-class families, there has been a 'shift from a life focused on the street to one focused on the home. ... [Moreover] this was accompanied by a change in the social organisation of the home. Parents, and in particular fathers, became less remote and authoritarian, less the centre of attention when they were present.'

From a media-centred perspective, the second trend rests significantly on the continual multiplication of media goods at home, for this can be seen to be fostering a shift in media use from that best characterised by the notion of 'family television' to one of individualised media lifestyles and, particularly for children and young people, of 'bedroom culture'. Notably, in the middle of the twentieth century, when television was first introduced it was placed proudly in the living room, with household members having to negotiate with each other how to use it. A key feature of today's domestic environment is the multiplication of goods, many of them increasingly owned by individuals rather than 'the household'. This multiplication of media in the home has little to do with technological innovation. Yet for the household the sheer multiplication of media is proving significant in social terms. The structuring of leisure spaces has altered, and domestic media are coming to play an ever more central role in these changes.

Focusing in on the home, then, we may observe that while in some ways the personal computer today is entering the home in a similar fashion to the television before it, there is a major difference. For the decision is no longer whether to have a video recorder, or a hi-fi system, but rather how many to have and where to locate them in the home. The single computer household, one may speculate, is similarly historically temporary. Having more than one computer at home, which may now seem as extravagant or unnecessary as the multiple television sets that appeared several decades ago, is already becoming commonplace among wealthier households. This *multiplication* of domestic media goods is facilitated by the reduction in price for media goods, by the growth of mobile media (e.g. mobile phone, walkman), by the continual process of innovation in the design and marketing of existing technologies, and by the *diversification* of media forms (which encourages the multiplication of goods through upgrading and recycling existing technologies through the household). As a result, children increasingly have their own television, video, computer, radio, and so forth, as we have seen.

In short, for many young people, a media-rich home is taken for granted. Certainly most children today grow up in homes which can be termed 'media-rich' by the standards of their parents' childhood. This has reached the point where children even lose track of their possessions. Thus one 6-year-old boy told us, 'I've got two computers in the house, I've got Sega, and a Nintendo. No, I've got three, Sega, Supernintendo and the normal Nintendo.' In another family, the children disagreed about the number of television sets they possessed, although they were clear that every room in the house contained a set:

Interviewer: Right, so how many televisions have you got in this house?
Sam: Millions!
Interviewer: Millions? (Laughs) Is that one over there, hiding in that cupboard?
Sam: Yes. One, two, three (pause). We have got about eleven or twelve.
Matthew: It's about nine isn't it? ... Well, most of them are quite old ones but we have got a new one in there and that is a new one as well.

(Middle-class boys aged 10, 13 and 14)

The two themes addressed in this chapter are linked, for both deal with the boundary between public and private. Specifically, as interviews with parents make clear, the creation of a media-rich home tends to be justified by parents in relation to the first theme, the decline of street or public culture, as they stress the supposed benefits that a media-rich home brings to the children in terms of both safety (as outside space is increasingly seen as dangerous) and education (as media use at home is increasingly construed as influential in supporting the role of the school), as well as simply being valued for enhancing leisure. However, given that much leisure time is spent at home, while tastes and interests differ across family members (see next chapter), there are also many practical advantages to the multiplication of media goods, and both children and adults often wish to use media uninterrupted by family members, as we shall see.

While the present attempt to contextualise children and young people's media use within the spatial arrangements of their daily lives is thus consonant with the ways in which social historical accounts agree that the twentieth century has seen a radical shift in children's space, the strength of the YPNM project lies in tracking the practices of everyday life which together constitute the basis for these larger trends. These micro-level practical and discursive factors may appear trivial. Yet the present exploration of this shift towards home-based leisure in general, and media use in particular, is also, necessarily, an exploration of how young people's leisure activities serve to connect, or separate, spaces inside and outside the home. For example, the traditional alignment of inside and outside with feminine and masculine is altered when boys stay home to play computer games. So too is the familiar association of home with entertainment and school or work with learning altered when mothers take up teleworking and children study using the Internet at home.

The Decline of Street Culture

Joanna: There's nothing to do really ... 'cause they've just gone and closed down [the club].
Debbie: Can't go down there no more.
Sophie: [The club] was a disco.
Joanna: For our age.
Debbie: But there's nothing here now.

(15–16-year-old girls living in a rural area)

We saw in Chapter 3 evidence of a reduction in the unstructured or informal time available to children, suggesting that it is media which now occupy this time. While in that chapter the purpose was to contextualise media use by considering the other, potentially rival, activities in which children and young people engage, it is also important to recognise that these activities vary in terms of the spaces they occupy.

The spaces for young people's leisure activities have changed in meaning over the past half century. James et al. (1998) draw on Beck's (1992) theory of the risk society in noting that parents increasingly identify the world outside the home as a source of risk from which their children must be shielded; by implication, the home is construed as a haven of safety. In a parallel vein, Hill and Tisdall (1997: 194) comment that 'our fears about children's crime in public places exemplify society's requirements for an "indoors child", which will not only keep children but also the public safe'. As one working-class mother commented: 'I think it's got a lot to do with society. In our day it used to be "Watch for the bad man", but now it's "Watch for the bad man, and the bad woman and the bad policeman and the little boys and girls". You cannot trust anybody. It's a horrible thing to say, but you cannot.'

Thus, while parents recall with nostalgia their own childhood freedoms to play, or hang out, out of doors, they are in strong agreement that conditions have changed for their children, so that the large amounts of unstructured time available to them which, in the eyes of children and parents alike, were best spent out of doors, are no longer available for their children. Hence, the mother quoted above went on to tell us that her 9-year-old daughter is 'not much outside during the week, because with the garage being outdoors and it doesn't shut until 6 and there's traffic that's constantly coming and going. … I'm not paranoid. I'm just extra protective when they're outside and most of the time I'm in here and I'm thinking, "All right, what's happening to them?".'

Significantly, when we asked these parents how this compares with the amount of time they spent out of doors when they were her age, their answers echoed those of many parents in drawing a strong contrast:

Mother: I was never in!
Father: Neither was I!
Mother: From 5 o'clock until 8.30 I was off.
Father: Yes and me. As soon as I woke up in the morning I was off.

These kinds of fears are not restricted to families living in urban areas. Parents and children in the most sheltered rural environments were affected by such concerns and reports of harms to children on television and in the newspapers often figured in parents' accounts. Indeed, the YPNM survey shows that only 11% of parents with children aged 6–17 say the streets where they live are 'very safe' for their child, compared with 56% thinking this about the neighbourhood where they were brought up (see Table 4.1). Describing the change the other way around, nearly one-third of parents think the local streets are 'not very safe' for their child, while fewer than 5% thought this had been the case when they were a child. And when asked to 'think about their child and what is affecting his or her life nowadays', parents of children in every age

Table 4.1 *How safe parent thinks the local streets are, by age of child*

	For parent at child's age (N = 969)				For child nowadays (N = 971)			
	6–8 (%)	9–11 (%)	12–14 (%)	15–17 (%)	6–8 (%)	9–11 (%)	12–14 (%)	15–17 (%)
Very safe	51	56	59	59	5	10	13	15
Quite safe	42	38	37	38	53	62	59	59
Not very safe	5	4	3	2	31	21	26	20
Not at all safe	2	2	1	1	11	7	3	6

Source: Livingstone and Bovill, 1999.

Table 4.2 *Parent's views about amount of time spent outdoors unsupervised by self at child's age (N = 942) and by child now (N = 965), by age of child*

	For parent at child's age				For child nowadays			
	6–8 (%)	9–11 (%)	12–14 (%)	15–17 (%)	6–8 (%)	9–11 (%)	12–14 (%)	15–17 (%)
All/most	27	34	37	34	8	12	11	27
More than half	37	32	25	29	17	20	23	21
About half	22	22	26	27	32	35	39	29
Very little	12	11	11	9	32	29	25	23
None of it	3	1	1	1	11	4	2	1

Source: Livingstone and Bovill, 1999.

group identify the availability of illegal drugs and the child being victim of crime among their top three concerns.

British parents' fears are not without foundation. Home Office statistics (1994) on child victims of crime report twice as many cases of gross indecency with a child in 1992 compared with 1983 and a fourfold increase in child abductions. Nonetheless, surveys conducted on both European crime rates and fear of crime show that while in Britain crime rates against children are relatively high, fear of crime is disproportionately high among British parents (Livingstone et al., 1999), suggesting the importance of cultural discourses surrounding childhood over and above the occurrence of actual physical threats.

Unsurprisingly, one-third of parents (31%) say that their child spends 'very little' or 'none' of his/her time outside the home or garden without adults around, while only 12% say this was the case for themselves at their child's age (Table 4.2).

According to their parents, girls, younger children and middle-class children spend comparatively less time playing or 'messing about outside'. The YPNM diary, completed by children, confirms this picture, showing that, when asked about *'messing about or playing outside'*, on weekdays only the 9–10 year olds mess about outside before school, and they are also the most likely to play outside after school, although they come inside by 8 pm. The 12–13 year olds go out a little less, but come in at the same time. The 15–16 year olds mess about outside even less but may stay out till 10 pm. While boys are more likely than girls to mess about outside after school, it is the working-class children who are slightly more likely to stay out later in the evening. On Saturdays, the main time to spend out of doors is across the middle of the day; otherwise the demographic patterns are similar as for weekdays.

In sum, it seems that considerable changes have taken place in recent decades in public perceptions of the dangers of the streets for children. Hill and Tisdall (1997: 12) worry that 'children are marginalised in adult thinking and actions, resulting in major restrictions on children's access to attention, places and resources. This marginalisation is often justified by children's need for protection, but can also be paternalistic in its effects.' Ennew (1994) goes further, arguing that much of British children's lives is ruled by 'the idea of danger', which she sees as having taken a new twist at the beginning of the 1990s.

A consequence of the growing fears regarding children's safety is a growth in adult management of children's leisure space and time. For example, for Himmelweit et al. (1958) the necessity of time spent travelling each day to school was regarded as one of the valuable unsupervised periods in children's lives. Today, as most parents accompany their children to school, certainly up to the age of 10 or so, this time has been lost, particularly in Great Britain. Hillman et al. (1990) found that while in 1971 80% of 7- and 8-year-old children walked to school on their own, by 1990 this figure had dropped to 9%. This change they ascribed mainly to increased car ownership and worry about safety on the roads, although one-quarter of parents was also worried about abduction. Comparing the UK and Germany, Hillman et al. (1990) also note that over three-quarters of German primary school children come home from school on their own, compared with only one-third of English juniors. When they compared children in the two countries for permission to cross roads, to come home from school alone, to go to other places than school alone, to use buses to go out after dark and to use their bicycles on the roads, German children were far less restricted than their English counterparts.

This retreat from street or public culture contributes to an increasingly clear demarcation between adult space and children's space. Where the street or public square was common land, in which young and old could intermingle, the spaces today reserved for children, both indoors or outdoors, are distinct and marked off from those for adults.[1] Indeed, in earlier generations children played outside both because outside spaces were seen as safe, for everybody, and because they were unwelcome at home, the home being a place for housework, to be kept tidy, with bedrooms certainly not to be played in during the day. Yet today, separate leisure spaces for adults and children, each equipped with media, are increasingly common.

Here two middle-class mothers, both with 10-year-old boys, stress the importance of such a separation within the home:

> *Interviewer:*   Would you say there are more advantages than disadvantages for him to have a television in his bedroom?
> *Mother:*   Yes, I think there's er, it's an advantage to me, um, basically 'cause it gives me a bit of free time. ... Er, you can, I can sit quietly down here – it's a small house.

The second mother agrees: 'I feel that as an adult I need adult time, and there's certain things on the television that are no-go to children. You don't really know what's going to come on.'

James et al. (1998) draw on Mary Douglas's notion of dirt as 'matter out of place' to suggest that increasingly 'children either occupy designated spaces, that is they are placed, as in nurseries or schools, or they are conspicuous by the inappropriate or precocious invasion of adult territory. ... [Childhood] is that status of personhood which is by definition often in the wrong place' (1988: 37). As any child knows, the informal codes of conduct regarding queuing in shops, crossing busy streets or even being visible in public places all assume adult status, and 'unaccompanied' children are routinely excluded. How society regards this division between adult and child spaces is contested: Postman's (1992) concern with the supposed role of media in undermining childhood innocence rests precisely on the way that television transgresses what he sees as a valuable division, thereby making 'adult' knowledge routinely available to children. These debates are as rife among parents as among academics and commentators, and whether one considers it best for children to know about the adult world or to be protected from it frames parental strategies of media access and use.

That occupying 'the wrong place' has a strong moral dimension is most apparent in the ways in which parents may talk about 'other people's children' who are not 'appropriately' contained. Here, the middle-class mother of a 12-year-old boy puts this moral anxiety into words:

> To be honest I'm too strict, but I would rather be strict now and have him grow into a decent adolescent teenager than one that was running round the streets creating havoc. There's a few at his school that are very – their freedom is never questioned, they're out in the morning and they go back at 9.30, 10 o'clock at night, and they have terrible, terrible reputations, and I don't

want that for Alex. I want him to have a reputation of being a nice child, and a nice human being, but I don't want him to have a reputation of being a thug and an out-and-out bully.

The perception of public space as relatively unsafe, under-provisioned and even immoral may be a particularly British view. Britain is often popularly described as a 'child-unfriendly culture', where many social codes exist to manage the separation of spaces for children and adults, and many others exist to regulate children's participation within those adult-designated, or adult-defined 'family' spaces. However, observing parallel trends in America, Coontz (1997: 17) comments that:

> People talk about how kids today are unsupervised, and they often are; but in one sense teens are under more surveillance than in the past. Almost anyone above the age of 40 can remember places where young people could establish real physical, as opposed to psychic, distance from adults. In the suburbs it was undeveloped or abandoned lots and overgrown woods, hidden from adult view, often with old buildings that you could deface without anyone caring. In the cities it was downtown areas where kids could hang out. Many of these places are now gone, and only some kids feel comfortable in the malls that have replaced them.

This characterisation of the change switches our focus in relation to public space from a parental to children's perspective, and the result is to make the picture appear rather different. While their parents are more likely to focus on the dangers of going out, our interviews showed that children instead stress the absence, as they perceive it, of activities and facilities in their neighbourhood, as illustrated by the discussion quoted at the start of this section.

Certainly, a substantial majority (66%) of children and young people aged 9–17 think there is not enough for them to do in the area where they live, as the YPNM survey showed. The number dissatisfied with provision of outdoor leisure facilities rises sharply after the age of 11, when attendance at the many organised leisure activities outside the home (such as swimming or dancing lessons, scouting organisations, etc.) tends to fall off (see Chapter 3). Indeed, three-quarters aged 12–14 and as many as four in every five of those aged 15–17 are discontented with leisure alternatives outside the home (Table 4.3). In a parallel survey, Matthews (1998) confirms that only 33% of children and young people say they find plenty of things to do locally, while 65% claim to be bored in their spare time. In addition, 82% claim they prefer being out and about to being inside, but the streets are perceived by half as fearful places.

Table 4.3 *Child's view of whether there is enough for someone their age to do in the area where they live (N = 984)*

	All (%)	Age			Gender		Social grade			
		9–11 (%)	12–14 (%)	15–17 (%)	Boy (%)	Girl (%)	AB (%)	C1 (%)	C2 (%)	DE (%)
Yes	33	54	27	19	37	29	37	36	35	27
No	66	45	73	80	62	71	63	63	64	72

Note: Percentages may not total to 100% as *c.* 1% answered 'unsure'.
Source: Livingstone and Bovill, 1999.

The message from children and their parents to policy-makers is clear – improve the provision of safe leisure alternatives for young people, particularly teenagers, outside the home. For where, they ask, are the affordable and accessible meeting places – the cafés, parks, swimming pools, cinemas, skating rinks, youth clubs that they so wish for? Cynics may reply that the young are always dissatisfied, but it is noteworthy that this level of dissatisfaction as expressed by young people in the UK is around double that of young people in other European countries. For example, in the UK 81% aged 15–16 are dissatisfied with the facilities available in the area where they live, compared with only 61% in Sweden, 49% in the Netherlands, 43% in France, 34% in Germany and 21% in Switzerland (Bovill and Livingstone, 2001).

Not only do young people bemoan the absence of places to go, but crucially, places of importance to children often exist on a micro-level which rarely show up on an adult street map – the back alley, the local waste ground, a small stream – and they are connected by informal or hidden routes. Hill and Tisdall (1997: 108) stress children's preference for 'real' over 'artificial' environments, for 'they like to create their own play environment, whether imaginatively or through using and moving materials provided by nature or left by adults'. Through such imaginative play, children come to feel ownership over their environments (Corsaro, 1997), although, as Hill and Tisdall (1997: 109) go on to note, 'children are not considered prominently, let alone consulted, in most decisions about the design and use of space'. It will be suggested below that children's most private space, their bedroom, represents a rare exception here, although the most that can be achieved is, in Coontz's terms, a psychic rather than a notable physical distance from adults. Having conducted three ethnographic studies in different types of urban or city environment, Lieberg (1995: 20) concludes that young people use public space 'because they often have nowhere else to go when they want to be among friends' and because 'an orientation toward friendship concentrates on "doing nothing" activities in mixed-gender groups (peer-groups) in public spaces' (1995: 22). This is seen positively, for 'one of the most important aspects of teenagers' use of public spaces is the possibility of controlling and shaping their own existence without adult control' (Lieberg, 1995: 33).

In short, children and young people live much more local lives than do adults, and this goes easily unnoticed by adult observers – researchers, policy-makers and parents alike. Hence the importance of taking a child-centred rather than an adult-centred approach to children's leisure. An area which appears to an adult to be run-down or loud with traffic noise may provide a friendly street with neighbouring children to play with, while an idyllic rural village is likely to lack an adequate bus service to the cinema or swimming pool in the next town. Listening to the rules that children told us about – concerning space, time and money – which circumscribe their access to outside spaces makes this local and contingent character of their access very apparent. Rules include particular spatial restrictions (e.g. only visit this street, only cross certain roads, only cycle a certain distance), temporal restrictions (e.g. be back by 7 pm, only go out after homework is completed, only go somewhere at the weekend), financial restrictions (relating to entrance fees, transport costs, etc.), and social restrictions (e.g. only visit certain known children, you can't go to certain public places, etc.).

Consider, for example, this interview with the middle-class parents of three boys aged 10, 13 and 14 who live in a large and comfortable house – the same family with the many televisions quoted earlier – in an unspoilt rural area two miles from a tiny village. When asked 'what the boys do around here', their mother painted a picture of diverse activities, albeit requiring considerable parental support:

> Well, we have done the usual things, like they have been in air cadets and they have been to scouts. ... I think we are quite fortunate here that we have a cinema up in [neighbouring town] ... we belong to a country club ... where we play golf and do clay pigeon shooting in the back meadow. Well, they have all got bikes so they meet their friends and perhaps go and get something to eat at [local village]. ... I think it is still quite unspoilt. We have a boating lake nearby so the facilities around here are quite good. But in the winter we have to take them to the cinema because there are no buses. We give them the mobile phone and then when the film is finished we come and fetch them home.

The three boys, on the other hand, feel isolated, notwithstanding the beauty of their rural surroundings, and the youngest and hence most restricted child was particularly critical: 'I'm not allowed on the road on my bike so I am usually stuck at home watching TV or something or reading a book. ... When we want to get out we try and get out but sometimes we have done everything and that's all that there is to do and it is just so boring. There is really nothing to do around here.'

The situation of this family contrasts with that of an Asian family living in a working-class area where unemployment, racial tension and crime rates are high. The family live in a shabby, small semi-detached flat above the corner shop where both father and mother work for long hours. On interviewing this second family, we found rather pessimistic parents but much more satisfied children. Thus, when we asked whether there was much for the children (a boy of 7 and a girl of 5) to do in the neighbourhood, the mother answered:

> Unfortunately there's not, no. There's a leisure centre, there's a YMCA as well. They feel kind of outcast though because there's not many Asian children around here. So really what I have to do is to do things with them in the house-hold and in the back yard, or take them down to the Metro Centre because they've got a good leisure centre there as well, so that's quite good for them. ... There's a new water park, but, er, I'm very reluctant to take them there. ... It's mainly with older children on their bikes and they are, er, hanging around and you don't get many other children there. And really the parks are not up to standard because there's loads of rubbish. ... It's quite frightening as well sometimes when I take them to the park. I've had one bad experience taking the children there.

The satisfaction of the children brings home the local nature of children's lives. Here, being able to play in their own street with friends makes all the difference: as Hassan himself tells us, 'I play out. ... I ride my bike. Sometimes I go round the block with my friends. ... I go up this road and if I am allowed I cross the road all the way up there. But the Nursery is at the top, so I stop and come back. I am allowed to do that if I ask my Dad or my Mam.' The situations of these two families confirm the argu-ment made in the previous chapter. For, as the middle-class family illus-trated, television and reading enter the conversation when describing restrictions on their activities – having to stay at home means spending time with the media. Further, as both families illustrate, what is particu-larly valued about going out is spending time with friends which, while not in itself new, confounds many public anxieties about the hypnotic attractions of the media. Moreover, what is often valued about the media is the ways in which they aid children in overcoming the obstacles placed between themselves and their friends (hence the rapidly growing interest in mobile phones and email).

Writing in the mid-1970s, Corrigan (1976) contrasted the potential unpredictability of street-corner culture with the (boring) alternatives of Mum and Dad in the front room or the known environment of the youth club. If those were the options in the 1970s, they had changed by the 1990s.

For many young people we interviewed, the streetcorner has been banned, the youth club has closed down and the front room has been replaced by a multimedia home and, particularly, a multimedia bedroom, as we see below.

The Retreat to the Home

The decline of street culture and the rise of the media-rich home are related. Both parents and children explicitly link restrictions on the child's access to the world outside to increased media use within the home. On occasion, this reveals some cause for concern, as when a 13-year-old boy, living in an area with a high level of unemployment and violence, tells us that 'Mum gets us a video or a computer game if we have to stay in because of the fighting'.

More often, though, the link between street culture and media culture is an implicit and subtle one. Clearly, it reflects not only a shift in perceptions of public space, but also in perceptions of the home. For while today it is going out which is heavily hedged about with rules and expectations, once the home was similarly restricted, with activities judged appropriate for particular people or particular rooms also heavily rule-bound, and in this regard children's desires or interests had little scope for expression.

Interestingly, in telling their often-nostalgic story of decline, today's parents are more likely to recall the freedoms of outside than the restrictions of inside.[2] Here a middle-class mother living in a rural location talks about her 10-year-old son:

Interviewer: You see television as playing a different role in Leo's life than it did in yours?

Mother: Oh yes, definitely. I can remember playing outside in the street for hours on end and having a lot more freedom to play out. They haven't got that as children now ... he's in more than we ever were as children.

Her son confirms the importance of media in his life, telling us that he spends a lot of time with the television, hi-fi and a games machine in his bedroom, and that while he would like to go out more often, the garden is too small and he is not allowed to play football there.

Interviewer: So what would you do before 9 o'clock on a school day?

Leo: Play on my computer and watch TV.

Interviewer: And what sort of things do you watch in the evening then?

Leo: On a school day I would watch *The Bill* and a few – other stuff. And then at the weekends I would watch anything and everything until 10 o'clock.

Interviewer:	What sort of things would you do in the mornings on a Saturday?
Leo:	Just get up and watch TV until about 12 o'clock. Get dressed and have dinner and watch TV again.
Interviewer:	Have you got a TV in your room?
Leo:	Yeah. I spend most of my time in there.
Interviewer:	Why is that?
Leo:	I prefer it. I like being on my own sometimes. Watch what I want to watch instead of watching what my sister wants to watch or what my mum wants to watch.
Interviewer:	And in your bedroom do you ever have your friends round?
Leo:	Yeah. They used to come and we'd play on the computer.

This last observation is confirmed by the YPNM survey, showing that a favourite leisure activity outside the home is in fact visiting friends in their homes, and these visits frequently encompass the use of media. Indeed, many young people are motivated to visit friends in order to use media that they do not have access to at home: two-thirds of boys aged 9 or more visit a friend's house to play computer or video games and half of 15–16 year olds visit a friend to watch a video. Around a quarter sometimes go to use a computer (not for games) or watch satellite or cable television. Such social uses of media challenge suggestions that the effect of the media is to isolate children from social interaction. On the other hand, if friends are not forthcoming, the media play a much more important role, and one about which parents have considerable misgivings, while when friends are available, the media play a lesser role. Consider the case of this middle-class 6-year-old girl who used to live in a rather isolated cottage. As her mother told us:

> She did watch a lot of TV then. She would watch everything that was for children. … I had a young and very demanding asthmatic baby so there wasn't the time for her. She would watch other children playing on *Sesame Street* and just almost interact with the children on the television because there was no one up there. You see I didn't have the energy to get out all the time, or to have people around all the time. … It was useful. … She just used to have a wee chair in that corner and sit there glued.

Since then, however, the family has moved to a housing estate in a small village where the children play regularly in the street outside. The children's social life, and therefore the place of the media in it, has been transformed, as the interview with Belinda shows:

Interviewer:	Imagine you've just got back from school. What would you do?
Belinda:	I like playing out the front or something.
Interviewer:	Who would you play with?
Belinda:	I like playing with Alice who's 9 and Carrie who's 8 who's Alice's sister, or Megan or my friend next door, Lucy.
Interviewer:	What would you do?

Belinda:	We would play on our bikes or something. Or I would play with Lucy next door on our bikes. We like playing 'follow my leader' on our bikes. (Laughs)
Interviewer:	And what's best – being outside or in the house?
Belinda:	Outside.

This interview was typical of many, demonstrating that 'outdoors' above all was a social space where the children and young people we talked to could be together with friends. It represented excitement, freedom from adult supervision and freedom to explore. However, one should caution lest discussions of the adult supervision of childhood slip into a celebration of childhood freedoms and innocence (or of young people's supposed resistance to the dominant culture; Widdicombe and Wooffitt, 1995). For example, the image that could be seen to result from the data presented in Chapter 3, of a heavily supervised and morally anxious middle class and a free, informal social life for the working class on the streets, tends to criticise the former and romanticise the latter. This leads in turn to a neglect of the problems which working-class culture may reproduce for those young people (Willis, 1977) as well as a neglect of the complaint clearly emerging from all young people, namely that there is insufficient public provision of leisure facilities, particularly for those who fall into the no-man's land between the definitions of 'child' and 'adult'. Moreover, if we replace the focus on supervision with a focus on resources, the picture instead becomes one of a well-resourced middle class – in terms of activities both outside and inside the home – and a less privileged working class which is comparatively deprived in both these respects. In short, we should neither over-glamorise leisure in public spaces nor underestimate the value of the new, high-tech bedroom culture. At home, the middle classes have more rooms, more media, as well as having more organised activities and more money to go out (although they are also subject to greater monitoring and restrictions; Livingstone and Bovill, 1999).

It has been seen that, given limitations in their financial resources and the age-appropriate facilities provided for them, as well as the constraints of dominant discourses around childhood, the long-term historical shift towards the privatisation of leisure (Williams, 1974) means that the home (rather than, say, commercial facilities available within the locale) as a locus for leisure becomes ever more central to young people. And while at home, for a variety of reasons television in particular, but also the media in general, are frequently acknowledged as the easy way of keeping the family entertained, notwithstanding the doubts parents have regarding the media as 'time-wasting'. In short, the boundary marked by the front door is sufficiently problematic for families that, motivated also by other factors operating within the home, there is now another boundary, this time marked by the bedroom door. On the other hand, the broad link being proposed here, between anxieties about safety outside the home and provision of media inside it does not apply straightforwardly at the level of individuals. In the YPNM project we compared those parents who were relatively more or relatively less fearful of their children's safety in terms of the levels of media provision in the home, looking both at household and bedroom media, and found no direct association between concern with safety in public and provision of media in the private realm. Rather, as already noted in Chapter 2, provision of media in the home or in the child's bedroom depends primarily on the factors of the age and gender of the child, and on the economic and cultural capital of the parents.

Home and family are not necessarily one and the same. Ironically perhaps, the privatisation of once-public leisure activities, combined with permitting children to spend their leisure time within the home rather than sending them out during the day, throws family members together precisely at a time when the cultural shift towards individualisation means that children and young people are ever more encouraged to pursue their own individual tastes and interests. Thus not only are their media preferences decreasingly shared with their parents, but there are ever more media contents and sources tailored to their age group. In short, while the privatisation of leisure increasingly keeps the family together at home, the cultural process of individualisation increasingly pushes them apart, resulting in a diversification of leisure lifestyles within the home, in which the diversification of media plays a key role. But this apparent conflict between family togetherness and separation is also reaching a spatial resolution within the home, thereby further transforming the spatial arrangements of the home. Specifically, the multiplication of media goods in the home supports, facilitates even, a diversification of tastes and habits at home which frees young people from following the lifestyle decisions of their parents, but this requires the development of a media-rich or high-tech 'bedroom culture' in order to allow for the expression of individualised lifestyles on the part of young people (and their parents).

FROM FAMILY TELEVISION TO BEDROOM CULTURE

Interviewer: Do you think that there are any advantages or disadvantages to Charlie having TV in his bedroom?

Mother: Advantages are that we can watch programmes in here when Charlie wants to watch something else and –

Father:	Disadvantages are that it, err, disencourages family life because it separates people. Errm, maybe not so much Charlie, but I do think that in general it encourages children to stay in their room. And it breaks off the contact.
Interviewer:	So is spending time together as a family important to you?
Father:	Yes, of course, the family is the most important thing.

(Working-class family with 12-year-old boy)

If in public spaces, the second half of the twentieth century witnessed both a decline in access for children, and an increasing demarcation between adult and child spaces, the private, domestic realm has been undergoing parallel changes. This period opened with the arrival of the television set into the family home, transforming the spatial and temporal rhythms of family life, and closed at the point at which it has become expected, and in many cases achieved, that each room, or each household member, would have his or her own space in which to view television with, perhaps, music, a VCR and, increasingly, a personal computer and mobile phone as well. To give an example, one that contrasts with the parents quoted above, when we asked the family with the many television sets whether this was because of the multiplicity of channels, the mother laughed and said, 'It's the multiplicity of children!' As she went on to explain: 'Everybody is very individual, and it also allows everybody to relax in their own way and in their own time.'

Historical studies of the arrival of television suggest that far from fitting into the home, television transformed the structure of the home by prompting a considerable rearrangement of domestic space (Spigel, 1992). As each room had pre-defined activities associated with it, there was a new problem, namely where to put the set. As one new television viewer recalls, 'I remember, you had to go into the front room to watch it, and in those days, the front room was really only used for "best" – for special occasions. The television changed that' (quoted in O'Sullivan, 1991: 167). In most UK homes, the decision was made to put this proud new object in the once adult-only front room or parlour of the post-war British home, transforming this room in the process into the 'living' room, this itself being part of a wider trend towards the creation of the open-plan living space (Oswell, 1999; Scannell, 1988). In interviews, we found few children for whom this formal notion of the privacy of the home was still relevant, although ten-year-old Kevin told us that, 'Well my Mum doesn't like people actually coming in ... umm, because they'd probably break something, 'cos we've got a lot of china ... and my Mum's teapots ... and she doesn't want them broken'.

In the main, however, only relatively wealthy homes now keep a room for 'best', and many family homes have 'knocked through' from the best room into the dining room to make a large multifunctional space – the 'family room' available to all. In this new multifunctional living space, the media play a central role. Walk into the modern living room and one is likely to find a décor inspired by the middle-class aspirations of the sitcom family or a prime-time home decorating programme, an arrangement of sofas and comfy chairs encircling the television set, an array of hi-fi equipment, video recorder, television-linked computer games machines and, covering most visible surfaces, a comfortable clutter consisting of television listings magazines, remote controls, newspapers, notes with URLs scrawled on them, compact discs, headphones, print out from web sites, toys themed from the latest Disney hit, and so forth. All such space is marked by informality, typically noted by the family as you enter through the routine request to the visitor – 'please don't mind the mess'.

Closely associated with the family room is 'family television' (Morley, 1986; see also Moores, 1988), a site of both conviviality and power plays, in which the family share interests, pleasures and conflicts. As recently as the mid-1980s, Morley described an image in which the family gathers in the main living room to co-view the family television set, this providing an occasion for the operation of traditional generation and gender inequalities. Dad monopolises the remote control, sport wins out over soaps in the struggle to determine programme choices, women's viewing is halted when the husband wants to see 'his programme', and children have to fit in with others. Some of this is still visible, as when a working-class 15-year-old boy explains, 'most of the time Dad watches what he wants 'cos he pays for the telly'. Yet he goes on to add, 'sometimes if there is something on Sky that we want to watch. ... He [Dad] sits in one of our rooms to watch it and we watch it downstairs.' In other words, partly in response to the domestic conflicts charted by Morley, just a decade later we find a very different pattern emerging.

As the media at home have multiplied, no longer representing a scarce resource for the family, the kinds of social practices which surround and accompany viewing have altered. An increasingly common solution is to transform bedrooms into private living rooms, transforming the meaning of both solitary and shared viewing, and leaving the family living room for those specific times when the family chooses to come together, enforced conviviality being a thing of the past for all but the poor. Thus today, most homes have been reorganised, the dominant principle no longer being that of 'front' and 'back' (Goffman, 1959), nor that of daytime use and night-time use, nor of adult spaces and child spaces, but rather that of family/communal space and individual/personal spaces. How far along this path to go represents a central dilemma for the family at the turn of the century, and in so far as parents and children construct 'family life' through their daily activities, their decisions to acquire multiple televisions, or where to locate the personal computer, push them towards either a more communal or individualised model (see Chapter 5). The 'living room wars' (Ang, 1996) were most obvious to those researchers of the one-set home, sensitising them to power inequalities based on gender and generation. Against that context, it might have seemed that multiple sets would resolve family conflicts by providing each family member with control over their own viewing. Yet as we come near to reaching that state, many British families now see themselves facing a new problem of dispersed living. As each person goes off in his or her own direction, this generates some nostalgia for the so-called togetherness once experienced in front of the set.

The long-term trend clearly involves moving new screen-based media – the television in the 1960s, the VCR in the 1980s, the computer in the late 1990s – away from the main family space of the living room where they generally start their domestic career, towards more individualised spaces, particularly the bedroom/play room. This spread is both spatial and temporal, for while the media are spreading throughout the home, they are also spreading throughout the day. As noted in the previous chapter, television schedules have changed to fit this more casual use, from mainly prime time availability to an increasingly 24-hour service, and doubtless the ever more informal mode of address on television (Corner, 1995) also supports this altered style of use. The computer – like most other media, but significantly unlike television – is unable to impose its timetable on its users (though the Internet is making some moves in this direction), but still one might expect a gradual shift from use in valued time, reflecting a positive choice to engage with favoured contents, to more casual time-filling uses associated more with boredom than with choice (one might even see the increasingly entertaining screensaver as a new version of the notion of television-as-wallpaper). Thus while the computer as a technology appears to assume a focused user, the screen does not require this, as the history of television shows.

Finding a Home for Media

Given the current stage in the diffusion of television and of the computer (Chapter 2), and having seen the expressed desires on children's part for yet more privacy in relation to their media use, let us consider further two of the choices currently facing households with children. The first is where to locate the computer; the second is whether to put a television in a child's bedroom. In just over half of all homes with children, these decisions have recently been made. Location is related to use, for children with their own computer spend some 20 minutes per day longer than those with access to one elsewhere in the household, resulting in almost twice as much use altogether, although the balance of time between playing games and using the computer for 'serious' purposes differs little (Livingstone and Bovill, 1999).

Whether or not to acquire a personal computer is, as we saw in Chapter 2, a matter of household income even more than it is one of parental education. For many families, however, the question is no longer whether but when: as one mother told us, 'all I know is that I can see computers being as much part of the home as the TV and video'. Once acquired, the decision of where to put it reveals some complex processes of appropriation by which parents and children negotiate their domestic environment. These decisions may follow the public/commercial discourse that accompanies purchase of these goods, but families also alter or resist these meanings, situating the goods so as to facilitate other kinds of practices. If the newly acquired computer is put in Dad's study, the child's bedroom, an older brother's bedroom, under the stairs or in the family living room, very different meanings are activated, relating the key dimensions of meaning – leisure/work, shared/individual, parent/child, masculine/feminine – in different alignments.

It has proved less obvious where the personal computer should be located than the initial location of the television, and the result has as yet made less impact on main living spaces, though the growing presence of computers in bedrooms or what were once spare rooms is altering the meaning and uses of these more peripheral spaces. Different households make different decisions. These decisions have dual implications, for both the meaning of the computer and computer use in the household and for the meaning of the space in which the computer is placed. One pattern in evidence is that families try the living room option first – following the location which succeeded for the television – but then subsequently move it into either the room of whoever turns out to use the computer in practice (this often deviating from anticipated use), or into a previously undefined space (box room, hallway, etc.), often then relabelled as 'the computer room'. Occasionally, the reverse process occurs, especially when parents decide that a computer, originally bought for one child, should be more closely monitored and so a more public setting is chosen.

Looking at those homes where the decision has been made to buy a personal computer, we see that class and gender differences determine its

Table 4.4 *Location of computer in the home, by gender and social grade (base: all households with computer, N = 556)*

| | All | Gender | | Social grade | | Gender by social grade | | | |
| | | | | | | Boy | | Girl | |
		Boy	Girl	ABC1	C2DE	ABC1	C2DE	ABC1	C2DE
Child's room and elsewhere	12	16	8	9	16	15	17	4	15
Child's room only	16	22	9	11	23	15	33	7	13
Elsewhere only	73	62	83	80	62	69	50	90	72

Source: Livingstone and Bovill, 1999.

location (see Table 4.4). Middle-class parents, and parents of girls, appear to prioritise sharing the computer within a communal space over personal ownership by the child. Working-class parents, and parents of boys, who invest in a computer appear twice as likely to place it in the child's bedroom, or to have a second machine in the child's bedroom. As a result, there are no social grade differences in the numbers of children having a computer in their own room, although, as we saw in Chapter 2, middle-class households are almost twice as likely to have a computer somewhere in the home. For gender, on the other hand, we see the reverse: while boys and girls are more or less equally likely to have a computer somewhere in the home, boys are twice as likely to have one in their bedroom. In other words, boys are twice as likely either to have the family's only computer located in their room, or to have an additional computer of their own. Interestingly, middle-class families are less likely than working-class families to invest in a second computer for their daughters, but in other respects the gender bias is just as marked in working-class families where 33% of boys have the only computer in the home in their rooms compared with only 13% of girls.

In accounting for the decision to put the computer in a family space or in a child's room, there are some cultural factors at work. Dutch and British children, for example, are equally likely to have a personal computer in their bedroom, but in the Netherlands they are twice as likely to have a computer in the home (van der Voort et al., 1998). In other words, Dutch families are more likely overall to favour a communal interpretation of the computer while British parents are more likely to see the computer as facilitating a child's homework (or, as freeing the family from the sound of games playing). On the other hand, Danish children are not only more likely than British children to have a computer in the home, but also proportionately more likely to have one in their bedroom for their personal use (Bovill and Livingstone, 2001), suggesting Denmark to be further 'advanced' on the path towards multiple, and thereby individual, computer ownership.

While the decision over where to locate the computer is described by parents and children as distinctive to the computer, it is noteworthy that similar patterns of provision for the bedroom occur for television. In other words, as we saw in Chapter 2, middle-class parents, and parents of girls, appear to prioritise co-viewing or sharing the television in a communal space over personal ownership by the child, while working-class parents, and parents of boys, are more likely to provide a television in the child's bedroom. Yet the justifications surrounding these decisions are rather different. In the case of the computer, parents talk of supporting the child's education, or of the need for several family members to share the computer or, less often, of the need to monitor publicly how the child uses the computer. In the case of television, parents talk of allowing different family members to pursue individual content preferences, and of providing privacy for both children and adults in the household. In both cases, they are subject to pressure from their children: when asked in the YPNM survey what they most want for their next birthday, 16% of children without their own television made this their top choice, and 14% of those who already had a computer elsewhere in the house nonetheless chose to have their own in addition. However, television, far more than the computer, is also popularly associated with dividing the family, and so parents' doubts about their children having their own set are associated with parental anxieties regarding their success in creating a cohesive family.

Media as Solitary or Social

In the YPNM survey we asked young people to estimate what proportion of the waking time they spent at home was spent in their bedroom. While few – especially among the younger children – claim to spend most or all of this time in their bedroom, by the time they are 15–16 the majority of young people say they spend at least half of their waking time at home in their bedrooms. This is especially the case for girls, although socio-economic status makes little difference, and it holds across diverse European countries (Bovill and Livingstone, 2001).

Ambivalence regarding the potentially isolating impact of the media is very salient for some parents, as one working-class mother of a 15-year-old girl describes:

> Joanne has her television on when she is sort of sitting in there [in her bedroom], which I didn't approve of. ... I feel that she is not in here with us that much then. I like us all to be together. I like that. But she has got to have

her space. And she obviously likes watching some programmes that we don't, the younger programmes.

Not all families are so concerned, for 'dividing the family' can be fairly redescribed as 'providing for individual interests'. For example, when we asked one middle-class mother of an 11-year-old girl what her daughter's favourite television programme was, she replied with apparent equanimity: 'I don't know if she has got a favourite programme. I am afraid that we are a family where we all go in our own rooms. We don't sit around together. … The children go up in their bedrooms and have their telly on and I am in here.'

  In general, while 63% of 6–17 year olds have a TV set in their bedroom, the YPNM survey showed that only 19% of parents think it 'mainly a good thing' for a young person of their child's age to have a television set in his or her own room, while 31% think it 'mainly a bad thing'. These views are strongly related to social class, with middle-class parents twice as likely to disapprove of their child having a television in their bedroom than are working-class parents. Nonetheless, one in five parents (drawn equally from working-class and middle-class backgrounds) who think it mainly a bad thing do allow their child to have a set in their bedroom.

  It is worth reflecting on the reasons for this. Partly, they concern the domestic regulation of access to media contents, and partly they reflect a public anxiety about 'being alone'. The present account, namely that children and young people primarily wish to be with friends, with media taking second place in their preferences, is one which parents and researchers alike are happy to hear. And in many respects, this account of young people's sociability is a fair one. For example, the description of the period after school offered to us by this 10-year-old girl is typical of many:

Rachel:	Well, normally I just choose to sit and watch TV.
Interviewer:	Right, when you're on your own?
Rachel:	Yes, and when a friend's there, we just play upstairs, then sometimes go out and have a walk round the village.

But both this account and its opposite, namely that children and young people are becoming isolated and addicted through excessive media use, tend implicitly to accept the assumption that being alone is problematic. Yet such an assumption does not accord well with the attempt to take young people's perspective seriously. For example, Ferrari et al. (1985) conceptualise research on the implications of home computing for children and families, in terms of an opposition between the computer encouraging isolation of users, or encouraging co-operative group use. Within this framework, computer experiences with other family members are construed as positive, while individual experience is seen as negative. By contrast, Hill and Tisdall (1997) review research which shows how much children value the right to be alone in general – to be quiet, independent and free from intervention (while, conversely, Emler and Reicher (1995) observe a relation between sociality and delinquency). If we take this 'right' seriously, it is clear that the bedroom answers admirably, for central to young people's pleasure in their bedroom is the way in which it represents a place of privacy. The association of being alone with being in one's bedroom is culturally variable. In Finland children are more likely to find they have the living room to themselves (Suess et al., 1998) as the school day finishes relatively early and the proportion of working mothers is higher than in the UK,[3] a situation which in the UK and US contexts is defined as the social problem of 'latch key children'. Notably, children describe finding they can have the living room to themselves with great pleasure.

Popular concerns about the media frame the adult judgement of the value of being alone, neglecting considerations of privacy, for now that bedrooms contain screen entertainment media, what was once seen as broadly positive – the child alone, lost in a book, losing track of the hours in a fantasy world – is seen as worrying.[4] As a culture, we do not think that the child alone, absorbed in a computer game, losing track of the hours in a fantasy world, is making a valuable use of their time. The growing endorsement of the 'time is money' metaphor makes us place a higher value on a mixed 'diet' of preferably sociable leisure activities than on any consideration of privacy, especially if it involves a lengthy escape into a fantasy world. Perhaps the main factor, though, is that in our culture being alone is a state of adulthood, meaning independence, making one's own decisions, learning from one's own mistakes, structuring one's own time, falling back on one's own resources, etc. A child alone in her bedroom may be seen, in some sense, not only as rejecting 'the family' but also as escaping the status of being a child, as exercising a certain independence.[5]

Whether we construe a child making use of media in the bedroom as positive or negative, there is little doubt that the more media are located in the bedroom, the more time children spend with those media – even once age, socio-economic status and gender are taken into account – and so the more time they spend in their bedroom (Livingstone and Bovill, 1999). From the perspective of the media and communication industries, detaching media goods from fixed domestic locations by making them either affordable in multiple versions or by making them mobile, is a successful strategy for increasing the use made of them.

Among 9–10 year olds, having screen media (television, games machine, or personal computer) in the bedroom is associated with the greatest increase in time spent. Across all age groups, children and young people with their own television report spending 37 minutes more per day viewing than children who only have access elsewhere in the home, while for the computer the equivalent figure is 21 minutes and for the TV-linked games machine, 19 minutes. Among older children, being able to play music in their own room makes the most difference – a matter of nearly half an hour per day, although having a television set remains important, particularly among those aged 12–13.

Across European countries surveyed, similar patterns hold (Bovill and Livingstone, 2001), suggesting that having a media-rich bedroom is associated with greater use of the bedroom. While it is tempting to conclude further that, as bedrooms become ever more media-rich, children are spending increasing amounts of time in their bedrooms, there is little past data on bedroom use to permit this, and the reverse interpretation – namely that those who spend more time with the media are most likely to acquire media in their bedroom – is also plausible.

In the YPNM survey, and again this holds true across the European countries surveyed (Bovill and Livingstone, 2001), there is also a negative correlation between spending time in the bedroom and spending free time with family and a positive association with mostly spending free time alone. Again, it is difficult to determine whether this should be interpreted in terms of the isolating effect of personal media or the desire of some more than others for privacy. While having one's own television means that children are more likely to watch their favourite programmes alone, we also found that 12–13 and 15–16 year olds are more likely to watch television and play computer games with friends if they have their own television or TV-linked games machine or personal computer. This suggests that what is key is the flexibility to balance time spent with family, friends and alone.

There are some cultural differences in sociability. Comparisons across Europe reveal that in Spain both boys and girls are particularly likely to spend time with the family and to spend comparatively less time in the bedroom (Bovill and Livingstone, 2001), while Swedish and Finnish teenagers are overwhelmingly more likely to spend their free time with a group of friends, also spending a smaller proportion of their free time in their own room. This suggests that wider cultural factors lead family life in Spain to remain largely communal, while in the Nordic countries youth culture is more peer-oriented.

Table 4.5 *Percentage of 10–16 year olds who watch/play more than half the time ...*

| | Television | | | | Computer games | | | |
	All (507)	10–11 (176)	12–14 (261)	15–16 (70)	All (403)	10–11 (136)	12–14 (210)	15–16 (57)
Alone	25	17	28	30	63	64	62	70
With friends	7	7	7	1	17	22	15	11
With siblings	53	59	52	39	24	25	26	18
With mother	46	50	45	40	3	3	5	–
With father	35	35	37	27	7	8	8	–
With other	13	16	13	3	6	11	4	5

Note: Multiple response options allowed.

Source: Livingstone, 1999c.

Not only do parents undoubtedly value having some space and time to themselves, this being a significant factor in their arrangement of their home and daily timetable, but children clearly desire such time alone. This preference represents one means by which children contribute to the structuring of domestic arrangements, for they are not only consumers but also, through their activities and desires, architects of the new style home with its multiple screens in multiple living spaces. These activities and desires were readily identified in the YPNM survey when we asked 10–16 year olds about the social contexts in which they watch television and play computer games.

Table 4.5 shows that watching television remains primarily a social activity – for three-quarters of these young people watch along with others more than half the time.[6] This is especially the case for the younger children, with siblings and mothers being the most common viewing companions. By contrast, computer games are a much more solitary activity, for nearly two-thirds generally play alone, while friends and siblings are the most common comparisons.

Notwithstanding the apparent social nature of television viewing, and as an exercise in trying not to impose assumptions on to our respondents, we also asked children in the survey to draw themselves watching television. Perhaps surprisingly, about half of them chose to draw themselves watching television alone, often in their bedrooms, suggesting a marked shift from the image of television as the family hearth, replacing the dinner table perhaps, but at least a social focus in the centre of family life. Having also asked them how they most enjoyed watching television and playing computer games,[7] it became apparent that these drawings were more likely to reflect preferred than actual viewing habits (Table 4.6), for the differences between Tables 4.5 and 4.6 reveal some interesting discrepancies between actual and preferred viewing.

Table 4.6 *How 10–16 year olds most enjoy watching television (N = 507) and playing computer games (N = 403)*

	Television						Computer games					
	All (%)	Boys (%)	Girls (%)	10–11 (%)	12–14 (%)	15–16 (%)	All (%)	Boys (%)	Girls (%)	10–11 (%)	12–14 (%)	15–16 (%)
Alone	40	42	46	31	45	44	44	48	32	43	42	51
With friends	19	36	18	16	19	12	28	19	20	25	31	19
With siblings	15	11	19	19	12	13	15	9	20	16	13	20
With mother	11	1	2	16	9	6	1	9	12	3	1	0
With father	3	2	5	5	4	0	4	4	2	5	4	0
With other	5	2	6	5	5	1	4	2	7	5	3	4
n/a	7	7	3	8	8	3	5	7	7	3	6	7

Source: Livingstone and Bovill, 1999.

Clearly, children would like to be able to watch television alone far more than they actually can at present. Indeed, viewing alone is the most popular option. This would seem to be strongly motivated by the desire to escape from co-viewing with siblings and with parents. The YPNM survey also showed that more boys than girls watch their favourite programme alone. While this may reflect a greater desire on the part of boys to be on their own, it may also reflect an association between the genre of their favourite programme and the context of viewing. Soap operas, more often the favourite of girls, appear to invite more sociable viewing, while sports, more favoured by boys, are more often watched alone. Indeed, four-fifths of both boys and girls who identify a soap opera as their favourite programme generally watch it in company, while one-third of boys and girls who choose sports for their favourite watch this alone.

In all age groups, but particularly among boys and teenagers, more would also like to watch with friends.[8] This preference for being more often with friends than is currently managed is repeated when we compare experiences and preferences for playing computer games. However, in contrast to their experience with television, more children are already playing computer games on their own than would opt to do so given the choice: almost two-thirds mostly play computer games alone, but fewer say they most enjoy playing this way. The converging evidence, therefore, is that television – traditionally conceived as a social medium – remains a family activity but a sizeable proportion of children and young people would rather view individually. This suggests a growing pressure from children and young people for having a television in their bedroom if they do not already have one. However, the emerging picture is less one of children's preference for isolation than one of a preference for escaping the family and for spending time with friends. This latter is itself heavily media-related, for while the preference for peer relations serves to put media 'in their place', it is also obvious that one can no longer imagine youth culture without music, computer games, soap opera, or chat rooms, and that multiple-screen homes are becoming increasingly commonplace.

These preferences for 'socialising' the media work to overcome some features of the technologies themselves. Notably, the computer, which generally supports a single user – there is often only one keyboard, one joy-stick, one mouse – and which is indeed a medium children are very likely to use alone, is also a medium which many would prefer to use with friends. Moreover, Pasquier et al. (1998) suggest that the computer (playing on it, talking about it, advising on use, comparing experiences) may provide a new opportunity for father–son discussions which previously were rela-tively absent within the typical family. Observations of children playing computer games suggest that children are finding ways of playing even one-person games with friends, issuing instructions to the one with the mouse, negotiating turn-taking, and so forth, as well as talking about computers at school or visiting friends to see their computer. LaFrance (1996: 316) notes that the games themselves encourage group involvement, for the stress on passwords, cheats and tips, represents a knowledge 'that one can find in cer-tain books or magazines, which children seldom buy but the content of which circulates, in informal networks of friends'.[9] Meanwhile, technologi-cal support for social gaming – in the sense of multiple, simultaneous game players using multiple networked computers – is growing. So too are email and the Internet being used primarily, and against popular expectation, to sustain face-to-face relationships more than to create virtual ones.[10] In short, while often played alone, there is also evidence that, contrary to the popular fears that computer games have an isolating effect on children, they are instead finding a series of strategies for 'socialising' the computer.

In general, the possible harms, if any, of 'solitary' use of media remain unproven. Moreover, in principle, as social psychologists have long argued, even if one sits alone with one's thoughts in an empty room, one is irrevocably social; there is no individual (or private) thought or action which is not constituted in and through the other thoughts and actions of the social realm. But being apart from others, physically, is clearly seen by children and young people themselves positively. The importance of bedroom culture for children and young people is now considered in more depth below.

The Culture of the Bedroom

We have seen that equipping the bedroom with media represents for parents and children an ideal compromise in which children are both entertained and kept safe. For parents are more fearful of their children's safety outside the home than of any media-related dangers, as the YPNM survey shows. And as many young people do not think there is enough for them to do in their neighbourhood, they are only too happy to receive their own new or hand-me-down televisions, VCRs, etc. Thus, by the end of the 1990s, many young people have media-rich bedrooms, not necessarily reflecting an intrinsic fascination for the media so much as the unsatisfactory nature of the available alternatives. We have also seen that parallel data from other European countries suggest that British children experience a comparative lack of leisure facilities outside, but this is compensated in part by a comparatively greater media provision inside the home (Bovill and Livingstone, 2001; d'Haenens, 2001). Of course, other social changes, including central heating[11], smaller family size, and continual upgrading of domestic technological goods all have their part to play (Allan, 1985), but the result is clearly a new kind of place for children's leisure which has been little explored to date, and one which is ever more filled with media goods for ever younger children – their bedroom.

The YPNM survey showed that in British children's bedrooms music media are the most popular: 68% have a personal stereo, 61% have hi-fi and 59% a radio. Screen entertainment media follow close behind: 63% have their own television and 21% have a video recorder, while 34% have a TV-linked games machine and 27% have a Gameboy. Two-thirds (64%) have books (not for school) and as many as 12% have their own computer, though only 4% have a CD-ROM and 1% a modem (see Chapter 2). However, one should not presume 'bedroom culture' to be homogeneous across all children and young people. In the YPNM project we divided the bedrooms of children and young people aged 6–17 into four types according to the media they contained:

- Media-rich bedroom
- Specialist bedroom (typically, books and music or books and computer)
- Screen entertainment bedroom
- Media-poor bedroom

The *media-rich bedroom* describes around one-quarter of children and young people's bedrooms. These contain a variety of old and new media, including greater than average ownership of screen entertainment, music, books and computers. It is more typical of boys, older and working-class children. This last may seem unexpected, as overall household provision is positively associated with household income; however, in provisioning children's bedrooms, as we saw earlier, different factors come into play, and many of the media-rich homes were found in relatively poor households. To be sure, media-rich bedrooms tend to be located in media-rich homes, where the contents of the child's bedroom tend to duplicate those elsewhere in the home; yet we encountered a proportion of relatively low-income households (often single-parent households) where the child's bedroom was equipped apparently at the expense of the home.

We saw in Chapter 2 that certain media have become more specialised in their uses. Similarly, some bedrooms (about one in three) specialise in particular combinations of media, eschewing other, particularly screen entertainment, media as a result. Hence, the combination of *books and music*, especially favoured by girls, or, increasingly common among teenagers, bedrooms prioritising *books and the computer* are more typical in middle-class homes with educated parents. A screen/ print trade-off is clearly observable here, for these bedrooms are also distinguishable by being particularly low on screen entertainment media, especially television.

By contrast, the *screen entertainment bedroom*, more common among working-class boys, especially between the ages 12 and 14, tends to prioritise the television, TV-linked games machine and, for some, a VCR, over books and music equipment. While screen entertainment represents a media specialisation of some children and young people (and, indeed, of some parents), it is rarely characteristic of the home overall and so does not emerge as a household type (see Chapter 2). This is because households rich in screen entertainment media also contain books and music and so are more generally media-rich. This type of bedroom – characteristic of one in five of the sample – is interesting in part because it is the focus of most popular concern. Indeed, these bedrooms – along with the media-rich bedrooms – are characteristic of children who claim to spend a higher proportion of their waking time in their bedroom.

Lastly, around one-quarter of bedrooms may be characterised as *media-poor*, being less likely to contain any of the media we asked about. Interestingly, these are not necessarily those of poorer or younger children, though these children do tend to be lower media users. Media-poor bedrooms are associated with a considerable variety of households. As pointed out earlier, there is no simple relation between household income and provisioning of the bedroom. Rather, two factors are relevant in accounting for the existence of media-poor bedrooms in average-to-high income households. First, this low level of provision may represent a disinclination to prioritise screen media within the family's lifestyle. Secondly, it may reflect a preference on the part of parents for shared rather than personalised media use within the family, so these homes may be well equipped other than in the child's bedroom. Perhaps because girls are less interested in acquiring screen media in particular, or because girls are more often expected to share with the family, media-poor bedrooms are more common among girls.

The YPNM survey also shows that media in the bedroom are heavily used, and that, generally speaking, those children with access to certain media in their own room spend more time with those media than do those who only have such access elsewhere in the home (this holds true even after controlling for the age, gender and social class of the child). It follows then that those with 'screen' or 'media-rich' bedrooms spend more time overall with media (especially with screen media) and those with 'book/music' or 'media-poor' bedrooms spend the least time with media overall (with the exception of reading) (Livingstone and Bovill, 1999).

The relationship between the type of home environment and media provision in the children's bedrooms is far from predictable. However, the emerging pattern suggests that there are two categories of parents who provide a 'media-rich' home: those who equip their children's bedrooms as part of a general strategy of high levels of provision in the home, and those who equip the home well for common use but provide less for individual use in the bedroom. A converse pattern may be observed in 'media-poor' homes: while some of these families provide relatively little media for their children's bedrooms, a similar proportion provides high levels of media in the bedroom for individual use. Of major significance, then, is the balance struck – depending more on family ethos than finances – between individual and communal lifestyles within different households. The nature of 'bedroom culture' for particular children varies in consequence.

This balance, and hence this emergence of what we might term the mediatised, or hi-tech, bedroom as a child-centred and private space, has its own developmental trajectory. Not only are media-rich bedrooms more common among teenagers, but interviews with children and young people confirm that the meaning of the bedroom as a leisure space alters with time. Three key rationales for the bedroom vary in importance for different age groups:

- For sleeping in and convenient storage of personal goods
- For escaping the family and for activities which require concentration
- For constructing and expressing one's individual identity and sociability

Convenience   In general, younger children prefer the family spaces, especially when parents are present – by contrast with teenagers who also like to use the space and facilities of the living room, but mainly when their family is absent. Consequently, children younger than about 9 years old are relatively uninterested in bedroom culture, although a well-equipped, 'media-rich' bedroom is occasionally provided as a way of ensuring the parents' privacy. When we asked Belinda (age 6) why she claims to spend little time in her bedroom, she answered:

Belinda:	Because I wouldn't usually play in here.
Interviewer:	Where would you normally play?
Belinda:	Errm, the living room, the back garden or in the front.
Interviewer:	So do you come up here and get your toys and take them downstairs?
Belinda:	Yes.

However, even by this age children's bedrooms will often contain (and protect) their collections – whether of china animals, Disney memorabilia, foreign coins, Pokémon cards or the paraphernalia of a Manchester United football fan. Ten-year-old Rachel tells us: 'I used to collect bees', while her little sister Hester adds, 'and I collect Owls, little china owls'. Significantly, when we asked Rachel, 'do your friends collect the same sorts of things as you do or different?' she explains, 'no, they collect different things', suggesting the link between collections and personal identity. Part of the convenience of the bedroom, then, is its role in the safe storage of valued objects. As her mother says of Shelly (age 9): 'She used to collect the Farthing Wood Animal models. She used to make the models and then put them out of reach so that no one else could touch them.' As this quotation also suggests, these collections are generally recognised as transient. Parents and children describe the collection as something engaged in for a while and then – like the image of the self it represents – grown out of. Hester's mother says, 'Hester used to collect little ornaments of owls. She hasn't collected any for a while now but she went through a stage of collecting them.' Consequently, children's bedrooms house evidence of not only the current enthusiasm but also that of previous enthusiasms, making for a series of partial collections which, while appearing *ad hoc* to the outside observer, represent the story of a child's development:

Leslie did collect, he's got loads of dinosaurs, little plastic ones and things, he did collect the football stickers, he likes the Power Rangers things but he hasn't still got all of them. Lucy – she has got a lot of Barbies but she's gone off them at the moment, she just, no she doesn't really collect anything.

One may see in these collections a legitimised form of consumerism. Generally encouraged or even initiated by parents, the practices associated with adding to and displaying the collection are construed by parents very differently from the irritating pressure for another computer game or the latest trainers, being seen instead as specialist, serious, engaged, knowledgeable. We see this positive assessment of 'the collection' in the narrative spun for John, aged 7, by his mother, a lower middle-class single parent. She first introduced the notion of the 'collection' to explain her son's video viewing through his interest in animals. In so doing, she establishes a series of associations between videos and education, knowledge, value and, ultimately, John's career potential:

> *Mother:* We have got a lot of the Walt Disney videos because we collect those because I think they are a collectable item and John is very much into marine life and the Free Willy video, anything to do with animals. … If there is a wild life programme on them, John will just sit there from start to finish. He is very into that. … John likes any aspect of it, like any programme, like wildlife programmes, or Animal Hospital, he loves things like that. But the videos, I mean the collection is varied. They have the wildlife videos, the Disney videos, and films that have come out or that they have seen at the pictures and wanted to have as a keepsake type of thing. When we were younger, we had a lot of Thomas the Tank ones. The Sooty video collection was good with the alphabet and stuff like that, and Rod, Jane and Freddy, when they were around. Those are videos that I have since passed on to friends with smaller children because I thought that they were quite educational at the time. … But sort of with the animals he has always been – he is a very sensitive child and with animals it is something from a very very small age, I mean like sitting in the dog box with the dog and if you say 'no' to a chocolate biscuit then you can see John just feeding the dog and stuff like that. In actual fact, the teacher in school said to him something about the whale that was in Free Willy and said to me 'if your son doesn't become a marine biologist then I will eat my hat'.

Already, through these collections, through their emerging fandoms, and through the associated theming of wallpaper, bed linen, decoration, etc., children's identities are being constructed and, simultaneously, commodified. In early to middle childhood, the objects collected vary widely, but with the exception of videos, are generally not media goods (though of course they are often promoted through the media). By the teenage years, objects being actively collected are nearly exclusively collections of music tapes and compact discs, videos, computer games, magazines, and so forth – all of them media goods. This transition is noted by 15-year-old Kathy's parents:

> *Mother:* Oh well, she used to collect all those little whimsies that we once got from a car boot sale (laughter) … little animals that she collected.

Father: She doesn't collect anything now though, apart from music, not seriously anyway.

As for John, above, Kathy's possession of some 200 tapes is judged 'serious'. However, possession, and safe storage, is no longer key to the enjoyment of these goods, for media require time spent with them. Associated with the transition to media goods is a transition in the use of the bedroom – no longer primarily for convenience but now also for escape (or individualised media use) and for identity (requiring an investment in media use to promote self-development and self-expression).

Escape   From middle childhood, children – particularly girls – become more interested in their bedroom, and start to want personal ownership of media. This is largely for pragmatic reasons, particularly being able to choose and watch their own programmes uninterrupted. Over and again, children described how irritating it is to be interrupted – when watching television for example – by siblings or parents, suggesting strongly that, for them, being alone means being able to concentrate. Here a 10-year-old girl explains: 'I like being on my own. ... [I can] watch what I want to watch instead of watching what my sister wants to watch or what my mum wants to watch.' The notion of the bedroom providing some 'peace and quiet' is much valued, and one can see why when we consider the experience of this exasperated 7 year old who talks of trying to watch his favourite television programme with his 5-year-old brother:

John: I can't hardly see the TV, he goes zoom, zoom, zoom, he's whizzing around, I can't even hear what it's saying.
Interviewer: Right, so does that annoy you a bit?
John: Yes, and then when I get really angry I have to, what I have to do is climb down – this makes me really mad – switch it off.

This value of the bedroom does not cease, at least for the 72% who do not share a bedroom with a sibling. Here a 16-year-old girl, living in a working-class family, expresses a similar sentiment:

[My bedroom] has got all I need in it. But it is nice because I have got like a stereo and a TV, so if I need some peace and quiet, or I just want to be on my own, I can just go up there and do what I want.

However, even though our European comparisons show that British children and young people generally own more screen media, especially than do their counterparts in other countries (with the exception of America; Roberts et al., 1999), they do not claim to spend more than average amounts of time in their rooms. The advantages of convenience do not necessarily, it seems, encourage isolation from the family (Bovill and Livingstone, 2001). However, the desire for escape – whether for peace or for engaging in individual media tastes – is precisely about finding value in the distinction between self and family. Wanting to escape, then, we can see as marking the transition from *having* personal 'stuff' and so needing somewhere safe to put it to *being* a distinct individual and so needing somewhere private to express this.

Identity   In adolescence, this concern with the self is of pre-eminent importance. The significance of the bedroom is now primarily centred on identity, as young people take a growing interest in how their bedrooms are furnished, arranged and equipped. By the early teens, these psychological reasons are easily as important as the practical ones as children and young people seek to identify, protect and embellish their own spaces distinct from adult scrutiny and intervention. The bedroom provides a flexible social space in which young people can experience their growing independence from family life, becoming either a haven of privacy or a social area in which to entertain friends, often listening to music, reading magazines, playing a new computer game or watching a video together. Corsaro (1997) notes that first and foremost peer cultures are organised so that children protect their interaction space – this is as apt in accounting for children's investment in their bedrooms as it is for the outdoor places that Corsaro has in mind. Rochberg-Halton (1984: 347) suggests further that 'transactions with cherished possessions are communicative dialogues with ourselves'. Listen to the satisfaction with which 15-year-old Joanne, from a working-class family, describes her room:

> I'm usually in my bedroom. ... I think that I like to be by myself really. I don't know. I suppose it's just because at the moment I have got all my furniture arranged like in a sitting room area, a study room area and my bedroom and it is just, like, really cool and I just like to go there because I know that that is my room. ... I mean I have decorated it how I want it and it's just like a room I don't think I will ever move out.

Similarly, when asked why she watches television in her own bedroom rather than in the living room, 16-year-old Rose tells us:

> *Rose:*   Well, usually because my Mum's down there. Don't want her listening to what I'm talking about. ... Um well I suppose, boys.
> *Interviewer:* So your bedroom's quite a private place, in fact?
> *Rose:*   Yes. My personality's expressed.

Personal ownership of media dramatically increases in the early teenage years, as part and parcel of the development of identity. From the perspective of the social psychology of adolescence, 'valued material possessions, it is argued, act as signs of the self that are essential in their own right for its continued cultivation, and hence the world of meaning that we create for ourselves, and that creates our selves, extends literally into the objective surroundings' (Rochberg-Halton, 1984: 335; see also Furby, 1978; Kamptner, 1989). Rochberg-Halton's (1984) account of the symbolic value of goods for the self stresses that while everyone values their old photos, their favourite records, their childhood teddy bear, for children and teenagers these 'special' objects are highly likely to be located in their bedroom. Yet curiously, Rochberg-Halton sees this as evidence of young people's egocentricity – their desire to have every-thing, and every activity, in the one room – rather than recognising that the bedroom is the main, if not only, place where young people can exert control over the arrangement of objects in 'their' space.

Notably, images of self-sufficiency and control figure strongly in young people's talk of their bedroom. Here a young girl describes her picture of her ideal bedroom:

> She's got all these comics on the bed, and she likes to read them, and she's got a computer next to her TV so if she gets bored she can just move around quick, and she's got like a computer booklet on computers and TV, and she's got a telephone with a hi-fi midi system sort of thing.
>
> (9-year-old girl living in a middle-class family)

In this context of self-sufficiency and control, unwarranted interventions by others can be experienced as a significant violation of privacy:

> Last year I went to Austria and erm, I came back and I nearly had a heart attack because my mum had completely cleaned my room. … She had com-pletely blitzed my room and I was so angry about it. … It is my own private space and I really don't like her touching it. … She just goes on and on about me cleaning it and I mean, I try to tell her that it is my personal space and let me have it how I want.
>
> (Middle-class girl aged 15)

Madigan and Munro (1999: 70) identify the particular difficulties posed by the structure of the home for women in resolving the tension between 'the socially sanctioned goal of family togetherness, sharing, equality and the goal of individual achievement, self-identity'. While they suggest that for women this is more often achieved through the management of time than space, for children the bedroom is provided as a spatial solution. Emler and Reicher (1995) explore how the management of spatial boundaries, and the constraints on this, frames the everyday management of identities. Behind this lies the social psychological argument that identities must be enacted, and the relationships through which they are enacted are situated in locations with particular spatial and temporal structures. Most simply, whether children can keep their friendships distinct in space and time from their family relationships is crucial to the sustaining of multiple, possibly distinct, identities. Hence, the widespread irritation occasioned by siblings intruding into spaces in which friendships are conducted, media are engaged with, or privacy enjoyed represents an irritation not simply due to the interruption of an activity or conversation but a clash of identities. At such an interruption one is drawn into being primarily a sibling, a family member, rather than a friend, peer group member, or whatever, and the identity thus foregrounded may, from the young person's point of view, pull them back to a familial identity possibly more typical of when one was younger, and one more defined by others, particularly parents, than by oneself. The irritation is thus not alleviated by the younger sibling promising to be quiet, or not interfere, for it is a symbolic intrusion, a clash of one identity with another, a loss of freedom to reinvent oneself for oneself. Similarly, the persistent untidiness of many children's rooms, and the high degree of tidiness of others, may reflect more than a concern, or lack of concern, with order. For an untidy room is hard for an adult to walk around, and a very tidy room will show signs of intruders. The effect is to make the room both child-friendly and adult-unfriendly. By contrast with the traditional hierarchies of the living room, the bedroom is fundamentally a heterarchical space – perhaps the only place where children can dictate the rules of engagement to their parents.

Bedroom Culture The culture of the bedroom draws on all three rationales or meanings of the bedroom. It provides a convenient location in which one's personal goods can be gathered and maintained. It provides a means to escape from the interruptions, interference and desires of others. The combination of these two constitute the basis for the construction of an individual identity, facilitating both a positive statement of oneself through one's possessions and activities and a negative statement of what one is not, of being elsewhere and of doing other things than with one's family members.

Steele and Brown (1994; see also Brown et al., 1994) describe teenage 'room culture' as the place where media and identities intersect through the bricolage of identity-work objects on display in young people's rooms, seeing adolescents' rooms as 'mediating devices' by which they express who they are and who they want to be – a safe, private space in which experimentation with possible selves can be conducted.

Frith (1978: 64) links the history of rock music to the then new culture of the bedroom, suggesting that it resulted from the emergence of music for young people tailored to youth while simultaneously defined against the tastes of their parents, thus effectively drawing on trends towards both the privatisation and the individualisation of media use. As Flichy commented later, the media-rich bedroom in the 'juxtaposed home allows teenagers to remove themselves from adult supervision while still living with their parents' (1995: 165).

Bachmair (1997) talks of the bedroom as a text within which the television programme is interwoven as one central element among others. From the sign on the door ('Parents, keep out!') to the popstar posters on the wall, the collection of Disney mementos, and the music on the radio or magazine programme on the television, together these constitute an interlinked and personalised text. As such, this complex text of the bedroom provides a key site for the construction of identity and a position from within which to participate in a shared peer culture. This participation takes two forms, for the bedroom is both a location in which children and young people can entertain friends and also a place in which they can experience their connection to the peer group even when alone, particularly through the use of media valued by peers.

The media are used in various ways to manage these boundaries of space and identity, especially by young people who not only sustain multiple identities but whose identities are often experimental, temporary, available for making over. The symbolic resources of the media provide the content – images, representations, themes – as well as the material means of managing these boundaries (the walkman, the loud music in the bedroom, the total absorption in a computer game). Hence, the 'deafness' parents complain about is more due to identity considerations than to media addiction. The skilful opening and closing of windows, depending on who is in the computer room, the use of screensavers or other means of personalising the screen, temporarily or permanently, are similarly means of marking the computer in terms of identity.

'Bedroom culture' in this sense is very much a Western phenomenon, being dependent on a high degree of modernisation and wealth. As such, it represents a new opportunity for targeted advertising and marketing, as the media-rich child's bedroom is both a site of reception for commercial messages and a location for the display and use of consumer goods. While the bedroom is thus a key site for the increasing commercialisation of childhood and youth, it also supports the development of identity in ways that may be, but are not necessarily, exploitative. Thus while McRobbie and Garber (1976) and Frith (1978) emphasised how teenage girls' search for identity through self-presentation and the development of 'taste' has been led by powerful commercial interests in the fashion and music industries, Fornäs and Bolin see mediated consumer images as providing the raw materials with which young people creatively construct 'their' style. Similarly, studies of the domestic appropriation of media (Silverstone and Hirsch, 1992) focus on the use of media products, like other consumer goods, to express individual and collective styles.

The Gendered Bedroom   It is no accident that the quotations included thus far come from girls. McRobbie and Garber (1976) noted how girls' subcultures are too often rendered invisible by academic and popular discourses, especially those that focus on problematising boys' appropriation of public spaces. Looking back to the 1950s onwards, they stressed the importance of the culture of the bedroom for girls, which they related to the greater attachment of girls to their family and to either a best friend or a small group of close friends, a circle which can be accommodated adequately in the bedroom.[12] Spending time in one's bedroom is not purely a matter of choice or convenience, but also reflects girls' more restricted access to public and often male-dominated spaces and the domestic duties expected of them which tie them to the home (Frith, 1978).

When McRobbie and Garber (1976) describe girls' bedroom culture as protected spaces, free from parental surveillance, in which style, identity and belonging can be expressed, little attention is paid to the possibility of boys' bedroom culture – presumably, they are seen as primarily engaged instead in 'street corner culture' (Corrigan, 1976). But these images of bedroom and street culture stem from a time – 1950s to 1970s – before bedrooms were media-rich. Today, with a growing concern about street culture and its associated dangers, together with the increasing provisioning of media in the bedroom, bedrooms are also of importance to boys; they too need space for identity and relationship work, and the pervasiveness of media in these spaces is significant. One may even speculate that for boys, some aspects of street corner culture may be reproduced in the bedroom, transforming historically feminine culture of the bedroom in the direction of the traditionally male culture of the street. Cunningham (1995) described the street corner as about waiting for something to happen (or even about making that unpredictable something happen), in order to alleviate boredom. As young people are, in his terms, 'repatriated' to the home, a new kind of making things happen can be seen, now focused on the screen: the logic of computer games especially is often about power and mastery, anticipation and eventfulness (LaFrance, 1996).

Gender differences are perhaps most salient when children outline their ideal bedroom. We asked children to draw us pictures of their ideal bedroom 'in the year 2000' (taken by our interviewees to refer to a rather distant future). While the importance of conspicuous media consumption was central to many pictures, girls tended to foreground the aesthetics of interior design while boys were more fascinated by technology and control. Here are two working-class girls, aged 13 and 14:

> It would be a big spacious room with loads of space and pine furniture with big wardrobes and drawers ... and there'd be a big TV with all the channels and everything and a big stereo with big massive speakers and there'd be a little room going off in my own bathroom with like marble floors and a jacuzzi and everything and in the room there'd be a big king-size bed and then there'd be another little room going off with my own little gym in it and a swimming pool.

> My bedroom's going to be black and gold and white. I'm going to have a cyber-wardrobe, when you walk through it it puts clothes on for you. It depends on what mood you're in. And then it's going to have a shoe wardrobe that changes your shoes for you. And then I'm going to have a sand bed with sand underneath it because I think that would be wicked. ... And then a TV like a cinema screen. And then a glass floor and a massive chest of drawers that looks more like a wardrobe but it's just got thousands of drawers, and then like a big window a massive window and my speaker boxes. I've not had time to draw my stereo in but it'll be on top of my chest of drawers.

These children greatly enjoyed this task, playing with the ideas of new media possibilities with great humour. As one 13-year-old girl noted: 'I'm drawing me mum, she's stuck in a time warp in my wardrobe!' And a 10-year-old boy calls out excitedly, 'Everybody! Look what you've forgotten! An interactive mum!' His friend replies in kind: 'I've got a Playstation 1 million. I've got a camcorder. I've got a fridge. I've got a slave. I've got me and my babe on my bed and I've got an emperor's bed what is king, king, king size!' While no future moment will make these fantasies come true, for children and young people, their bedroom is a key site in which their fantasies of who they are and who they might yet be are perhaps most readily expressed.

LIVING TOGETHER SEPARATELY

The growth of a market for personal ownership of television sets, videos and computers is multiply determined. Crucially, children and young people value using the media alone, despite adult worries about 'isolation'. Yet this privatisation does not necessarily mean that social contacts are being replaced with social isolation, for media can offer new means for social interaction, albeit often peer- rather than family-focused interaction. Much of this privatised use of media is focused on the bedroom, once rather chilly and uncomfortable, sometimes forbidden, places in which to escape the demands of family life, but now positively valued opportunities for socialising and identity work, saturated with media images, sounds, technological artefacts and other media products. As leisure becomes increasingly media-dominated, and as rooms (or people) rather than the home (or the household) increasingly become the unit for acquisition of screen media, today's parents cannot rely on their own childhood experiences to guide them in managing the spatial and temporal structures of domestic and family life. Rather they must figure out for their own household how to accommodate, regulate and enjoy the plethora of media goods now widely available. This they generally do together with their children as part of a sometimes co-operative, sometimes conflictual negotiation, within a broader context which pits the discourse of new opportunities and consumer choice against that of the parental duty to manage appropriately their children's social development in the face of increasing potential harms.

We have seen that media-rich bedroom culture can contribute to the shifting of the boundary between public and private spaces in several ways. Within the home the multiplication of personally owned media may facilitate children's use of individual, privatised space, as opposed to communal family space[13]. However, such a relatively privatised bedroom culture is also developing as a result of the apparently progressive exclusion of children and young people from public places in society, together with a growing priority placed on 'the home' as the centre of a screen entertainment-focused, privatised and individualised leisure culture. At the same time, the nature of such private space within the home may be transformed as the media-rich bedroom increasingly becomes the focus of peer activity, and as the media themselves, through their contents, bring the outside world indoors. Staying at home is framed, to a significant degree, by the meaning of 'going out': for parents, going out is risky while staying home is safe, being with others is healthy while being alone means being isolated or antisocial, organised time is time well spent while free time is easily wasted, and so forth. Whether the metaphors come from the realms of health or finance, time with media is rarely neutral, and it is within this cultural context that both parents and children make their choices.

Notably, all this is merely the latest chapter in a long history of communication technologies, one that can be told as a story of the increasing privatisation of leisure. One can trace the transformation of the public show – first at the theatre and then, in the twentieth century, in the cinema – from an occasion for 'collective listening to the juxtaposition of a series of individual listening experiences' (Flichy, 1995: 153). A number of factors, including the architecture of the theatre, the social status of both audience and performers and, in relation to the cinema, the introduction of sound (Hansen, 1991), effected the broad shift from 'collective listening' – which was about 'noisy listening', joining in, shouting out, being seen – to a new form of spectatorship – as silent, dark, alone, non-participatory.

Historically, these transformations from public to private, and from collective to individual, were rarely anticipated. Boddy (1985) quotes a variety of commentators who failed to anticipate the casual uses of television. The following, taken from *Harper's* in 1940, is typical: 'Television, like the motion picture or the stage, and unlike the radio, requires complete and unfaltering attention. If the eye wanders for a moment from the television screen a programme's continuity is lost' (Boddy, 1985: 131). And although Flichy traces this history for the radio – from collective to individual, from centrally located to mobile and dispersed, from shared to fragmented experience, from restraint to free use – even he, writing in the early 1990s, finds it hard to anticipate a similar future for television, arguing first that television's mode of address is to the group not the individual and, secondly, that the evidence for multiple set ownership is far slower than that of radio. Yet as Williams (1974: 26, original emphasis) observed several decades ago, broadcasting 'served an at once mobile and home-centred way of living: a form of *mobile privatisation*'. We may reasonably continue Flichy's (1995: 159–60) narrative, namely that, 'whereas in the 1940s the family had gathered together around the radio, in the 1960s each family member pursued his or her own activities while listening to a separate radio', by suggesting that from the 1990s onwards in Europe, and rather earlier in the USA, the same has occurred for television. Perhaps a similar story is already emerging for the computer.

The 'lonely crowd' of the theatre and cinema may be less visible in the home, the space where most twentieth-century mass media have developed, yet the same fear of isolated media use on a mass scale has fuelled a series of moral panics which have followed in turn the introduction of television, video games, computers, the Internet, and so forth (Buckingham, 1993; Drotner, 1992).[14] Broadly speaking, today's domestic media are following a similar path to that of public leisure spaces. The now familiar case of the telephone also illustrates this trend, for this was originally thought of as a means of listening to theatre or concerts at home, thus failing to anticipate the more private, one-to-one use which became dominant. Flichy describes the social history of radio, from the collective listening in the family living room to 'living together separately', facilitated by the new portability and cheapness of the transistor radio, which allowed the multiplication of radios within the home, as well as by the introduction of a new centre for family life – the television set.

In analysing the cultural significance of this shift, there is a tendency among commentators to conflate the process of privatisation, the primary focus of this chapter, and individualisation, an analytically separate but historically coincident process also relevant to, for example, the multiplication of domestic media. Privatisation typically refers to the move away from publicly accessible spaces where people are conceptualised as citizens (e.g. Meyrowitz, 1985) and the simultaneous move towards domestic spaces, where people are conceptualised as consumers or audiences. This in itself is often unclear in so far as there is a tendency to confuse the common usage of the term 'private', which maps private and public spaces onto inside and outside the home and family (or even, which construes public as visible and private as solitary or unseen by others) with the analytically precise use of the term seen in the work of Habermas (1969/89) and others (e.g. Poster, 1997: 208). Here the realm of the private refers to commercial interests, whether part of the system (specifically, the economy) or the lifeworld (the home), as distinct from the disinterested concerns of the democratically conceived and institutionalised 'public good', again whether part of the system (the state) or the lifeworld (the public sphere). This usage clarifies certain ambiguities regarding the key spaces of children's lives. The mall is located outside, and so, seemingly public but actually private (i.e. commercial or commodified or exploitative). The home is valued for its privacy (the 'sanctity' of the home) yet this is increasingly intruded upon by private (i.e. commercial) interests. The bedroom is the object of concern not because it offers privacy but because it appears to isolate young people from participation in the public (i.e. disinterested) sphere.

In short, underlying the common and sometimes obfuscating uses of the private/public distinction, we can identify four key oppositions which frame debates over young people's media use. Thus debates may refer to notions of private in the sense of:

- commercial or commodified (versus disinterested or public) leisure;
- withdrawal or isolation from others (versus connection to/participation in public culture or the public sphere);
- privacy or the evasion of surveillance (versus being 'in the public eye');
- individual, as in 'acting as a private individual' (versus social or communal, with a focus on a shared and socially grounded or traditional set of knowledge, conventions or values).

The very confusion among these different uses of the private/public distinction in popular discussion tends to fuel the moral panics regarding 'home alone kids', Net-addicts, the McDonaldisation of kids' culture, and so forth. Morley cautions against understanding privatisation as a withdrawal from social relations, for instance, when he notes that '[t]elevision viewing may be a "privatised" form of activity, by comparison with cinema-going for example, but it is still largely conducted within, rather than outside of, social relations – in this case the social relations of the family or household' (1986: 14), and this holds true even when viewing is further privatised into the bedroom.

Notably, the places in which children and young people spend their leisure cut across these various notions of public and private culture – the home is apart from the public sphere yet grounded in tradition, the bedroom offers privacy yet is increasingly commercialised and media-rich, the shopping mall is both connected and commodified, the street corner is in the public eye yet may represent a defiance towards public culture, the youth club is part of the public domain yet supports an individualised youth culture. Once these four oppositions are separated, it becomes clear that different responses are appropriate. For instance, concerns over the commercialisation of kids' culture (e.g. Kinder, 1999), and over the loss of a public sphere which positively encompasses children, certainly mark a historical shift and are likely to be widely supported. But this should not be taken to threaten children's right to privacy or freedom from surveillance. Nor should we assume that the loss of tradition is necessarily against young people's interests. Indeed, the social movements stimulated by a growing politics of identity may be seen to work for their interests. However, our responses to particular leisure spaces will remain complex, not least because, as the private realm of the economy increasingly penetrates the disinterested public sphere, and as the institutional realm of the state increasingly penetrates the lifeworld and the domestic sphere, the meanings of these places are, as Habermas has argued, historically contingent and changing.

One should note at this point that the last opposition above is more correctly theorised not in terms of public/private but in terms of individualisation, the broad Western trend in which everyday experience and practice is becoming detached from traditional sociostructural determinants (such as socio-economic status), resulting in a concomitant diversification of lifestyles freed from the social ties and traditions that have hitherto defined identity and taste (see Chapter 3). In practice, however, when we examine the domestic media uses of children and young people, we find these processes working together (as encapsulated in the notion of 'living together separately'; Flichy, 1995). The traditional conception of public life focuses on the community and on what is communal, so that civic life reflects choices and habits shared with others. In other words, there is a link between activities conducted in public, as part of the public interest, and the social structures and traditions that we inherit and which bind us together. Meanwhile, the driving force of private interests is towards the multiplication of markets, the diversification of taste categories, with the result that private life is increasingly centred on markers of distinction and difference. Popular anxieties over the solitary nature of new media use draw on both these conceptions, linking anxieties about the loss of citizenship participation with those concerning the loss of community tradition and values. Thus, privatisation supports individualisation and vice versa. Similarly, models of public or civic media have traditionally been tied to national regulatory frameworks, while only a global media market, commercially funded, is proving able to support the diversity of individualised lifestyle preferences.

Our common-sense language, in which many social ideals (and anxieties) are framed, tends to presume a clear separation of lifeworld and system. Yet if one accepts Habermas's analysis of modernity in terms of the penetration of the lifeworld by the system world, with deleterious effects on both public sphere (increasingly managed in the interests of economy and the state) and on the home (increasingly commercialised and a site for commercial management and manipulation) (Habermas, 1987), options often posed as either/or alternatives surely become both/and options instead. Society asks: Is the policy of introducing Internet into schools about enhancing public knowledge communities or enhancing the competitiveness of a national workforce? Is the family viewing of a Disney film an expression of private pleasure or of successful commercial exploitation of a once non-commercial domain? And so forth. To answer 'both/and', however, is not to offer a bland rejection of new media hype and hope, but to invite a considered evaluation of the opportunities and dangers which arise.

This chapter has traced the shift from public to private in relation to both the decline of 'street culture' and the retreat to the home, and in relation to the decline of 'family television' and the rise of 'bedroom culture'. Many of these issues raised in this chapter in turn raise more general questions regarding the meaning of childhood and family life. For although of course the present generation of parents were not, in the main, children during the 1950s, the culture of family values and child hood expectations dominant at that time, as well as the challenges to this culture posed then and since, has framed the struggle over the meanings of childhood throughout the decades which followed (Coontz, 1997; Osgerby, 1998). The notion that the privatisation of leisure (and in part, of childhood) has gone hand in hand with the democratisation of the family is taken up in the next chapter.

NOTES

1   This separation can be traced back to the sixteenth century and the origins of childhood itself: 'The discovery of childhood created childhood and adult society where only society had existed before. The creation of childhood simultaneously separated children from adult society, limited their freedom among adults, and imposed severe disciplinary controls on children and youth by home, school, and church' (Luke, 1989: 23). See Hoggart (1957) for a lively and insightful account of the texture of home and street life for families in the post-war period.

2   This may be partly a matter of generation. Today's parents grew up in the 1960s and 1970s, a time of increasing liberalisation, rather than the more formal and restrictive 1940s and 1950s, during which a very different conception of 'home' was institutionalised.

3   For a comparison of the conditions of childhood across Europe, see Livingstone et al. (2001).

4   It is difficult to determine whether attitudes to children's solitary activities were once more positive, or whether society has always regarded the desire to be alone with suspicion. Certainly, it is screen media that today serve as the focus for such concerns.

5   Increasingly, a large proportion of children and young people use personalised media such as the walkman, allowing them to create a private and individualised environment for themselves even when in public places.

6   From the broadcasters' YoungView panel, children aged 10–16.

7   From the broadcasters' YoungView panel, children aged 10–16.

8   Those with their own television set are almost twice as likely as those without to watch their favourite programme on their own, they are a little more likely to watch with friends, and they are particularly less likely to watch with opposite gender siblings (Livingstone and Bovill, 1999).

9 LaFrance describes this as an absorbed, emotional, uncritical sociability – 'experienced as the abandoning of the personality rather than as the enhancement of individuality' (1996: 315).

10 *'Families and the Internet'* Research Project; Livingstone and Bovill (2001b).

11 In 1970 only 30% of UK households had central heating; by 1999 this has risen to 90% of households (Down, 2000).

12 Certainly, our recent YPNM survey confirms that girls spend more of their free time with one best friend or with their family while boys spend more free time with a group of friends.

13 Rompaey and Roe (2002) call this the increasing 'compartmentalization of family life' as a result of the individualising effect of ICT combined with teenagers' desire for privacy within the family context.

14 With the growth of specifically domestic media, as opposed to those in public places, concerns have been expressed not only over the privatisation of what was once public, but also over the intrusion into a traditionally private place of common, national or even global images. As Silverstone (1999) has noted, a new and highly significant 'door' within the home has been introduced, with the electronic screen providing or preventing access to the wider community. In general, this new 'door' is proving as controversial as we have seen the front door and bedroom door to be for children and their parents, albeit one that is increasingly being opened when, or even because, the physical doors are often closed.

5

LIVING TOGETHER SEPARATELY: THE FAMILY CONTEXT OF MEDIA USE

FAMILY, HOUSEHOLD, HOME

Family life in the twentieth century saw an increasingly focus on the home (Allan, 1985), so that now using media at home means, for many people, using media in the context of family life. Despite the ordinariness of this observation, in writing about the family one must acknowledge how emotive and contested the notion of 'the family' has become (Muncie et al., 1999), and this complicates any analysis of the media. Assigned the task of nurturing and reproducing society's highest moral values, both through sustaining 'traditional' living standards and through the 'responsible' socialisation of children, the family is simultaneously the focus of high expectations and considerable anxieties. At least since the sixteenth century, 'a cohesive family unit was considered an imperative precondition for a stable and cohesive society' (Luke, 1989: 63). Today, 'the family' is popularly conceived in just these normative terms (as nuclear, cohesive, inherently good) in opposition to the individual (conceived as alienated, divisive, dangerous). Anything seen to threaten this ideal of the family – and the media are a common target – is subject to criticism.

This normative framing has tended to lead both research and public discussion to conflate three key terms – 'the home', 'the household' and 'the family'. Discussion of 'private' or 'domestic' space may add to the confusion, the effect being to align family with home and to create these together as a black box for which further subdivisions or analysis are rendered inappropriate. We have already looked within the home in Chapter 4. From this, we can take forward the following points:

- The apparent decline of public leisure facilities, after school facilities and 'street corner culture' accessible to children and young people means that leisure is significantly focused on the home.
- Houses are increasingly 'media-rich', this reflecting both a common provision of media for the family (a shared culture) and a personal provision of media for children in their bedrooms ('bedroom culture').
- Thus one must consider the media environment as a whole rather than ask about the use of each domestic medium separately.
- Moreover, as media spread throughout the day and the home, time at home today means time with media, and it is often a matter of choice rather than necessity whether this is spent also with other family members.

In consequence, and stimulated also by the decline of the public sphere, the home represents a key site for the privatisation of leisure. However, while the provision of multiple media in individualised leisure spaces fosters an explicit culture of individualisation, the home remains only partially a site for individualisation. The existence of considerable gender and socio-economic status differences in media use and leisure time, noted in Chapters 2 and 3, suggests that the daily routines and practices of domestic life also support the reproduction of normative social distinctions and stratifications, transferred from parents to children. Many parents are ambivalent about these trends, often setting out to support both individual preferences and 'family life', even though – in so far as the former are centrifugal and the latter centripetal in their effect – these on occasion conflict. This ambivalence regarding the individualising potential of the media points up the difference between asking about media at home and media in the context of family life, for the latter raises expectations regarding not only privacy, familiarity and comfort, but also communality, relationships and mutual expectations.

For families themselves, these cultural notions of family life may be experienced as highly normative or idealistic. Researchers are more likely to stress a non-normative definition of the family. For example, Hill and Tisdall (1997: 66) argue that 'the idea of family is to some degree a fluid one, with a mix of concepts at its core – direct biological relatedness, parental caring role, long-term cohabitation, permanent belonging'. Even so, this contrasts with the use of the term 'household', which avoids the normative or moral constructions of 'the family', remaining neutral regarding household composition and dynamics. Yet it is the concept of the family that foregrounds not the shared space and common economy but the relations among the individuals as primary. As Goodman (1983: 408) notes, adopting a family systems perspective, 'a family is not just a collection of individuals; it is greater than, and different from the sum of its members. ... A systems approach views the family in the context of its social milieu and in the context of its life cycle'. Interestingly, Hill and Tisdall (1997) review evidence suggesting that children's own perceptions of 'family' change as they grow older, with older children being more likely to include emotionally significant relationships within the term 'family' while younger children place more stress on co-residence.

The concepts of family and household are both of value and it is worth contrasting their meanings. A household may contain men, women and/or children of various ages; a family contains mother, father, sons and daughters, or various combinations thereof. The time scale of a household is usually defined by when the grouping moved into a particular house; the time scale of a family is far more elaborate, usually but not necessarily defined according to a normative notion of the lifecourse (couple, parents and children, parents and teenagers, parents in the 'empty nest'), though also extending backwards and forwards through the generations. Thus, even the nuclear family may be seen to extend over several households, while the extended family, as well as the family divided by divorce, obviously encompasses multiple households. Lastly, the household is, as a space for consuming goods, part of the market economy. It is in relation to this geographic and economic unit that the acquisition of, and inequalities in, media and consumer goods, the management of domestic space and time, and the construction of 'home' are more usually discussed, whether in the realms of market research or the sociology of consumption (e.g. Silverstone et al., 1991). On the other hand, the family is, as a locus for social relationships and social reproduction, central to discussions of social change. Here too the media are of growing importance, as part of the concerns regarding regulation, education, participation and culture.

In consequence, while the household has no established narrative, the family is all but overwhelmed by the burden of the narratives constructed for it by culture and history – narratives of dependence and interdependence, moral obligation and autonomy, tradition and progress. While researchers may choose to side-step these moral complexities, families themselves cannot, and it is within this narrative context that they make use of media and within which the media play a constitutive role in family life.[1] This role may be of greater or lesser importance for different aspects of family life and in different families. However, the moral tensions and anxieties about 'family life' are salient to many people as they make decisions regarding home-building and parenting. In consequence, this moral agenda frames families' use of media. As any parent can tell you, good parents read to their children, proper families talk to each other rather than staring at the box and, at worst, happy families watch soaps together rather than playing computer games on their own. One may regard these claims as mere rhetoric. But after listening to people's extensive and readily proffered accounts of the many dilemmas of parenting, all part of the project of bringing up children in accordance with the aspirations, values, interests, and skills that are important to them as parents and 'as a family', I am more inclined to conclude in favour of Varenne's claim that 'a great part of the energy used in everyday life is spent in an attempt to put ideology into practice' (Varenne, 1996: 431).

Historically, family and household have been overlapping but not identical constructs. What Coontz (1997) labels 'the 50s family experiment' was perhaps the moment when they most strongly coincided, not least as a popular ideal. In asserting that the household should contain the whole family and nothing but the family, this period of normative consensus-building drew heavily on the re-invention of the so-called 'Victorian family'. It is against this ideal that the post-war agenda of researching media and children, as well as popular expectations regarding parenting, was set (Buckingham, 1993; Oswell, 1998a). As we now look forward from the 1950s and its construction of the traditional nuclear family, we see the emergence by the start of this century of a new and equally idealised image of the family, namely that of the 'democratic family'. The social trends of the twentieth century can be read as undermining the Victorian family, creating an economic and legal hiatus between dependent child and independent adult, and resulting in considerable tensions between the discourse of dependency and needs and that of individualism and rights. The democratic family may be seen as offering some resolution, advocating that one provide for children economically for an extended period of time while simultaneously recognising their independence in terms of sociality and culture. This of course creates difficulties in balancing the requirements of parents and children, difficulties to be resolved through the process of democratic discussion and debate (the 'family forum' or equivalent).

However, these ideals regarding family, parenting and childhood have a far longer history than a purely twentieth-century lens reveals, and therefore the domestic mass media – notwithstanding their status as contemporary scapegoat for the ills of society – only enter the picture relatively late. Indeed, as early as the end of the seventeenth century, one could identify 'the privatisation of families from each other, and the individualisation of members within families' (Luke, 1989: 39), trends which continue today not only to frame 'family life', but also to frame the public anxieties which surround it. Hence, that Victorian conception of the family – significantly predating the domestic mass media and instead placing considerable value on 'making one's own entertainment' – can be seen for what it is, not the 'good old days' but the reinvention of tradition (Hobsbawm and Ranger, 1988).

Historians of the family 'argue that the shift from the premodern extended family unit to the modern nuclear family occurred over a three-century period from 1500 to 1800' (Luke, 1989: 1). Stone (1977) identifies three key stages in the development of the family:

- The Open Lineage Family, dating from antiquity to the mid-sixteenth century
- The Restricted Patriarchal Family, dating from the mid-sixteenth century to the end of the eighteenth century
- The Closed Domesticated Nuclear Family which emerged in the late seventeenth century

This last, premised on personal autonomy and affective ties rather than patriarchal authority, coincides with the modern notion of childhood. Here Aries's (1962) 'discovery of childhood' between the sixteenth and eighteenth centuries is perhaps the most famous thesis regarding childhood and the family, although historians have since qualified many of his contentions, noting that 'concepts of childhood changed unevenly and gradually across the social strata in a given society at different times in different societies' (Luke, 1989: 15). Crucially, where before the transmission of knowledge and culture was achieved through the participation of children in everyday life, the creation of a separate realm created the requirement of a new set of tasks for parents, and especially the state, namely those of socialisation and education. In developing this analysis of the family as a unit of political importance, Foucault identifies a key historical shift around the middle of the eighteenth century, centring on the emergence of the concept of 'population' and, with it, administrative social science. As he notes, 'prior to the emergence of population, it was impossible to conceive of the art of government except on the model of the family' (Foucault, 1991: 99). However, after this development, 'the family becomes an instrument rather than a model: the privileged instrument for the government of the population and not the chimerical model of good government' (1991: 100).

Varenne (1996) updates this historical account to encompass the contemporary Western (for her, American) family. She argues that what has characterised the family since the 1950s is the increasing diversification of household arrangements, largely but not solely resulting from the marked rise in divorce. Thus, while the love relations that underpin Stone's third stage of family development remain crucial to the modern family, Varenne argues that they are increasingly separated from reproduction, legal marriage ties and cohabitation. Rather, these love relations are framed by notions of freedom and, within this, of chosen – and felt – community or solidarity. Particularly, the love relation between parent and child hinges on the relative 'freedoms' which each can provide for the other, this being central to the 'good parent' and 'good child'.[2]

Of course, divorce is not the only factor here impinging on the modern family. Hill and Tisdall (1997) review a number of social trends affecting children's lives since the 1960s, including most notably, rises in:

- the proportion of births to unmarried mothers
- the number of households headed by a lone parent
- the number of marriages ending in divorce
- the numbers of remarriages and reconstituted families
- ethnic diversity
- male unemployment
- the proportion of mothers in paid employment

Notwithstanding a concomitant fall in fertility (resulting in reduced average family size, fewer siblings, and children comprising a smaller segment of the population), the outcome is a considerable diversification in household composition and family structure over the post-war period. As a result, the mapping of 'family' onto 'household' is more complex, requiring an account of both internal and external household relationships. This chapter centres on the distinction between 'family' and 'household' in order to analyse the place of media in relation to two basic senses of 'family':

- Family as relations of in/dependence between parents and children
- Family as a network of relationships within and beyond the household

Thus, first we consider those families constituted of parent(s) and dependent children. Here the key dynamic is that of dependence/independence, a dynamic that is negotiated through the management of domestic rules and through the social construction of age and expertise. The media, and especially ICTs, enter this dynamic in particular ways. While parents and children are defined in their roles of independence and dependence through their relations with each other, we can secondly consider the family in terms of a network of individuals connected by relations of blood, marriage or convention. This network makes the family more than a household, both in the sense of sharing – to a greater or lesser degree – common resources and a common culture within the household, and in the sense of their connections – more or less actively pursued – with other family members beyond the household. Such networks cannot always rely on convenient, daily face-to-face interaction and so mediated communication becomes important to sustaining the family network; in the YPNM project we focused on relations between children and non-cohabiting fathers to explore this. In relation to both senses of family, as we shall see, sharing media experiences has become a key ritual through which family members come together 'as a family'.

THE SOCIAL CONSTRUCTION OF 'INDEPENDENCE'

> To some extent, all societies encompass a gradual or graduated shift from pro-tection to autonomy as children grow older, but the nature of this progression is socially constructed in myriad ways. In each case, notions of childhood, adulthood and hence the 'transition to adulthood' are inextricably connected. (Hill and Tisdall, 1997: 19)

The dominant narrative of childhood, and hence of relations between parents and children, concerns the balance between dependence and independence. This balance varies developmentally, altering as children get older, sociologically, being struck differently by different families and in different domains of the lifeworld, and culturally, for understandings of maturity cannot be separated from the particular historical and cul-tural requirements placed on the adult population. This balance also varies historically: as Gadlin (1978: 253) notes, 'the most important characteristic of contemporary child rearing is the continued diminution of parental authority and responsibility'. Indeed, childhood commenta-tors are broadly agreed on a series of significant changes in the status of childhood during the twentieth century. Notably, recent decades have witnessed a growing contradiction in Western notions of childhood and maturity: put simply, in the cultural and psychological domains, children seem to be growing up faster; in the economic and educational domains, children attain adult status ever later than before. Overall, the twentieth century has seen the following interrelated trends:

- The shift from children having a productive role in the economy to that of children as consumers, an occasion for parental expenditure (Cunningham, 1995).

- An extension of formal schooling, evidenced through a substantial rise in the statutory school leaving age (in the UK, from 14 in the 1950s to 16 today, although many young people now expect to remain in education or training until 18 years old at least) together with a significant increase in the proportion of the population entering further and higher education (Cunningham, 1995; Hill and Tisdall, 1997).
- As a result of this increase in the educational demands placed on young people, they enter the workforce later than ever before (Lagree, 1995).
- With the demise of 'jobs for life' and of the traditional career, it has become increasingly difficult for young people to predict with certainty how their employment prospects will develop (Flores and Gray, 2000; Pollock, 1997).[3]
- In consequence, the average age of leaving home has increased steadily to the age of 23, thereby altering the composition and life-course expectations of households with children (Coleman, 1993).

These trends are resulting in a variety of challenges for the family, making age and maturity contested issues. Most significant is the emergence in the mid-twentieth century of the category of adolescence,[4] a result of the transformation of the category of 'youth' from that of young people in the labour market to that of young people as a largely economically inactive consumer market.[5] As Cunningham puts it:

> The essence of the vision of childhood at the beginning of the [twentieth] century was the powerlessness of children, their dependence; good parenting consisted of preserving and prolonging this, in part at least by the exercise of parental authority. What has happened in the second half of the century is that parental authority has declined, and children have demanded and received an earlier access to the adult world; they have not been willing to accept the attempt to prolong childhood to the late teenage years. In some ways this represents a return to a historical norm in which childhood did not extend beyond fourteen at the maximum. The difference is that in earlier centuries at the age of fourteen a person was economically productive whereas in the late twentieth century he or she will have a minimum of two years and quite probably a further seven or more years of non-productivity. Not surprisingly 'adolescence' has come to be seen as a time of stressful conflict between parents and children. (Cunningham, 1995: 185)

The media enter this process of contestation and conflict in a number of ways, for the media are of growing importance to children and young people in all these domains – identity, culture, education and consumption. When Himmelweit et al. (1958) studied the introduction of television into the lives of children, the upper age included was 13–14 year olds, this representing the final school year, after which these young people became workers, removed from the control of teachers and, to a lesser extent, parents. As we saw in Chapter 1, it was possible to say then that the 13–14 year olds in the sample could be treated as similar to adults in their tastes and reactions (Himmelweit et al., 1958), pointing up the emergence since the 1950s of adolescent or teenage 'subcultures', with distinctive tastes and with at times problematic relations to adult culture.

Indeed, the social psychological consequence of extending formal education, delaying entry to the workforce and so extending the period of financial dependence on parents, is that young people's identity, sense of self-worth and participation in peer relations must all be constructed in this period of 'non-productivity', as Cunningham describes it, thereby centring not on their participation in the workforce but on their somewhat more problematic status in society as 'youth' (Osgerby, 1998). To the extent that youth is conceptualised, in both popular and expert terms, using the metaphor of progression – youth as a step on the road to adulthood – this status is made more problematic in so far as this 'attainment' of adulthood is increasingly postponed:

> The 'youth' life stage is said to be becoming longer and longer through a combination of increased economic dependency on the family which forces young people to delay their full independence as autonomous citizens and a 'youth market' whereby the leisure opportunities for young people have exploded into a multitude of possibilities and have taken in both older and younger people in doing so. (Pollock, 1997: 55)

This postponement helps explain why teenagers feel there is little for them to do in their neighbourhood (Chapter 4). As one working-class 16-year-old girl explained to us: 'We're too young to go to night-clubs, and too old to go to, like, the young things. We need something that would interest us.' While the insufficiency of public leisure facilities is indeed a problem for young people, this may not be the major challenge. As it has become the main responsibility of children to prepare themselves for adulthood through education, this being their main contribution to society (albeit in the future rather than the present), and as the remainder of their time is legitimately occupied in leisure ('just being a child'), it is hardly surprising that their dissatisfactions are focused on these activities. But the problems which result from prolonging the period of childhood are not necessarily best resolved by making this period more entertaining. Coontz (1997: 13) argues, for example, that 'what many young people have lost are clear paths for gaining experience doing responsible, socially necessary work, either in or out of the home, and for moving away from parental supervision without losing contact with adults', and public policy should instead, or in addition, address this challenge.

However, while society may or may not provide more opportunities for young people to interact with others in a valued way, there is little doubt that the growth of the youth market for media and other consumer goods is growing to fill the gap between childhood and adulthood which has arisen as the age of economic maturity rises and the age of physical maturity falls. In this context it is perhaps inevitable that, as Coontz (1997: 15) goes on to note, 'any segregated group soon develops its own institutions, rules, and value systems, and young people are no exception', particularly as 'they have more access to certain so-called adult forms of consumption than ever before' (1997: 17). Thus it is unsurprising that children and parents do not always share preferences for television programmes or tastes in music; hence so the home must provide opportunities for 'living together separately' as well as for doing things 'as a family'.[6]

To put this another way, the picture emerging from the previous chapters regarding the 1950s–70s is that young people divided their time between socially valued, publicly visible activities (varieties of paid work, community participation, domestic labour) which involved a productive interaction between adults and youth, and unstructured play or hanging out in the interstices, this being more or less invisible to, even possibly resistant to, the adult world. The picture for today's children and young people is very different. Now their time is primarily divided between activities valued for their future rather than present worth (primarily formal education but increasingly encompassing varieties of informal education, often centred on ICT), involving a highly formalised engagement with adults, and unstructured play or hanging out in the home and with the media, this being a very visible way of – to adult onlookers – wasting time.

The Meaning of Age

> Youth *qua* youth is a cultural symbol, a population group, an age category, and a definition of what it means to be someone under 22 years old.[7]

Age is a central social stratification in any society, though the boundaries, the meanings and the process of negotiating the different age categories vary with history and culture. As James et al. (1998: 71) note, for modern Western societies, 'emphasis is placed on the individual's movement between status positions in the life course, with adulthood being seen as the pinnacle to which children and adolescents aspire and as the position of power from which older people find themselves gradually displaced'. The negotiation between parents and children regarding a child's growing independence from his or her parents is central to the cultural construction of age as a socially meaningful category, and it is historically conditioned in accordance with education policy, labour market requirements, family composition, and conceptions of childhood and children's rights. Talk about 'age', therefore, relies on a lay appropriation of legal and psychological theory in order that parents and children can reach decisions over what activities are considered appropriate for which age groups.

Discursively, no clear consensus over the meaning of age categories exists. Notably, there is no single term to describe people between the ages of birth and 18 (or whenever adulthood is held to start). 'Child', especially in the singular, tends to imply dependent, incomplete even, and hence vulnerable and in need of protection. Conversely 'youth', typically plural, tend to be seen as deviant, out of control, different, so that 'we' may be in need of protection from them. The awkward formulation used throughout this book, 'children and young people', reflects our societal uncertainty about how to categorise (and hence, understand and regulate) those of different ages; thus it is not just a matter of semantics.

The legal framework, which works primarily through the setting of age thresholds, offers little clear guidance to families, for it is confusing in just that newly-extended domain of late adolescence. Thus, in the UK, civil law specifies that at the age of 16 one can leave school, obtain full-time employment, have sexual intercourse, buy cigarettes and get married (with parental permission). By 17 one can fight in the army, join a trade union, buy a firearm, and drive a car or fly an aeroplane. Yet many mainstream films are restricted to those over 18. So too are voting, gambling and buying alcohol, while the age of criminal responsibility is only 10. Many economic milestones (obtaining a bank account, credit card, mortgage, etc.) are reached at much later ages, depending on education and employment status.

Implicitly, the legal hurdles to adulthood rest on a set of assumptions about maturity in different domains of life. But these receive rather little grounding from psychology. Instead, psychological theories of cognitive, emotional and social development are seemingly locked into a debate between stage theorists, in which children are conceptualised as passing through a predetermined and invariant sequence of distinct stages of development towards adulthood, and their opponents, who instead focus on the many empirical exceptions to the hypothesised sequence of development, the evident inconsistencies in defining key achievements and difficulties supposedly associated with each age or stage, and the cultural variations which undermine the assertion of any universal developmental path.[8]

While parents often express considerable worries regarding the freedoms they should allow their children, as we saw in the last chapter, as well as in their ability to regulate these, children themselves have a clear idea of the ages associated with different signifiers of maturity and they are generally impatient for the next 'stage', thereby giving an indication of the kinds of argument children and parents have. The way in which the adult world regulates leisure through rules about age seems to result in a considerable dissatisfaction with their own age, whatever it may be, and an enhanced desire to grow older (though, significantly, rarely a desire to be adult). In interviews, children and young people very commonly expressed a desire to be around two years older, whatever their current age, so as to have access to those opportunities and facilities which they may wish for but are instead told they are too young for. They want to be old enough to go out further, and later, than they are allowed to at present. At 6 they want to be 8 so they can ride their bike in the street. At 11, they want to be 13 so they can earn some money. At 15 they want to be 16 so as to earn more and stay out later. At 16 they want to learn to drive. Here a group of 12-year-old girls tell us why they think 12 is better than 10:

Jessica: You get treated your age.
Emma: Stay out later.
Clare: You can stay out until 9 now, 9.30 and that at the weekend.
Jodie: You can go to different places with your new friends.

One of them remains frustrated, however, saying 'I wanted to get a job doing half 6 to 8.30 but I couldn't because I'm not 13. … Because I need to get a job to get some money and that.'

In the following discussion among a group of 6–7-year-old working-class boys, the media are specifically introduced by the children as one of the freedoms that accompany growing older:

Interviewer: Tell me boys, what is it like being six years old?
Alan: Nice, but I'd like to be ten years old, I always do.
Interviewer: How will it be different being 10 years old to being 6 years old?
Alan: Because you can stay up later.
Interviewer: And what would be the point of staying up later?
Alan: So we can watch TV.
Fred: And play computers.
Paul: And put videos on.
David: And so you could go to more places, so you could go from Basingstoke to India.

Clearly, the media serve as significant markers of age. For the youngest it is being allowed to stay up later to watch television or to watch more 'grown up' programmes. For teenagers it is being allowed to watch 'adult'-rated videos or films. For many children, growing up means getting their own television, computer, etc., while being the one in a group whose parents regard them as sufficiently 'sensible' to gain access to drink, videos, transport, and so on is worth a lot. As they see it, childhood represents a series of hurdles to be crossed between their current restrictions and independence and freedom.

The symbolic significance of age frames children's preferences for media content. Across the age range 6–17, only one-quarter of named favourite television programmes is broadcast as a dedicated children's programme. This drops sharply by age from 58% of 6–8 year olds' favourites, to 27% of 9–11 year olds', and only 10% of 12–14 year olds' (Livingstone and Bovill, 1999), undermining the tendency of regulators, broadcasters and researchers to associate child viewers with children's programming. Indeed, we may interpret children's marked preference for generalist or adult programmes as a kind of resistance – here children are making visible their confidence in their own understanding and maturity.[9] To watch a horror movie is seen as a sign of maturity; at around 12, children begin to take an interest in informational programming ('it's good to know what's going on in the world'). They talk differently about television as they get older, becoming more critical of unrealistic plots, happy endings etc.,[10] and though they don't necessarily stop watching the programmes they criticise, voicing the criticism allows them to continue doing so without loss of face. Moreover, media content targeted at their age can seem patronising to them, as they resent reminders of what being their age is actually like.[11] Their marked preference for soap opera (and, for girls, the talk show), portraying adults anguishing over their very personal and 'adult' problems, is particularly interesting in this respect. In addition to their preference for such grown-up material, which also holds true for books (Boethius, 1995), we can also note here young people's preference for boundary-blurring material of diverse kinds – the crime-reality show, science fiction, horror – and for shows where teens act like adults and where adults act like kids (sitcoms and other comedy, game shows).

The media are far from neutral in this struggle over age and maturity, as is evident from the recent identification of the lucrative youth market, and the associated marketing push to reach ever younger consumers. They also play a second role here, for not only are the media markers of maturity, but they occupy the time of those designated immature. If not allowed or not able to go out, children watch television, play a computer game or read a book, and for teenagers, positioned for the lengthy period between childhood and adulthood, media use is considerable, as we saw in Chapter 2. Interestingly, young people are themselves not unaware of the role the media supposedly play in their lives:

> I don't think my mum's really got any rules. It's just like when I see like gangster videos or the movies like that, I want to be like the girls on there, it's just making me into a mini adult, serious, when I come to school I just take that attitude, like a mini adult, man. ... I'm growing up too fast, I've got to slow down. It's TV's fault you know, serious, because if half that TV wasn't there right, I wouldn't act the way I act sometimes.

Youthful Experts

It is ironic, then, that while children are focused on the negotiation of adult barriers to their activities, adults are seen to be losing the authority which justifies such barriers. As the historian Gadlin (1978: 253) puts it, 'there is less and less that parents can pass on to their children, with any certainty that it will help them in the future'. In other words, the increasing pace of modernisation has resulted in the post-war generation of parents having to bring up their children in a world significantly different from the world of their own childhood. Buchner et al. (1995: 47) concur, observing that 'the prevailing ideals and norms governing the child's behaviour have shifted noticeably since the time when today's parents were children'. Hence, frames of reference derived from their own experience are invalidated, and parents become involved in a process of negotiation with their children over mutual identities, rights and responsibilities. Notably, one way in which young people are now negotiating their 'maturity' with parents and teachers is through the construction of expertise, centred upon those domains in which children and young people have the time to devote to the exercise of this knowledge – youth culture, leisure and, increasingly, ICT. As Gadlin (1978: 240) also points out:

> As modernisation proceeds there are more people who simply do not know what kind of world their children will have to face. There is no room for persons who will replicate the past, obsolescence is built into all aspects of people's lives – their personality traits and values as well as their skills and commodities. Rather it becomes necessary to produce individuals who will create new familial and cultural patterns.

The cultural importance accorded to ICT competence (see Chapter 6) is at odds with this being one domain in which parental authority is seen to be diminishing in many households. Parents believe in the importance of ICT in facilitating their children's educational and employment opportunities, as we saw in Chapter 4, but being able to provide such support requires an expertise which they may lack, even one in which their children are better equipped than they. When we asked this working-class mother of a 7-year-old boy whether she thought technology will be important for her son, her answer reflected not only her conviction of its importance but also her doubts about her ability to support him:

> I think it will be very relevant and he will have to keep up with it. I think that in the coming 20 years there will be so much technology and so he needs to have a good knowledge of it. And err, personally I feel that I need to work with him in that field as well. With our busy lifestyle I feel that I don't spend as much time with him as I should do, and with his interests. That's something that's lacking, I think.

Without such skills, the technology may simply go unused. As one middle-class 12-year-old girl told us: 'We've got the Internet and stuff, but my Dad doesn't know how to work it so we can't use it.' On the other hand, many children are gaining such competencies rapidly, sometimes to the amazement of their parents:

> *Interviewer:* So who would you say knows more about them, you or Daniel?
> *Father:* Daniel. Definitely.
> *Interviewer:* And do you know much about that he's doing on computers in school? Does he talk about it?
> *Father:* He doesn't talk about it but the headmaster, at one parents' night, he did point out that on – it's an Apple Mac they've got – and he asked Daniel to do something, and I didn't think for a minute he would be able to, and he was 'Look at this. Wow, look at this'. Well, that would be double Dutch to me. You know, like, I didn't want to look stupid in front of the headmaster, you know, and I was saying 'Oh right'. So he must obviously be able to work it you know, do something with it, but it really is double Dutch to me. I just never took an interest in them at all.

(Working-class father of a 10-year-old boy)

Margaret Mead (1978) argues that in rapidly changing societies one witnesses 'reverse heritage'; put simply, in these circumstances the child teaches the parent. At a time of rapid technological change, children now encounter ICT innovations before their parents, reversing traditional status hierarchies and resulting in popular talk of 'the digital generation' (Tapscott, 1997). Thus they may well be in a position to teach their parents, though the evidence that this occurs in practice is sparse. Certainly, teachers talk of making use of an 'expert' pupil as a helper in the classroom (Livingstone and Bovill, 1999), thereby providing the pupil with a measure of social power and, perhaps, social mobility.

Whether the relative inexpertness of parents (and some teachers) results in the empowerment of young people, or merely means that these young people lack informed parental support, remains a moot point. Just to illustrate this latter point, consider the situation of this working-class mother who, talking about the second-hand Amstrad they had bought for their 7-year-old son, told us, 'I'm still a bit wary because basically I don't understand what's going on with computers. The more understanding that I have then the more confidence I will have.' What is interesting here is that her lack of ability to support her son means that for him, too, there is a problematic relation between access and use. When we interviewed Hassan, he appeared to enjoy playing games on the computer. But when we asked him to show us his favourite game, the skills required proved beyond him:

Interviewer:	I would like you to show me your favourite game …
Hassan:	I need a chair.
Interviewer:	Do you normally have a chair when you play it?
Hassan:	Yes I have to concentrate. … It's not working!
Interviewer:	Right. So now you're showing me how you play *Scooby Doo*.
Hassan:	It's rewinding. … Oh what am I doing? The tape has finished – it's not going round.
Interviewer:	Is this meant to go somewhere?
Hassan:	Oh yes. There.
Interviewer:	Here we go, is that right now?
Hassan:	Now it should work. [Pause. Takes out *Scooby Doo*]. I'll just put a different one on because this one isn't working.
Interviewer:	Oh, you're not going to play me *Scooby Doo*?
Hassan:	No, because it isn't working or something.
Interviewer:	Is it always so difficult to get it started?
Hassan:	Yes.
Interviewer:	Oh it is? So you really struggle to get it started, don't you?
Hassan:	Yes. It isn't working for some reason.

In the YPNM survey we asked the question, 'Who in your family knows most about computers?', of both parents and children, and found overall very close agreement between them: 31% of parents and of children name the father, 29% of children and 27% of parents name the child, 16% of parents and 12% of children name the mother, 14% of parents and 17% of children name a brother (Table 5.1).

Gender is key to domestic ICT expertise. Boys are twice as likely as girls to name themselves as the experts at home. Fathers are considered

Table 5.1 *Child's view about who in the family knows most about computers, by demographics (N = 1286)*

	All (%)	Gender		Age				Social grade			
		Boy (%)	Girl (%)	6–8 (%)	9–11 (%)	12–14 (%)	15–17 (%)	AB (%)	C1 (%)	C2 (%)	DE (%)
Myself	29	38	19	11	29	38	37	16	26	33	34
Mother	12	10	14	16	9	12	10	13	15	12	8
Father	31	30	32	44	38	23	21	55	37	24	20
Sister	5	3	8	6	6	5	6	3	4	8	6
Brother	17	15	20	14	14	18	23	13	12	20	22
Other/no difference	6	4	7	10	5	6	3	2	5	4	11

Note: The variables of gender, age and social grade are all statistically significant.
Source: Livingstone and Bovill, 1999.

more expert than mothers, brothers are considered more expert than sisters. Children whose mothers are in paid employment consider their mothers more expert than do children with mothers at home, suggesting the importance of the workplace for women's perceived expertise. Social class is equally important, however. Younger children and those from middle-class families are particularly likely to name their father, while older children, working-class children, and children from single-parent families are more likely to name themselves. When children name themselves the expert, this is often because there is no PC at home and so they are aware that through their access at school – this being near-universal, at least at a minimal level of provision[12] – they are gaining a knowledge which is new to the household.[13]

Thus, in many households, children are the recognised experts, and doubtless they do know more than their parents, with interesting consequences for family authority relations (e.g. Pasquier, 2001; Ribak, 2001). But this situation most likely reflects a household in which little is known about computers generally. Certainly it is likely that these children receive less informal support in gaining ICT 'literacy' (see Chapter 6) than do those in households where parents are competent computer users, typically gaining such knowledge through a middle-class occupation. In the YPNM survey, 68% of middle-class (ABC1) parents said they used a computer either at home or at work, but only 38% of working-class (C2DE) parents do so. Further, among these users, 26% of middle-class parents classed themselves as 'very comfortable' with the technology, compared with only 16% of working-class parents.

This problematic skills gap between ICT access and use, concentrated as it is on girls and in working-class households, raises some significant challenges for those who would promote informal parental support for children's education through home-based learning. As both schools and parents are finding, providing opportunities for access is easier than is providing knowledge or guidance for use (see Chapter 2). Where such knowledge exists, therefore, it is most likely to reproduce rather than undermine social inequalities.[14] In effect, through the provision of social, economic and cultural support for education and its values, parents exert an indirect but powerful influence over their children's development. The provision of a PC at home, as well as parental support for its use by children, may be seen as part of this process. Indeed, Varenne argues that while many of the traditional functions of the family have been stripped away, 'there is only one area that strongly argues for continuing to think of the family as a central institution: education in its relationship with the reproduction of social stratification' (Varenne, 1996: 440).

THE MEDIATION OF FAMILY NETWORKS

The importance of the family lies not only in the management of dependency but also in the creation of a more or less common culture, supported by common resources. It differs from the household in that it may be geographically dispersed both across and within households. As both these forms of dispersal are becoming more commonplace, given diversification in employment trajectories and family structure, it would seem that 'living together separately' is becoming ever easier, and as we have already seen in Chapter 4, there are many ways in which family members pursue their interests as individuals, including using media. In the following discussion, the aim is not to set up any ideal expectations or judgements regarding family life, for each of the models – from communal to individualised – has its advantages and disadvantages. Rather, the point is to understand how, whether family relations are characterised by connection or dispersal, the multiplying channels, forms and contents of ICT now play a significant mediating role, linking relatives who live apart, while sometimes dividing and other times uniting relatives who live together. The key dynamic is the balance between communal versus individualised leisure – in terms of decision-making, shared experience, individual preferences, and so forth. One consequence, it seems, is that coming together 'as a family' becomes a deliberate choice, often driven by parents' normative expectations of how families should be as well as by the positive desire of both parents and children. Those occasions on which people do come together 'as a family' are of particular interest not because they tell us about competition for scarce media resources, but because, in an increasingly media-rich environment, they reflect the choice to use the media so as to sustain a shared space rather than symbolically to mark off one's personal domain.

Research on the embedding of media within family life has proved most insightful when it adopts an ethnographic, contextualist, symbolic interactionist or family-systems approach. Palmer (1986), for example, views the child as social actor, meanings as socially constructed, and the media as rendered meaningful through processes of symbolic interaction. And Goodman (1983: 408) argues that 'the family is a small boundary-maintaining, natural group in which the behaviours of any one member affect the behaviours of other members and the system as a whole'. Following these approaches, research[15] has identified a wide range of ways in which media and the family are interconnected, rather than being simply mutually exclusive, centring on:

- Provision of a *common leisure activity* which may both stimulate or allow avoidance of family communication (especially, co-viewing television may provide a non-contentious joint activity for conflicted family members)
- Provision of *symbolic resources* for family myths and narratives – from simple communication facilitation through provision of a common topic of conversation to the more complex negotiation of rules and expectations (this in contrast to the notion of media as supplanting family conversation)
- The *mediation of reception* (e.g. parents frame children's interpretation of media contents or encourage social learning from such contents, while children may invite interpretative guidance from parents, etc)
- The *regulation of family time and space,* whether as structured or casual, and whether together, in various combinations, in parallel or apart
- The *mediation of family subsystems* within the household, where, depending on patterns of power within the household, as well as motivations to be independent or communal, the media may be used in any of a number of ways (as a scapegoat, boundary marker, time manager, stress reducer, bartering agent, babysitter, companion, etc.)

Doing Things 'As a Family'

Much discussion of the family is based on the assumption that talk, togetherness, group activities are good and, by implication, being alone, separate, individual is problematic for 'the family'. Yet the evidence suggests that family togetherness may be as much constructed discursively as it is enacted through physical co-location in time and space.

In the YPNM survey we asked parents how frequently they shared a variety of activities with their children (Table 5.2). The media figure very highly in the overall list of activities, with television being the most

Table 5.2 *Percentage of parents doing activities at least once a week with child (N = 830)*

	All	Age of child					
	6–17 (%)	6–7 (%)	8–9 (%)	10–11 (%)	12–13 (%)	14–15 (%)	16–17 (%)
Watch TV/video together	87	92	90	97	90	84	70
Have a good talk	77	84	83	78	74	73	59
Help with homework	71	84	77	81	76	60	28
Listen to tapes/records/CDs	61	70	62	63	58	53	44
Discuss books	56	88	69	52	38	32	22
Help make something/do a hobby	54	70	61	62	50	40	16
Listen to the radio	52	57	54	61	50	45	37
Read to child	40	83	58	27	12	6	2
Play cards/board games	32	51	42	26	23	11	8
Play a computer game	29	40	34	30	22	19	11
Play or watch live sport	27	28	27	23	32	26	19
Play 'let's pretend' games	21	51	42	26	23	11	8
Spend time on computer (not games)	19	26	19	17	17	14	11
Take to the park/countryside	18	27	24	18	9	6	3

Source: Livingstone and Bovill, 1999.

commonly shared, despite the advent of newer media and despite the media-rich environments of many homes. Moreover, the majority of children – of all ages – say they watch their favourite television programme in company (68%), usually with a member of their family (Livingstone and Bovill, 1999). In this sense, 'family television' remains strong, stronger indeed than many other activities perhaps more culturally valued as a means of spending time 'as a family'. As one mother enthuses:

> I quite like that actually in the morning time for them, because I think that makes it a family time, where you're mucking about in your dressing gowns and they're all in their pyjamas. They stay in their pyjamas, they watch the TV, they have different bits of toast, you know, I like that, I love that, it's a family time.
>
> (Working-class mother of a 10-year-old boy)

Yet only a minority of children (9%) say they watch television 'just because the family is watching', suggesting that it is the common interest in television which brings the family members together, rather than the desire to be together which determines viewing. On the other hand, these common interests must be generated, and so younger children are still more likely than older ones to watch in order simply to be together, as this 10-year-old working-class boy says:

> Interviewer: Do you prefer the programmes that are for children after school, or do you prefer programmes that are, er, more in the evenings?
> Kevin: Hmm, evening ones, because I – I like watching them with my Mum and Dad.

In thus coming together, the family's decision-making is changing. Here a working-class teenager explains the informal mix of patriarchy and democracy that determines what he gets to watch on television:

> Whatever my Da want to watch, if they're downstairs. We take turns each what we want to watch after something's finished, say my Da wanted to watch cricket or something, and watch the cricket and then when that finished some-one else would choose what they watch. It goes on like that.

New computer-based media, to the extent that they have entered the home, play a far less significant role in child–parent relations, though they are a weekly, shared activity in one in three families. Rather it is the traditional media – books and music – which, being well established in domestic routines, come second in the list of common media activities. Here a working-class father, with a 9-year-old daughter and two younger children, describes the importance of music in his family:

> We all like music so we play a lot of music. We could easily sit in that room and go through the whole CD rack and they'd dance to it. We can all sit and enjoy it, all of us, even the littl' un. We all love it. So we do that a lot.

Thus for many families, 'family time' is also media time, hence calls to reduce viewing, therefore, may also reduce time which parents and children spend together, serving to increase the individualisation of family life. On the other hand, the normative value placed on 'family time' may lead parents to overclaim its occurrence, as with 12-year-old Charlie's father:

> *Interviewer:* Are there any television programmes that you all watch together as a family?
> *Father:* Yeah.
> *Mother:* Yeah, films we do, some films we do.
> *Interviewer:* Can you think of anything you've watched together recently?
> *Father:* No, I'll have to think about that. (pause) Errm, what was that programme that was on years ago and we were watching it and then Charlie suddenly came in and said 'Oh this is good'? (pause) I don't know.

Other families make a positive choice to use media separately, even when they share interests in common. I interviewed one family in which all six family members watched the Australian soap opera, *Neighbours*, every day, but on separate sets or at different times, and they did not regard this common experience as an opportunity for conversation (Livingstone, 1992).

In the balance between communality and individuality, age matters.[16] Table 5.2 also shows that, with the exception of participation in sports

Table 5.3   *Frequency with which children say they share selected activities with their parents (N = c. 1300)*

	All	Age			
	6–17 (%)	6–8 (%)	9–11 (%)	12–14 (%)	15–17 (%)
Eat a main meal					
Most days	75	71	77	79	74
Once or twice a week	18	23	17	15	17
Less than once a week	5	6	4	4	5
Never	2	1	2	2	4
Watch television					
Most days	68	65	70	74	61
Once or twice a week	23	28	23	16	26
Less than once a week	7	5	5	7	10
Never	2	2	1	3	3
Talk about something that matters					
Most days	36	44	33	31	35
Once or twice a week	34	29	36	35	33
Less than once a week	24	20	24	25	26
Never	7	7	6	9	7

Source: Livingstone and Bovill, 1999.

and using a computer for non-games purposes, all leisure activities shared between parents and children decline significantly with age. While one would have expected some activities to decline (e.g. reading to the child), one might also have expected that other activities would take their place (e.g. having a good talk, or playing computer games, or listening to music). But, to put it the other way around, as children grow older we find that they share ever fewer activities with their parents, with only television, having a good talk and, to a lesser extent, listening to music remaining prominent. Thus, by the teenage years, watching television together has become one of the few activities parents and children can share.

Sharing activities at least once a week may not capture the everyday nature of child–parent relations. Table 5.3 compares how frequently children and their parents watch television together with the activity this is sometimes thought to have displaced, namely eating a main meal together (although we cannot tell, from this survey, how far the two activities coincide).

Eating together still has the edge, just, at least in middle-class families (the daily sharing of television viewing is higher in working-class families – at 73% – than in middle-class ones – at 61%), and at least for the older and younger age groups. Both meal times and television viewing

Table 5.4 *What regularly causes arguments between parents and children? (Parent's view, N = 978)*

	All (%)	Gender		Age			
		Boy (%)	Girl (%)	6–8 (%)	9–11 (%)	12–14 (%)	15–17 (%)
Helping in the house	59	58	61	44	65	68	59*
Homework	49	57	40*	39	49	59	47*
Going to bed	48	50	45	69	58	43	19*
Television	34	36	31	44	31	31	16*
Going out	32	30	33	33	31	34	29
Money	31	33	29	27	35	34	26
Telephone	30	23	36*	17	23	35	45*
Computer games	15	23	7*	19	16	17	9*
Videos	14	17	11*	22	14	10	8*
Music	8	7	9	5	7	7	15*

*Statistically significant difference.

Source: Livingstone and Bovill, 1999.

may be more or less casual or deliberate in providing occasions for family interaction (Goodman, 1983). 'Talking about something that matters' is necessarily deliberate, and the comparatively high level of frequency with which children say this occurs suggests that communication is a key feature of most families, being a daily occurrence in one-third of families and a weekly one in a further third.

We should not assume that shared activities are harmonious activities, of course. Yet it seems that television is more a means of facilitating positive family interaction than conflict.[17] Asked to say which subjects regularly cause arguments with their children, parents name helping in the house almost twice as often as they name watching television or using the telephone (Table 5.4). Both homework and going to bed are also more contentious than any media use. Watching television and using the telephone, however, are on a par with going out and money as a source of family disputes – 3 in 10 parents say they cause regular arguments with their children. Only around half that number of families quarrels about watching videos, playing computer games and even fewer about listening to music.

The causes of arguments change as children get older. Watching television or videos and playing computer games cause arguments most often when the children are very young, while arguments about use of the telephone and playing music increase as children grow older. There are also more arguments in families in straitened financial circumstances. Arguments about money, going out, telephone, computer games, videos and music are as much as twice as common among the poorest families.

As Goodman (1983) noted some time ago, it is apparent that of all the media, watching television together represents a particularly convenient and comfortable way for families with diverse interests or perhaps unresolved conflicts to spend time together. For as Bausinger (1984) has pointed out, turning on the television may not mean one wants to watch television so much as that one wants not to talk to the family.

While patterns of content preference tend to be strongly divided by gender and generation (Livingstone and Bovill, 1999), certain television genres, typically those conceived as 'family viewing', explicitly set out to appeal across gender and generation lines. The soap opera, the situation comedy, and the game show are all prime examples of genres which aim to provide an occasion on which the family will wish to come together to view, either because the appeal – drama, humour, competition, etc. – is designed to be more or less universal or because the genre contains 'something for everyone', as with the character mix in a soap opera. Consequently, as with more dramatic occurrences labelled 'media events' – whether the World Cup, a royal wedding or an election, all events which bring the nation together in a moment of ritual togetherness and shared commitment to a common culture (Dayan and Katz, 1992) – these more modest but also more frequent events establish daily rituals which bring people together 'as a family' (see Lull, 1990).

Carey (1989: 18) argues for the importance of ritual to our understanding of the media thus: 'a ritual view of communication is directed not toward the extension of messages in space but toward the maintenance of society in time', the point being 'not to alter attitudes or change minds but to represent an underlying order of things, not to perform functions but to manifest an ongoing and fragile social process' (1989: 19). While usefully redirecting attention from the media's role in the transmission of information towards its contribution to the daily rituals which constitute the lifeworld, this notion of ritual, in so far as it centres on participating in 'fellowship and commonality' (1989: 18), may appear both normative and overly static. For many of the rituals in today's household serve to mark off boundaries, separating individuals as much as providing the occasion for their coming together.

Mediating Family Subsystems

How shall we characterise the balance between communal and individualised activities? Overall, this picture of the media within the family thus far tends to underplay the extent to which families differ in their relational dynamics. Problematically, the research literature offers few accounts of family diversity other than those that derive from, or are reducible to, socio-economic differences, and thus it provides few notions of how families might vary in terms of their communal/individualised family dynamics. Moreover, while there is a sizeable literature on family systems (e.g. Stafford and Dainton, 1995; Street and Dryden, 1988), this is largely from a therapeutic perspective and makes little connection with the sociological approach. Some indication of diversity within the household can be derived from the YPNM project, for the survey included questions about family interaction patterns (Livingstone and Bovill, 1999). Using just a few such questions, and notwithstanding the caution that family interaction is hard to determine through closed-ended survey questions, we used the statistical technique of cluster analysis to seek out sub-groupings according to patterns of association between responses.[18] Although probably best interpreted as only indicative of the diversity among families, we identified six family 'types', as follows:

- Low interaction families
- Conventional families
- Intimate families
- Talkative families
- Democratic families
- High interaction families

Perhaps the most noteworthy point is that beyond a few age differences, we find no consistent association between demographic variables (especially, gender and socio-economic status) and family type. This suggests that families vary in their lifestyle preferences and interaction styles that are not simply to be reduced to socio-demographic categories. However, there are a number of interesting links between children's use of media and the occasions for, and types of, communication in their family.

Low interaction families do few of the activities we asked about on most days, and they are also noticeably less democratic in their decision-making than all the other types except the conventional family (i.e. parents are more likely to reach decisions themselves than to involve their children in a joint decision-making process). These children are the least favourable in their attitudes towards their parents, being more likely to say they do not 'get on well with their parents' and less likely to agree that their 'parents know when they were upset or worried' or that they 'want them to do well'. The children are somewhat more likely to be low media users, they least often watch television with their parents and their mothers are least likely to talk about media with them. If they play computer games, they are more likely to play with a friend than with a member of their family. They may therefore be seen as highly individualised rather than communal in their orientation to family life, although being relatively low media users, the media can hardly be blamed – should blame be required – for this.

High interaction families have the most frequent and varied types of interaction, and are more common among families with 6–8 or 15–17 year olds. Not only are they much more likely than the other family types to play or make something together (especially for younger children), almost all say they eat together and three-quarters say they talk about things that matter most days (especially for teenagers). They are moderately democratic, according to the parents, and among the most satisfied with their relations with their parents, according to the children. Of those who play computer games, they are more likely to play with their family (especially, father and siblings). They may therefore be seen as highly communal rather than individualised in their orientation to the family, and as they see it, this is associated with a considerable satisfaction with family life.

Other kinds of family are situated somewhere between these two in terms of their degree and type of interaction, tending rather to come together for some activities but not others.

Conventional families make a point of eating together most days, but they do very few of the other activities together and they are the least democratic, parents being more likely to say they alone make big decisions. The computer-game players among these children tend to play alone.

Intimate families talk about something that matters to the child most days, many eat together every day, and they are moderately democratic. Many of these children – typically between 9–14 years old – also describe themselves as liable to worry about things and to 'get fed up' with their parents telling them what to do. It seems that talking about things that matter to the child may produce some unwanted advice. As regards media use, these children are more likely to be 'screen entertainment' fans and to watch television with their parents.

Talkative families are most likely to discuss things that happen in the news. They are also likely to eat together and nearly half talk about things that matter to the child most days, and this talking includes talking about a variety of media; they too are moderately democratic. These are more typical among families with 15–17 year olds.

Democratic families are most likely to make big decisions together, and they eat together most days, though they talk about things that matter to the child less often than intimate, talkative or high interaction families. More common among 12–14 year olds, these children describe themselves as having good relations with their parents.

From this one may conclude that families sustaining different kinds of communication or interaction patterns incorporate the media into these relational dynamics in particular ways. Further, for the high and low interaction families, use of the media is consistent with patterns of engagement in other activities, while in other families the media may prove more exceptional (perhaps providing the main occasion for time together or time out). Moreover, while self-reports of satisfaction with child–parent interaction are not the most subtle of measures, when looking across the profiles of all the family types there is a hint that multiple kinds of interaction, including not just opportunities for conversation but also for democratic family decision-making, are associated with a positive view of family life. In this context, it is interesting that research finds that the main things children want from their parents are more open communication and more attention – specifically, more time spent with them, greater reliability in keeping promises, more predictability and more supervision.[19]

Keeping in Touch

Kin-keeping and the Extended Family   Families have never been straight-forwardly contained within the household. While the legal and other formal frameworks of the family assert the primacy of the nuclear family, families work systematically to establish a wider network of kinship and friendship ties, ties which, not always being underpinned by the state, are idealised all the more as a matter of choice, though they may also be experienced in terms of obligation. As Varenne (1996: 433) points out, 'each household must maintain a body of familial lore through telephone calls, requests for help, exchange of pictures, reunions specifically designed to bring the family together'. Such informal communication activities are easily trivialised as women's work, and as part of the leisure of the family. In a series of interviews reported in Livingstone (1992: 122), I contrasted men and women's views of the telephone. In a typical interview, one man said of his wife: 'She may use it because she wants to talk to a friend – there's no need to talk to her friend, but she will use it to talk to her friend. Whereas for me, it is not a tool of entertainment, it's just simply used because I need to use it.' The language of 'need' here is being used to distinguish relationship-maintenance (a feminine concern deemed by the husband to be unnecessary) and information transmission (i.e. as he saw it, the necessary making of arrangements).

Moyal (1995) replaces this discourse with the distinction between instrumental and intrinsic telephone calls, where the former are for making appointments, shopping, seeking information, etc., and the latter centre on kin-keeping, achieved through personal communication with friends, relatives, counselling and other kinds of intimate discussion and exchange. The result of these often invisible and easily underestimated communications, is what Moyal terms 'telecommunication neighbourhoods', and she shows how these are of significant social and economic value for the public welfare of a society. Through such routine exchanges, communities are welded together, problems resolved, identities and relationships sustained and, as a result, those marginalised by mainstream society – the poor, the elderly, recent immigrants, young mothers, single parents, those in rural circumstances, the disabled – are supported in their homes but so maintained within the community.[20]

We observed in the YPNM project that parents often deliberately encourage children to learn the skills of telephone use and, increasingly, email in sustaining relationships with grandparents, beginning with instrumental calls and graduating to the more complex skills of intrinsic calls. Unsurprisingly, we found that use of the telephone is significantly predicted by gender, age and social grade, with girls, older children and those from middle-class families using it more often. The role of family and friends in the child's social life also plays a part, for children who spend most of their free time with their families make less use of the telephone (Livingstone and Bovill, 1999). Indeed, communication media are increasingly used by children and young people to sustain not family but peer relations. Yet it is likely that the skills learned and habits acquired in relation to peers will be later used in relation to kinship networks. One may speculate whether, because the introduction of new, computer-based communication media means that boys are already joining in more than was shown by previous studies of the telephone or letter writing, men will play a greater future role in kinship communication.[21] On the other hand, it seems that following in a parent's footsteps remains significant, and for this reason, the telephone may remain gendered in its use for some time yet. One working-class mother tells us that she loves the phone and 'couldn't do without it', phoning friends and even neighbours daily, while her 7-year-old daughter tells us with equal enthusiasm what she talks about on the telephone:

> We talk about school, we talk about maths and we talk about if we like each other. We talk about if we're still going to see each other, talk about if we're going to die before the other one does and all that. We talk about when do you want to come over to my house, what time do you want to stay, when do you

want to have lunch, when do you want to have tea and dinner and when do you want to do some drawing. Oh yes – and when do you want to play out the front on the bikes and when you want to watch a video and when you want to watch TV or when you want to play a maths game, when you want to read.

This use of the phone is far from uncontroversial, given the costs in Britain of lengthy calls. As one working-class mother informs us:

Rose is in trouble over my last telephone bill, um, Sam isn't. He's very, just to the point. He just rings up and says what he wants and puts the phone down. He doesn't, I mean, he's not at all worried about using the phone, um, but he's not a chatterer on the phone, whereas normally you can't stop him talking ... (laughs). I used to do the same thing. And she will come home from school, walk home with a friend that she's been at school with all day, although they might not have been in the same classes all day ... but they'll have met at breaktime and lunchtime and then walk home from school together, and she'll be in fifteen minutes and she'll ring the same friend up and be on the phone for half an hour.

Kin-keeping After Divorce   The rise in divorce and separation means that more children move between two households and hence two media environments. Consequently, divorce represents a growing means by which families are, from the child's point of view, extended across households. In the YPNM survey, and more or less in accord with statistics for the UK as a whole, the majority (83%) of children lived at home with two parents (and of these, nearly 10% were 'reconstituted families') while 16% lived with one parent at home (this being their mother in 90% of cases); most (87%) also had siblings.[22]

That children may have two homes poses some methodological challenges. Nearly all quantitative research, and the YPNM project must be included here, tends to ask about just one media environment per child. Yet when in interviews, we attempted to summarise a discussion among 12–13-year-old girls by saying, 'and you've all got cable and satellite, is that right?', everyone chorused 'Yeah', with the qualification from one that 'I've got it at my Dad's, I don't have it at home'. Similarly, the question, 'So, how many of you have got a bedroom of your own?', produced answers which included, 'but at my Dad's I have to share with my sister' and 'I've got, yeah I've got my own bedroom at my Dad's house'. While more research is needed to establish how children move between these media environments and the different pleasures, expectations and rules that may pertain in each, what is already apparent is how the extended family increasingly draws on communication media to sustain its network of relations.

The diversification of forms of communication – telephone, mobile phone, email, Internet, etc. – enables children to transcend the separation of space in sustaining relationships across households, which is particularly important in the case of parental divorce. For example, Corinne (aged 16), whose father lives too far away to visit often, nonetheless rings her father once or twice a week. She tells us that, 'when I ring my Dad I'm always on there ages'. Her mother confirms the importance of these phone calls, noting that 'before he got married he used to come and see her here', but since his remarriage, meetings have become few and far between, partly 'cos the area's very bad, I won't, I won't let her travel down there on her own. So if he wants to see her they can come up here, you know?' Clearly, sustaining these relations is not always easy for either parents or children. Twelve-year-old Alex's mother provides a similar account, although here even the phone calls have become contentious. The financial difficulties are significant: as she sees it, 'probably if you're married you have the income to warrant having one – I sail pretty close to the wind every month of balancing the books, so having a telephone is to me quite a luxury.' But the emotional tensions are equally difficult:

> His father lives in the middle of Africa, and it's a bone of contention with both of us. He wants to see his dad, I don't think it's up to him to actually make the first contact, I just, rightly or wrongly, I don't see that a child should have to get in touch with his own parent, and I'm not particularly bitter about it any more, but I do draw the line at thinking that he should pick up the phone, 'hi dad it's your son'.

As is often the case on breakdown of communication in relationships, we realise the significance of everyday practices only during their absence.

Mediating Peer Relationships   Significant as the media are for kin-keeping across households, it is nonetheless the mediation of peer relations rather than family relations which is most enthusiastically embraced by children and, especially, teenagers. And through the mediation of both kinds of relationship, media use cannot be confined to the household but more generally permeates young people's social connections.

Not only does young people's social life frame their actual use of media, but it is also, in part, constituted through their talk about media. As was shown in the YPNM project, the great majority of children and young people (93%) say they talk about media at least sometimes to their friends, this being most often television, then music, then, for boys, computer games. While talk encompasses all media, it is newer media

Table 5.5 *Percentage visiting a friend to use media they lack at home, by demographics (N = 970)*

	All (%)	Gender		Age of child			Social grade			
		Boy	Girl	9–11	12–14	15–17	AB	C1	C2	DE
Play a computer game	43	61	24*	47	44	37	36	41	45	46
Watch a video	43	42	44	35	44	50*	35	42	45	46
Watch cable TV	26	28	23	25	23	29	18	22	27	31*
Use the PC (not for games)	23	28	19*	21	25	24	16	25	23	27
Use a CD-ROM	16	19	13*	14	18	16	14	18	15	16
Use the Internet	8	10	5*	5	9	9*	9	11	6	5

*Statistically significant difference.

Source: Livingstone and Bovill, 1999.

goods that are most commonly swapped, perhaps because they are most expensive to buy. Music and screen entertainment items top the list: around one-third swap music tapes, CDs or records (37%) and videos (33%). Computer games come third overall, for although the most common item swapped by boys (43% do so), hardly any girls (9%) are involved. Books and magazines, on the other hand, are exchanged by only around one in five. The media also play a role in friendship by acting as a spur to visit friends who own media which children themselves do not have at home (Table 5.5). Like swapping media goods, this represents another way in which children circumvent their lack of finances and broaden the variety of media they have access to. This is particularly significant as a means by which those currently without access are gaining experience of the newest media, such as the Internet.

Screen entertainment media attract most: almost two-thirds of boys sometimes go round to a friend's house to play a computer game they don't have at home and two in five boys and girls sometimes go to watch a video. Only around one-quarter go to a friend's house to watch cable television or to use the PC (not for games). At present, few visit friends to use a multimedia computer (16%) or the Internet (8%). Significantly, more boys are involved in both computer game-playing in friends' houses and in serious computer use. Significant age-related differences exist for watching videos and using the Internet. However, only in the case of watching cable television are there significant social grade differences, this being almost twice as common among children from DE families as among those from AB families.

Friends, therefore, represent a key means by which the variety of new media becomes available to young people, supplementing their access through their family. Conversely, the media play an important role in routine contacts between friends, including talking about media, swapping media goods and visiting each other's homes to use media together.

THE EUROPEAN FAMILY CONTEXT

Whether formulated as idealised aspirations or recognised as part of the routine lived-reality of daily life, expectations constructed for 'family life' are fundamentally cultural and hence open to variation. As Duncan (1998: 120) puts it, without in any way proposing 'invariable spatial relations', it is crucial to recognise that 'as spatial differences have been constituted, then all social objects and relations will be spatially variant'. In relating family life to media use, consideration of the variation across cultural contexts in both social relations within the family and key dimensions of the changing media environment allows a recognition of what is particular and what is general about any one country.[23]

In comparing children and young people's media use in the domestic context across twelve European countries, Pasquier (2001) identifies few cross-national differences in patterns of media *use* within the family home, although, as we saw in Chapter 2, there are some noteworthy differences in ICT provision even within European and North American contexts. Indeed, some expected differences were not found. For example, gender differences in computer use at home are no less evident in the Nordic countries, where gender relations in the society are more equal, than in the Mediterranean countries, where the social and employment status of women is very different. On the other hand, though more modest than some of the differences which emerge from comparison of more diverse nations (see Lull, 1988), the European comparative project did identify some cross-cultural differences in the relationship between private and public leisure, with implications for the family's use of media. For example, though without wishing to be overly reductive in the use of these categories, Suoninen (2001) contrasts 'traditional family-oriented cultures' (for example, as seen in Spain, France and Italy, and so apparently more typical of Catholic countries) and 'peer-oriented cultures' (more typical of, for example, of Protestant countries such as the Nordic countries and the Netherlands). Other countries are somewhat hybrid, being more strongly multicultural in their population (for example, Germany and the UK). The primary importance of this distinction is the interaction with age. As Nurmi (1998a: 246) points out, 'there is substantial variation in the timing and sequencing of various transitions adolescents face across contemporary Europe'. While the transition from a family-focus to a peer-focus in the child's relations with others is crucial to social development, in peer-oriented cultures it appears that this transition is made during late childhood, while in family-oriented cultures, the shift comes only in the teenage years.

In part, the issue here is one of differing conceptions of 'childhood', particularly in relation to the degree of autonomy deemed appropriate for young people of different ages. However, similar cross-national differences emerge when we explore the extent to which a media-rich bedroom culture depends not just on domestic space and parents' working practices, but also on the culture of childhood (Bovill and Livingstone, 2001). In Spain, for example, we found evidence for a strongly family-oriented culture where children spend comparatively little time watching favourite television programmes alone in their bedroom. In the United Kingdom and Germany, on the other hand, we found more privatised media use, partly because of cultural restrictions on children's freedom to meet friends in public locations. To help us understand such variation, in the pan-European survey, children and young people were asked which values they thought would be most important to them when they grew up. Across all countries and ages, 'having a happy family life' was pre-eminent. However, in several of the Northern European countries, there was relatively little consensus, and several values rivalled that of family life: in Germany – having 'lots of money'; in France – having 'an interesting job'; in the United Kingdom – having 'lots of money' for the youngest group, 'a good education' for 9–13 year olds, and 'an interesting job' for 15–16 years olds; and in the Netherlands, 'lots of money' matters most for the youngest group, to be replaced as they get older with 'a good education' in addition to 'a happy family life'. By contrast, in both Nordic and Mediterranean countries, 'having a happy family life' was straightforwardly the dominant value, which is perhaps curious given that on the basis of key demographic and media use variables these countries appear more contrasting than similar.

Although broad-brush characterisations of countries should be treated cautiously, we have suggested a characterisation of European trends in terms of three cultural patterns (Livingstone, 2001b). First, and more typical of Mediterranean countries where there is a comparatively high degree of family stability, albeit with relatively few children per family, and traditional gender relations as regards child-rearing, children seem to be regarded as the rather precious centre of a 'traditional family' which is taking advantage of the new lifestyle choices offered by a consumerist and globalised culture. It is perhaps no accident that in these countries we also find a media environment primarily oriented towards the varied diet which their national television, given their sizeable language communities, can sustain. By contrast, particularly in the Nordic countries, distinctive for having relatively more working mothers, higher divorce rates, more wealth, greater population homogeneity, the 'democratic family' represents a safe base within which children are regarded as valued citizens with the rights and the freedom to determine their chosen, often significantly peer-oriented, lifestyle. These cultural factors shape the context within which the relatively more pioneering stance of these same countries as regards ICT access and use has its effect. Last, we find a heterogeneous group of countries where the cross-cutting demands of late modernity – in terms of gender relations, population diversity, wealth inequality, and so forth – offer a more diverse or hybrid set of values for children and their families to live by.[24]

MEDIA AND THE 'DEMOCRATIC' FAMILY

This chapter has identified several ways in which families at the turn of the twenty-first century might be said to be embracing a democratic model of family relations, with parent–child relations increasingly centred on the mutual expectation of love, freedom and intimacy, rather than parental (especially, paternal) authority and children's respect. As noted earlier, the model of the democratic family offers a resolution between the lengthening period over which parents are expected to provide economically for their children and the cultural value placed on individual rights and individualised lifestyles, albeit a resolution which places centre stage the process by which family members negotiate their various rights and responsibilities towards each other. And while it might be appropriate to describe the history of childhood as 'a history of ideas, of institutions, and adult practices that circumscribe the child', it is no longer, even if it once was, plausible to add that 'young children in any era, unlike adults, do not have the cognitive or social maturity to evaluate, alter or resist the circumstances into which they are born' (Luke, 1989: 17).

Among a number of key cultural institutions, the mass media are central mediators of this new model of the family, both because they convey powerful and appealing imagery of family diversification and of the individualisation of lifestyles within the family, and because the negotiation of media use within the family is itself an increasingly significant means through which commonality and individuality among family members is constructed. This relation between family life and media use may underpin a shift towards a democratic model in several ways.

- As society has become more affluent, for the majority (though not all) of the population, this affluence has underpinned the growth of the media-rich home. Families are only now coming to terms with the individualisation of leisure which the multiplication and personalisation of media goods affords. Even under one roof, family members can develop and sustain different forms of knowledge or expertise and, in key respects (for which ICT is an obvious example), it is ever less the case that parents can assume they know more than their children.[25]

- Perhaps as a consequence, while a series of structural socio-economic changes are impinging on the boundaries between childhood, adolescence and adulthood, in daily life these boundaries are negotiated between children and adults through the setting of age limits, many of which centre on, and so are contested in relation to, leisure activities and media use.

- It has become commonplace for discourses of individualism (and, as part of this, of children's rights) to be used in support of a diversification in leisure and lifestyle choices. When the decision is made to 'come together as a family', this is increasingly a positive choice, rather than a routine requirement, and so is more often than not stimulated by shared interest in particular media contents.

- In many families, this chosen togetherness is more often centred on television than on the dinner table (itself once a locus for the hierarchical regulation of children's participation). Similarly, parents' explicit discourse of media use places decreasing emphasis on regulating harmful media contents and more on trusting their children's good sense, on sharing mediated experiences with their children and even on sharing values and interests, although media use is itself more individualised.[26]

- The distribution of family members across more than one household fosters a network model of family communication underpinned by such new communication media as email or the mobile phone. These media are as much, perhaps even more, the province of the young than of their parents.

- Within one nation, the variety of family forms suggests that some more than others are adopting the democratic model of family life. The same can be said across nations, with both the value placed on 'family life' and the democratic or traditional meaning of 'family life' varying across Europe and, doubtless, other parts of the world also, according to long-standing cultural, religious, economic and political factors.

But what does it mean to identify the 'democratic family' as the new ideal to replace that of the 'traditional' or 'proper' family of the 1950s? Even though socio-economic trends have increased rather than decreased children's dependence on their parents, ideological shifts over recent decades have increasingly asserted children's rights and, hence, the democratic family, following the broader rise of individualism in Western democracies. This shift is now evident in the policy framework for children and children's rights. Most notably, the United Nations Convention on the Rights of the Child (1989) stresses the need to respect and listen to children, to act in the child's best interests and not to discriminate against children. Hill and Tisdall (1997: viii) quote a child, herself on the Steering Group of Article 12 of the convention, who characterises this as a shift from 'children should be seen and not heard' to 'children should be seen *and* heard'.[27]

According to Giddens (1993: 184), we are witnessing 'a democratisation of the private sphere'. He claims that, through the historical transformation of intimacy, children – just like any other (i.e. adult) participants to a relationship – have gained the right to 'determine and regulate the conditions of their association' (1993: 185). Meanwhile parents have gained the duty to protect them from coercion, ensure their involvement in key decisions, be accountable to them and others, and to respect and expect respect. This democratisation is not simply a positive shift away from the autocratic and patriarchal Victorian family, but rather has come about as part of a complex set of social changes. Thus, Giddens describes a post-traditional order in which past certainties and habitual practices have been replaced by the radical doubt engendered by multiple and contested authorities together with the need to make multiple and uncertain choices. As social life is arranged bureaucratically at a distance, further undermining traditional practices and authorities, people become more aware of the risks they face, trust is increasingly placed in abstract systems of knowledge, and everyday life becomes ever more mediated and globalised. As a consequence, intimate relations are also transformed, being ever less defined according to kinship, obligation or other traditional structures and ever more dependent on the intrinsic quality of the 'pure relationship' which, far from providing a buffer against the outside world, is itself 'thoroughly permeated by mediated influences coming from large-scale systems' (Giddens, 1991: 7).

Buchner et al. (1995), focusing particularly on children and young people, argue that children face the expectation of taking responsibility for their own 'leisure career' or, ultimately, their 'biographical project' or 'project of the self'. This responsibility requires them to anticipate future uncertainties and deal with risk and status insecurity, in the context of a loss of traditional forms of family and community support. Hence, children increasingly participate in explicit discourses of identity and identity construction, facilitating their transformation into independent consuming citizens with their own rights and responsibilities. If there is indeed a new responsibility to construct an explicit project of the self[28] in socially regulated and approved ways – and for ever younger children – the media play a part in its construction. It is this shift into an independently managed leisure career, itself subject to pervasive market forces and peer pressures, which leads many parents to judge that children are being encouraged to 'grow up faster and earlier', and so requiring a democratic or partnership, rather than a patriarchal, family model.

There is some historical support for the apparent democratisation of the family, following the debate stimulated by Aries' *Centuries of Childhood* (1962). Gadlin (1978) offers a fascinating historical overview of child disciplinary practices and the cultural rationales that underpin them at different stages in the history of modernity. He argues both that discipline and training are the cornerstones of socialisation practices more generally and, more widely still, that 'parental control of young children is a microcosm of the methods of control appropriate to a given society, at a different moment in its history' (1978: 234). Beginning at the end of the nineteenth century, and becoming widespread by the middle of the twentieth, the democratic family emerges in distinction to the more authoritarian, conformist, hierarchical model which preceded it.

As Gadlin's review of family history makes clear, this new post-war model of the family is child-centred and heterarchical, concerned with promoting growth rather than imposing obedience. It is also, as part of the same development, individualistic, turning away from the norms set by the community towards the personal criteria of happiness, success and growth. In 'the modern family ideology [we promote] families in which the goal of individual self-realisation overshadows community solidarity and stability' (Gadlin, 1978: 236).[29] The relation between encouraging self-actualisation, to use Maslow's term (1970) – itself a new duty for parents – and permitting indulgence generates a certain unease among today's parent generation, and at the same time they express some anxiety over the apparent rise in disobedience and dis-respect for authority. As we found in a cross-generational analysis of responses to crime media, public discussion of the media, particularly in relation to children and young people's access to it, is exactly couched in terms of the potential link between individualised self-actualisation and indulgence/disobedience/disrespect (Livingstone et al., 2002).

How far is the optimism encouraged by the rise, at least in Western contexts, of the democratic family appropriate? Although children are indeed being ever more seen and heard, and while this shift is influenc-ing social policy in Britain and elsewhere in several ways, there are limits to this influence:

> In law and policy, increased prominence has been given to children's rights and especially to their entitlement to influence decisions affecting themselves. So far, this has chiefly meant greater sensitivity to hearing and understanding the viewpoints of individual children. There has been little preparedness to confer a greater role for children as a social group to influence policy and practice in schools, local neighbourhoods and society. (Hill and Tisdall, 1997: 2)

We have already encountered some of these limits when considering young people's sense of inadequate public provision for leisure activities (Chapter 2). The limits placed on considering the views and interests of young people are often motivated by economic considerations. A more subtle limitation on their social participation in both public and private domains is, instead, psychological. The earlier discussions in this chapter have shown how important to young people are adult judgements of their age and, implicitly, maturity. Note then the qualification in Article 12 of the UN Convention, which says, in effect, that 'children's views must be considered and taken into account in all matters affecting them, subject to the children's age and maturity' (Hill and Tisdall, 1997: 28). While only an extreme view would advocate that young children share in all adult rights and responsibilities, the assertion of a psychological judgement of maturity as the barrier, or gateway, to social participation is crucial; yet it is unlikely that shifting the debate into the psychological domain will make matters more straightforward.

Although historians confirm the underlying trends described above, the interpretation of these trends remains open. When Cunningham (1995) characterises the twentieth century as 'the century of the child', his is not the optimistic account which this label might suggest. Based on empirical analysis of historical trends in the popular parenting advice literature, he argues that in the twentieth century 'making the life of the child a technically controlled science was completed by attempting to make the parent–child interaction into a science' (Cunningham, 1995: 175), premised on the assumption that 'child-rearing was supremely important for the future of the child and of humanity' (1995: 176). In the first half of the century, advice centred on the establishment of regular habits – parenting by the clock – but this was superseded, at least to some degree, in the post-war period by the new duty of 'enjoying parenting'.

Arguably, we are witnessing contradictory trends, both towards the autonomy of children, domestic democracy and individualisation of childhood and towards increased regulation and risk management of children by adults. Rather than interpreting these as contrary trends towards independence and dependence respectively, Rose (1990) suggests that childhood is undergoing a process of bureaucratisation rather than of democratisation, through a combination of strategies which constrain children's participation in public while capturing their private, individual world of identity and agency.[30] Drawing primarily on Foucault's account of discipline and governance (1991), Rose (1999: 4) argues that:

> It is possible to differentiate the exercise of power in the form of government from simple domination. To dominate is to ignore or to attempt to crush the capacity for action of the dominated. But to govern is to recognise that capacity for action and to adjust oneself to it. To govern is to act upon action. This entails trying to understand what mobilises the domains or entities to be governed: to govern one must act upon these forces, instrumentalise them in order to shape actions, processes and outcomes in desired directions. Hence, when it comes to governing human beings, to govern is to presuppose the freedom of the governed. To govern human beings is not to crush their capacity to act, but to acknowledge it and to utilise it for one's own objectives.

In short, the shift towards the child as agent, as citizen, need not be understood – as it is in lay discourse – as one of giving children more autonomy. Rather, the disciplinary focus has shifted from that of external to internal controls. In terms of child development, parents are conscious of norms – targets even – appropriate to each age, and as activities in the home are increasingly drawn into educational policy, for example, parents are becoming accountable for their performance as parents. In terms of discipline, we are shifting from a shame culture concerned to control the moral character of children to a guilt culture concerned to control the personality of children (Gadlin, 1978). Thus, while nineteenth-century children were controlled by force and punishment, children at the end of the twentieth century are controlled internally. It becomes parents', and children's, responsibility to ensure that they grow up able to self-regulate, according to approved values and expectations, so that they precisely no longer need this external control. This analysis makes sense of an apparent paradox in the moral panics over children and media: as has often been noted, adults often express concern that other people's children should be subject to external regulation (hence the calls for censorship, V-chips, age-limits for videos, etc.) while their own children are not seen to require it (Davison, 1983). In other words, one's own children are seen as successes in the new game of self-regulation: they are sensible, and can be relied on to exert appropriate controls over their media use, watching only contents they are 'ready' for, and so forth.

More generally, however, the ways in which the media particularly become caught up in these processes remain to be disentangled. Age – or maturity – is crucial, and so too is gender: here the disciplinary struggles over young people's media use centre on sexuality for girls, violence for boys; importantly, both are popularly construed as matters of morality and self-control. However, we can perhaps recognise that parents are actively taking on, for better or for worse, this notion of governing (in Foucault's sense), by attempting to recognise the capacity of their children to act, and so adjusting to this assessment of their developing capacities. The aim, then, is on the inculcation of positive values rather than on the imposition of constraints. In other words, and often in explicit pursuit of the new ideal of the democratic family, parental discourse is framed, not in terms of parental regulation and children's acquiescence (or otherwise), but rather in terms of the parents' attempt to recognise, and where possible shape, their children's capacity for action. Children's actions, in consequence, are conceptualised less in terms of submission or evasion, conformity or deceit, but rather in terms of falling in with parental expectation or independence from these expectations, anticipated or not. However, through their confident yet often non-conflictual display of alternative or parallel interests to those of their parents, it does appear that in several ways today's children are simply side-stepping these attempts to govern their activities. The adolescent's resistance to the official adult conception of the family remains, of course, but many parents we interviewed in the YPNM project simply said that, after the age of around 14, they must hope their children are sufficiently sensible to make the decisions they as parents would wish them to, for they are all but beyond restrictive regulation. In this they tacitly recognise the role their children play in constructing, through their everyday actions and opinions, the family script and the domestic culture in which it is embedded, with consequences for the family budget, for the structuring of household time and space, and so forth.

This is not to say that parents no longer resort to the negative role of placing limits, and this is still often a conflictual struggle over definitions of dependence and independence, but they appear to be placing considerable emphasis on what might be termed positive regulation, first through the provisioning and arranging of the physical and symbolic space of the home and, secondly, through inviting their children to share a common activity or interest and so to generate the occasions of 'family life' through positive choice. In so doing, it seems that parents are more or less sensitive to establishing and maintaining a particular 'communication infrastructure' of the home (see Chapter 2). This does not, however, take us far in – and perhaps there is no empirical resolution to – the debate over the democratisation versus the bureaucratisation of the family. As lifestyles diversify, as families may be increasingly described as 'living together separately', parents and children resolve their coincidence or conflict of interests by espousing a discourse of democratisation. Yet critical observers may find this in itself evidence of the bureaucratisation or governance of the hitherto private home.[31]

NOTES

1 Byng-Hall (1978) identifies the importance of 'family myths' or family scripts, for example, in analysing how families themselves conceptualise their mutual relationships. Certainly, in accounting for patterns of media use in the YPNM project, families often found themselves telling us, implicitly or explicitly, about themselves and their family scripts.

2 As Varenne (1996) notes, 'freedom' is a 'contingent symbol', a set of cultural practices which are negotiated and displayed – a discourse of want rather than need, of preference rather than constraint.

3 Pollock uses the British Household Panel Study to show that the increase in major transitions experienced, and hence uncertainty over labour market prospects, represents the enhancement of opportunities for some and the loss of security for others. Moreover, the situation is strongly gendered, for 'while young women are still experiencing more labour market diversity than young men, the young men are beginning to catch up with them' (Pollock, 1997: 62).

4 Coleman (1993) argues, after reviewing the literature, that the widespread view of adolescence in particular as centred on a serious identity crisis involving a radical clash of values with parents is more myth than actuality. However, for a variety of reasons, this myth remains powerful and the categories of adolescence – or youth – are popularly constructed through discourses of deviance and disruption (see also Cohen and Young, 1981; Emler and Reicher, 1995; Pearson, 1983). Nonetheless, Coleman identifies contrary pressures on adolescents: 'sometimes these external pressures carry the individual towards maturity at a faster rate than he or she would prefer, while on other occasions they act as a brake, holding the adolescent back from the freedom and independence which he or she believes to be a legitimate right' (Coleman, 1993: 138).

5 The very nature of youth is hotly contested among youth researchers. For some it is obvious that 'young people today must prepare themselves for adult life. ... This task of youth is made more difficult by the fact that this is a period of transition, full of contradictions: on the one hand they are breaking with their childhood and their parents, while on the other they are qualifying and integrating themselves into the adult world' (Lieberg, 1995: 20). Others, however, reject the developmental notion of youth as an immature social stage, arguing that this represents a discursive means of justifying the exclusion of young people from the adult world, a linguistic classification through which 'youth competence can be denied, legitimized, and/or otherwise controlled' (Baizerman and Magnuson, 1996: 51). For Lieberg, the categories of adult and youth are externally set categories with which individuals must work as best they can; for

Baizerman and Magnuson, these categories are set by adults against the interests of youth and so should be resisted.

6 It should be noted that locating young people's media use within these broader socio-historical trends results in an account which contrasts markedly with technological determinist views such as those of Postman (1992). In *The Disappearance of Childhood*, he argues that today's children are seen to share activities, food, fashion, consumer expectations and, most important, social knowledge with adults, and that this is because of the demise of a culture of print and its displacement by a visual culture which requires no extended period of learning and which is therefore readily accessible to children as well as adults.

7 Baizerman and Magnuson (1996: 48).

8 This debate has become sufficiently familiar for many outside the discipline of psychology to use the critique of stage theories as a reason to reject a psychological account of childhood altogether (e.g. Buckingham, 1993; James et al., 1998; although others are more balanced, e.g. Hill and Tisdall, 1997). This leaves the difficulty of specifying how the competencies of children differ from those of adults; hence sociological or cultural accounts are unable to provide more than a purely descriptive account of childhood across the age range from infancy to adulthood.

9 Thus, as most children over 8 years old prefer to watch family/adult rather than children's programming, and as many are watching in their bedrooms, they may slip through the net of protective regulation at both ends of the communication process – production and reception.

10 See Livingstone and Bovill (1999), and also Buckingham (1991) and Hodge and Tripp (1986).

11 Moreover, children and young people are more likely to believe that people older than themselves share their taste in favourite programmes than do people younger than themselves (Livingstone and Bovill, 1999).

12 In the YPNM survey, 88% of 6–17 year olds were found to use a computer at school, for an average of 1–2 days per week, compared with 42% who use one at home (Livingstone and Bovill, 1999).

13 The nature of this 'expertise', and how judgements of expertise themselves may be changing, is pursued in Chapter 6.

14 One can draw here on the experience of work on the 'knowledge gap hypothesis' (Tichenor et al., 1970), where the deliberate provision of

knowledge is found to advantage differentially those whose knowledge and motivation is already high over those for whom the intervention is primarily intended.

15 See, for example, Alexander (1994), Bausinger (1984), Bryce (1987), Desmond et al. (1985), Goodman (1983), Liebes (1991), Lull (1990), Morley (1986), Palmer (1986), and Pasquier (2001).

16 Social grade differences are less strong, though it does appear that middle-class parents are more likely to spend time with their child discussing books, using a computer and taking them to the park or countryside while working-class parents more often listen to music with their children.

17 See, for example, Alexander (1994), Goodman (1983), and Johnsson-Smaragdi (1983).

18 These questions asked children about the frequency with which they eat together, play a game or make something together, talk about something that matters together, or talk about things in the news together with their parents. They also asked parents how decisions are made within the family as well as the topics that trigger arguments in the family.

19 Gibbons et al. (1995) cited in Hill and Tisdall (1997).

20 Interestingly, Segalen (1996) argues that during the Industrial Revolution wider kinship networks provided a buffer, a form of resistance even, against the otherwise hugely difficult conditions that framed family life during that period of rapid change. The functional importance of kinship networks in terms of what we would now term social capital (Putnam, 2000) is, she claims, discernible in the labour, housing and demographic patterns of the period.

21 Already, even within the home, Pasquier et al. (1998) find that fathers and sons can 'come together' over the computer in a manner not generally so stimulated by media.

22 Contrary to the notion of father at work and mother at home, one might also note that 22% of all mothers in the sample were in full-time paid work and 42% were in part-time work, leaving one in three mothers at home full-time (Livingstone and Bovill, 1999).

23 The rationale for comparative research in this field is developed in Livingstone (1998a). For an account of the dimensions of family life and media environments that distinguish different European countries, see Livingstone et al. (2001). Comparative research on childhood and family

life across Europe can be found in Biskup et al. (1984), Hawes and Hiner (1991), and Nurmi (1998b).

24 Duncan's (1998) analysis of gender and welfare relations within the family confirms these differences across European nations. Discussing the various dimensions of comparison, which inevitably lead to somewhat different groupings of countries, he classifies Southern European countries as 'transitional from private patriarchy' and the Netherlands and Nordic countries as moving towards the 'equality contract'. In his classification also, the UK and Germany are hybrid, though for different reasons.

25 Cause and effect are not easily disentangled here. In charting patterns of television use by the family from 1950–90, Andreasen (1994) suggests that the broad shift from family co-viewing towards individual viewing was facilitated both by technological developments – the purchase of multiple sets, the individualising effects of multichannel cable television and of the remote control – and by the emergence of more democratic families with non-traditional views about parent–child power relations.

26 This may be historically contingent, for UK parents at the end of the twentieth century are still more focused on television than on the Internet, for example, and television is, in the main, still highly regulated as regards potentially harmful content. It is also in many ways pragmatic, for from the parents' standpoint, the very factors which make the new media environment nationally less easy to regulate also make it domestically less easy to supervise. Faith in one's children is thus a workable strategy (Livingstone, 2000).

27 It is ironic that pressure is mounting to treat children and young people as citizens with rights (Hill and Tisdall, 1997) at the very point in which adult citizenship is seen by many as in crisis, undermined by the depoliticising effects of consumerism (e.g. Putnam, 2000).

28 For Giddens (1991: 5), 'the reflexive project of the self, which consists in the sustaining of coherent, yet continuously revised, biographical narratives, takes place in the context of multiple choice as filtered through abstract systems'.

29 Hence 'we find an increasing tendency to justify or rationalise techniques of socialisation in terms of their putative value in helping to actualise the potential of the child' (Gadlin, 1978: 244).

30 The contrary trends lead to paradoxes such as the way in which 'play and spontaneity have also become parts of the curriculum of nursery schools' (Qvortrup, 1995: 195); in Britain we have noted the apparent coincidence of parental restriction of children's access to public spaces and their liberal provision of media within the private domain of the child's

bedroom (Bovill and Livingstone, 2001). Rose's resolution is to argue that the more there is talk of children's rights, children's participation and children as agents, the more is society moved to regulate the conditions of this participation.

31   There is an interesting parallel here with the debate over the power of the text to determine audience reception in media research. Specifically, Foucault's domination/governmental distinction may be seen to parallel Eco's (1979) distinction between closed and open texts, for while the former attempt to impose their meanings upon a passivised reader, the latter are seen as anticipating the capacities, resources and motivations of the viewer and then mobilising these so as to channel interpretation in the desired direction. Hence, in this parallel, the value judgements are reversed: Eco prefers the open to the closed, Foucault instead appears to fear the triumph of the governmental for here the action of power is more insidious and incorporates our very souls in its own interests. The question of interest is of course crucial here.

6

CHANGING MEDIA, CHANGING LITERACIES

ACTIVE AND INTERACTIVE MEDIA USERS

In this book I have considered a variety of explanations for why the home has become media-saturated, why family life has become so thoroughly mediated over the past half century. As part of a longer social history, key cultural shifts in the construction of home, family and leisure have been identified, each of which contributes to the shifting nature and importance of media use in everyday life. These must be seen against both the background of a relentless economic trend towards ever newer, ever cheaper information and communication technologies as well as a persistent agenda of anxieties about childhood and youth. Notwithstanding intriguingly different inflections in different countries,[1] the present volume has explored why and how a childhood without media is now almost unthinkable, at least within Western countries. Why does this matter?

The social contexts of media use are inevitably also the everyday contexts within which we live out our social relationships and construct our social identities. The foregoing chapters have thus identified the consequences of a media-saturated childhood primarily in terms of contexts of use, analysing these in relation to the dimensions of space, time and sociality. In so doing, I have attempted to side-step the hype surrounding new media by embracing a wide definition of 'what's new', centring on three of the four features of new media outlined in Chapter 1:

- The multiplication of personally-owned media, encouraging the privatisation of media use
- The diversification of media and media contents, facilitating wider trends towards individualisation
- The convergence of traditionally distinct media, resulting in a blurring of traditionally distinct social boundaries

I end, in this last chapter, by pursuing the fourth aspect of new media identified in Chapter 1, namely the expansion of interactive forms of media, and the resulting potential for transforming a once-mass audience into engaged and participatory users of information and communication technologies. The focus is thus on the intellectual or symbolic consequences of a pervasive engagement with the particular forms and contents of the new media.

Newhagen and Rafaeli (1996) identify the following features as key to what's distinctive (if not entirely new) to forms of representations in new media and, especially, on the Internet:

- A *multimedia* text combining text (print), sound, pictures, animation, virtual reality, etc., requiring a multimodal engagement with Internet communication and hence supportive of a diversity of literacies, rather than a prioritisation of traditional reading skills.
- *Hypertextuality* – the text becomes non-linear and so infinitely open and plural in allowing for multiple paths, each of which is, when online, constantly updated and so continually changing, and thereby radically disrupting the traditional mass communication model of message flow from sender to receiver.
- *Anarchy* – the 'deliberately non-organised' organisational principle for routing traffic inhibits the operation of preferred paths, gate-keepers, and other forms of authority.
- *Synchronicity* – communication is now faster than ever, occurring over longer distances than ever before, and yet it may also be significantly time-delayed, introducing time warps into the flow of communication.

While there are some perhaps utopian assumptions built into this account, especially in terms of the political claims for heterarchical, even anarchic, forms of knowledge management, these four features together underpin the much discussed interactivity of new media, at least in terms of its potential. Specifically, given these new features of representing and transmitting information, those producing content for the Internet can offer a new or enhanced interactive relationship with or among users. These new possibilities are usefully subdivided into three types of interactivity to avoid some common confusions (see McMillan, 2002):

- User-to-user (as with computer-mediated interactions as email, chat)
- User-to-documents (providing technological control over content selection, as with hypertext documents on the world wide web)
- User-to-system (including a variety of human–machine interfaces such as games, search engines, educational software)

Once distinguished from each other under the broad umbrella of 'interactivity', one can see that somewhat different features of the Internet provide the underpinning for each. Most obviously, the distinctiveness of user-to-documents interactivity rests on its widespread (though not necessary) use of multimedia hypertext, the typical comparison being with the linear, *printed* texts that it appears to be displacing. If we take games as typical of user-to-system interactivity, all of multimedia, hypertextuality and synchronicity are vital to this mode of engagement, the offline comparison being with *play*. User-to-user interactivity, on the other hand, is most often compared with face-to-face interaction, and again the popular fear of displacement – this time, of *conversation* – is in evidence. Rarely as yet making use of hypertextual features, the key feature of user-to-user interactivity rests on the introduction of synchronicity into written communication, though the anarchic potential of multi-participant communication without gatekeepers has also attracted interest.

The role of the user differs in these different forms of interactivity. User-to-user interactivity positions the user as participant to an ongoing interaction with another user, engaging in a conversation, and thus resembles both speech (as on the telephone) and writing (albeit often in a newly informal and visually playful register). While many possible communication formats exist, the model here remains that of one-to-one, bi-directional communication among equals, with the user drawing on the social skills of everyday conversation. User-to-documents or system interactivity represents instead an update on traditional forms of mass communication in the sense that, first, the key players are culturally positioned as producer and consumer, and secondly, the communication flow is from one to many. Analysing the role of the user here can draw on analyses of the flow of mass communication in terms of the balance between the producer's power to structure and transmit messages and the audience or user's activities in interpreting the message in accordance with his or her cultural position and social circumstances.[2] In both models of the user, practices of message encoding and decoding are central, though one is rooted in verbal communication and the other in mass communication.

As new ICT formats and emerging genres increasingly combine different forms of representation and communication, we can expect the combination of different types of interactivity, and hence different models of the user, within one text.[3] At present, however, the interfaces used for online communication and information, particularly in the design of world wide web sites, continue to struggle to meet the vast expectations conjured up by the term 'interactivity'. While some express scepticism that people even want to engage with media interactively (W.R. Neuman, 1991), many more express disappointment that the kinds of contents currently available fall far short of the ambitions conceived for the Internet. Some of the frustrations arise because of a widespread confusion between user-to-user and other forms of interactivity, for there is a common expectation among ordinary users that, somehow, someone is 'listening', and that difficulties with documents or systems could be resolved if the system were 'truly' interactive (i.e. if there was a person at the other end listening and able to help).[4] The widespread 'email us' promoted by producers of television programmes, computer games and web sites perpetuates this confusion, presenting interaction with a document or system as if there is indeed someone waiting to respond to feedback.

To give an example from an observational study, consider how the question-and-answer format of a search engine like AskJeeves simulates conversation (user-to-user) while in fact providing user-to-system interaction, thereby confusing, and so failing to serve, its user. Megan, aged 8, was observed diligently typing complex and personalised questions to a 'Jeeves' who could only respond to simple, standardised questions, thereby making apparent what was intended to remain implicit, namely that in fact no one is actually listening.[5] Perhaps this would matter less if the 'implied user' (Iser, 1980) of many Internet interfaces did not so lamentably underestimate the intelligence and originality of their actual young users.[6] The consequences are as yet uncertain, but in the case of Megan, it is noteworthy that she was subsequently observed to give up on her complex questioning of AskJeeves and to learn to reframe her thoughts in terms of everyday key words and 'tell me more about…' follow-up questions. Shall we call this becoming more literate?

In practice, such experiences lead the Internet frequently to disappoint. As one child commented to us, the very 'freedom' of the Internet can be unhelpful:

> It can be more reliable to go to the library, because when you think about it anybody can write something on the Internet, and it could basically be a load of rubbish written by a 2 year old, and like with books they have to go through a publisher and everything, so what's actually written down is true.

In the context of such hopes and disappointments, it is worth examining more closely the claims that new media, particularly computers and the Internet, are accompanied by new forms of literacy (Kellner, 2002; Tyner, 1998), that our very ways of understanding, representing and communicating knowledge are being transformed through a sustained use of new information and communication technologies. What does this mean for the media audience? Or for young people's education? And what are the implications for the regulation of media access and use?

THE UNCERTAIN PEDAGOGY OF THE DOMESTIC COMPUTER

Since the advent of mass compulsory education, children's lives have been divided broadly into spaces and times for education and spaces and times for leisure. While education represents children's preparation for adult responsibilities in the future, leisure has hitherto consisted of activities centred on the here-and-now, often ignored by adults, unevenly provided for in terms of leisure facilities, and so occupying the marginal spaces in society, from the street corner to a bit of waste land. All this is changing, and ICT contributes to the process of cultural mediation that both distinguishes and connects different aspects of children's lives. We have seen that leisure has 'come home' in recent decades, that it has become centred on the domestic media and that, for reasons of growing commercialism and privatisation, its costs in time, space and money have made children's leisure increasingly visible to adults. It is thus no coincidence that we have witnessed a parallel rise in attempts to determine the value of leisure, and to limit the harms supposedly derived from 'misspent' leisure, notably as assessed not in the here-and-now but in relation to future adult responsibilities.

Perhaps the most significant way in which this occurs is through the blurring of the work/leisure or, for children, the education/entertainment boundary, so that entertainment is increasingly evaluated in relation to its potential educational benefits rather than its provision of immediate pleasure. Many 'leisure' activities, from ballet classes to the Saturday football match, have become incorporated into this pedagogic discourse. Central to our concerns here, and itself the locus of considerable uncertainty, is the part played by the arrival of the domestic computer and, more recently, the Internet, in this inter-penetration of 'just having fun' by the discourses, institutions and ideals of education. The institutional aspect of this inter-penetration of entertainment by educational goals should not be underplayed, for although leisure has traditionally been relatively private, part of the lifeworld, education by contrast has long been central to the project of the state, a centre-piece to the production of a future competitively skilled workforce.[7]

Overwhelmingly, the case for young people gaining access to ICT at home or at school is presented across public and policy fora as an educational one. As we have seen, parents are making a considerable investment in ICT at home, and schools are making an even greater investment in ICT within education.[8] At home, the growing importance of education in leisure occurs in the living room, changing the roles and responsibilities of parents and children. But with the advent of interactive media, this blurring and shifting of social relations occurs also in the construction of, and engagement with, the media text itself. In many ways, there is nothing especially new about this. Buckingham (2002) reviews the evidence that television, like computers today, was initially promoted to parents as an educational medium, and some research on the value of television in children's education tends to support the claims for educational benefits.[9]

But, as Buckingham goes on to note, little is known as yet about 'the pedagogy of computer use in the home'.[10] This uncertainty encompasses both the practical and technical issues of how children and parents are introduced to computers and become skilled in certain aspects of their use, and the more ambitious educational questions of how computers advance knowledge and understanding in particular curriculum subjects and/or 'empower' children to become 'active learners'. When we ask parents and teachers exactly how they suppose the introduction of ICT will facilitate education, there is often a pause while people struggle to account for that which has become taken-for-granted and yet which has been insufficiently argued in public, drawing as it does on a contentious and inconclusive research base (Hawisher and Selfe, 1998). It does not help that, as noted in Chapter 5, in the realm of ICT many adults believe children to be more at home, more expert than they, even though traditional models of education construct the adult as expert and child as learner. Is expertise being transferred from the adult who accompanies the child to the informational resources available on the screen ('ask an expert' is now an online slogan appealed to by all users, adult and child)?

Throughout our interviews with parents and teachers, less so with children, we encountered expressions of uncertainty, ambivalence and anxiety regarding the relation between education and entertainment.[11] This can be seen in the dismay expressed when an expensive investment made to support children's education turns out to be 'merely' a new way for them to play games. It is evident in the uncertainties expressed over so called 'educational' software, a way of relating to the screen which is marketed as the 'fun way to learn', though its research basis in supporting education is proprietary and so rarely made available to public scrutiny. Parents wonder whether to put the computer in a quiet bedroom or study to aid concentration on homework, even though this makes its use for entertainment purposes more difficult to monitor and regulate. Teachers face similar difficulties not only in determining which software could in reality advance their educational agenda but also in deciding whether ICT facilities should be made available for games-playing at lunchtime, email and chat after school, and so forth. While various trial-and-error solutions are provisionally settled upon, perhaps the biggest remaining challenge concerns their management of the home–school relationship, as teachers are encouraged by educational policy to incorporate parents into the framework for learning, increasingly relying on parents to create an appropriate learning environment at home which goes far beyond the space at the kitchen table once considered sufficient to support homework.

Research on new media, especially the Internet, is at an early stage and so, despite widespread acceptance of the importance of incorporating computers into education, teachers and parents – and perhaps also policy-makers – remain unclear about the nature of the supposed bene-fits. When asked, parents identify a range of possible educational bene-fits, from being able to use a Windows environment or being able to manage a data base to getting ahead at school and so improving one's job prospects (Livingstone and Bovill, 1999). For example, the working-class mother of 11-year-old Sam and teenage Rose, clearly believes computers are educationally beneficial. Yet she reflects a wider uncer-tainty over just how this benefit results from so substantial a family purchase:

> I would love to buy one of these, you know, like a multimedia PC, but I just don't have the money. Not necessarily for them to play games on. ... I think they're educational, I mean, Rose uses them at school a lot. She does a lot of her work on school computers, and it would be nice for her to be able to do it at home. ... I'd quite like one for him [Sam] because he doesn't read very much. I think he'd be more inclined to if we had the sort of encyclopaedias that you can get on CD-ROM. I think he'd be more inclined to use that rather than go to a book and look things up. ... But again, they can be a bit of a dis-advantage, because they just find what they want and print the whole page out and don't actually bother to read the thing.

While she thinks a computer at home will complement her daughter's use at school and will encourage her son to read and gain information, she worries that they will play games instead, and this for her is not an educational activity, or that they will print information without reading it, again conflicting with rather than facilitating educational goals. This contrasting of the unproven benefits of the computer with the proven benefits of books, and the uncertainty resulting from the ambiguity inherent in a machine which supports both educational and entertain-ment uses, precisely illustrates the cultural uncertainty over the educa-tional value of the computer.

Teachers are often similarly uncertain; for them too the case is not proven. While one primary school teacher we talked to felt computers offered future employment benefits, saying that 'we have to teach children the skills that they will need in society, i.e. the ability to be able to use computers confidently and in a useful way', others feel that this is distorting the educational process. Here a secondary school teacher feels that things have gone too far:

> *Teacher:* It is just another medium to deliver education through. If anything they have gone overboard. The computer should be used purely as a tool. They have got things on the syllabus that are really silly.
>
> *Interviewer:* Have you got an example?
>
> *Teacher:* Yes, some of the depth of computer logging. It is nice for the pupils to have an awareness of things, but they do not need to be able to use data logging equipment. And yet there it is in the national curriculum. Controlling external devices is nice but it is not essential and if you are doing that, then it is at the expense of something else. ... But if you were to go into industry the first thing that they will say is 'forget what you learnt at school'. They completely replace it with what they want, their way.[12]

Nonetheless, a growing body of research is charting a beneficial effect for introducing computers into educational settings. For example, one study compared playing a computer game about the brain with listening to a lecture about the brain and found the game generated both increased motivation and increased learning, suggesting a positive relation between learning and motivation.[13] A study by Loyd et al. (1987) confirmed that the more experience children have with computers, the more interest increased and anxiety decreased, suggesting that if home computers merely provide familiarity with computers, making computers seem fun and interesting, this alone is an advantage.[14] Indeed, ever since Greenfield (1984) reviewed evidence that computer games have many positive, even educational, aspects, encouraging a range of cognitive skills that include problem-solving, spatial awareness, hand-eye co-ordination, etc., many of the doubts have been rebutted. For example, computer games are popularly accused of undermining children's ability to concentrate, and yet, as Calvert (1999) notes, if a child stops attending to a television programme we worry little, and the child can return to viewing later. Hence, Anderson and Lorch (1983) showed that such persistent inattention is in fact a routine feature of children's television viewing; it is so managed by both programmes and children, through the use of perceptually salient features at key points in the narrative, that the programmes are generally well understood. Moreover, one may argue that computer games encourage children to concentrate, for if they stop playing, the game ends. On the other hand, Cordes and Miller (2000) review a body of evidence critical of the claims that use of computers in schools improves educational achievement, suggesting rather that computers undermine creativity, isolate children from face-to-face communication, and distract educators' attention from children's needs by focusing instead on technology. Frustratingly, it seems as if, very like the debates over the effects of television some decades earlier (Livingstone, 1996), more evidence adds to rather than resolves the confusion, partly because while presented as a purely scientific debate, contentious issues of policy, politics and morality are also centrally involved.

Much of the debate focuses on the improved delivery of a traditional curriculum, an aim seen as key by some teachers and educationalists, but seen by others as underestimating the potential of the new media. Buckingham's research (2002) suggests that while children understand the potential of computers in principle, they rarely engage in relatively more creative or technically complex activities themselves, tending as a result to under-use the potential of the computer quite considerably. While doubtless a similar claim could be made for more traditional forms of representing knowledge, arguing that children significantly under-use the potential of books, encyclopaedias, libraries, and so forth, the point is that one must always inquire into actual uses of a medium rather than relying on at times utopian accounts of the technical possibilities of a medium. Such an inquiry is especially important in so far as the forms and contents of ICT being developed for children and for the home market are in flux, in some ways ambiguous or confused in their ambitions, and crucially open to further social shaping depending on evidence as becomes available regarding children's preferences, interests and practices.

In sum, the existing research literature is not yet sufficiently developed to determine the specific advantages brought about by access to new information media. As a society we believe that familiarity with computers, the Internet, etc. supports learning and competitiveness in the job market – but as yet there is little clear evidence of this. While this hardly legitimates a sanguine attitude towards continued social and economic inequalities in ICT access and use, greater consideration is needed to the very question of what 'good' – access to which policy 'should' make public and fair – is at stake.

TRANSFORMING KNOWLEDGE

Uncertainties regarding the social uses and consequences of ICT for young people rest on two factors: first, the continued development and inherent interpretative flexibility of entertainment and educational technologies themselves (Bijker et al., 1987); and secondly, the parallel cultural and social changes affecting relations between home and school, family and state, private and public institutions. Most conservatively, one might argue that, especially as new media tend to rely heavily on the contents and forms of old media (McLuhan, 1994), ICT simply makes familiar contents available through additional means. On this view, the educational benefits are primarily those of increased convenience for rote learning or 'drill-and-skill' tasks (especially to 'catch up' remedial students with basic numeracy and literacy instruction), of increased access to and coverage of information, and for serving to motivate children during their experience of education.

This traditionalist position assumes that the use of multimedia and Internet texts requires only some technical facility with the interface, but involves no radical shifts in interpretation skills or knowledge representation. Such technical skills (mouse control, keyboard skills, managing a windows environment, etc.) are widely seen as particularly easy for young people to learn, as they are not set in the ways of old technology. Even where these prove difficult, the gain in motivation obtained from introducing computers into learning environments represents a benefit that outweighs the disadvantages of any skills gap. Moreover, as the educational materials employed are themselves often little transformed by being rendered accessible through the screen, the perceived educational benefits of such ambiguous activities as playing computer games or surfing popular culture web sites are restricted to gaining minimal technical competence, and may serve as a distraction from 'real' educational contents. This view is widely asserted by parents and teachers, and can be seen as an attempt to reassert the boundaries between education and entertainment that the shift from print to screen appears to undermine. As one teacher noted scathingly, 'I see no place for computer games on a tool that cost £1000 which a kid could be word-processing their essay on at lunch time'.

By contrast, however, the alternative position holds that screen-based media offer significantly new forms of representing knowledge which in turn require new forms of literacy to interpret them.[15] As Kress (1998: 74) observes, even 'notions of language *use* – that is, use of existing resources without changing them – will have to be replaced by notions of the constant remaking of the resources in the process of their use, in action and in interaction'. It is this position that we now explore below. However, one may note first, that if the traditional view is to hold sway, that ICT merely supplements existing forms of communication and information, and so merely extends the range of educational tools available, then there would be little to say, from the perspective of a study of media and their users, in contributing to this agenda. But if the alternative vision of ICT and its implications for the transformation of knowledge, education and communication is found to be convincing, then leaving education to the educators while others research media use in leisure time would be highly unsatisfactory. On this view, 'technological literacy' is only the beginning of the story, and the more exciting challenges lie in the realms of inquiry-based or student-centred teaching and learning, of creativity and of critical literacy. As Tyner (1998: 8) argues, and as discussed in the last section of this chapter, 'the literacy of schooling, based on a hierarchical access to print literacy, is increasingly at odds with the kinds of constructivist practices necessary to accommodate the more diverse, interactive, and less linear media forms made available by digital technologies'. Any challenge to this literacy of schooling will come as much from the world beyond the school as from changes within it.

Developing the earlier discussion of what's distinctive to forms of representations in new media and, especially, on the Internet, I now explore three key claims on which the alternative, or perhaps radical, case rests: multimodality and the turn to the visual; hypertext and the end of linearity; the shift to conceptualising representation as centred on processes rather than products.

Multimodal Representation and the Turn to the Visual

The first claim for a transformation of knowledge is that the multimodal nature of new media contents brings together multiple forms of engagement hitherto considered distinct forms of production (writing, drawing, designing) and reception (reading, listening, viewing, learning), as well as activities commonly distinguished from the reception of mass media (playing, talking, researching, performing)[16]. Yet both social commentators – and the public – still tend to conceptualize media and activities which are converging as if they were in competition with each other (e.g. television versus computer games, books versus screen, watching versus doing). In short, these technologically-mediated convergences seem to blur traditional, and valued, social distinctions; 'books versus screen', for example, representing a coded version of the high versus low culture debate. Yet even when such social distinctions are perpetuated, technological development is undermining them. Calvert (1999: 242) writes that 'seamless environments will develop as the moving audiovisual images of television merge with the interactive capabilities of computers in an increasingly realistic format. Children will be able to explore the Internet on their television sets, or watch movies, play video games, write stories, and perform innumerable other tasks on their computer screens.'

As those struggling to promote concepts of visual literacy fairly complain, Western society has long prioritised verbal, print-based literacy over any other (Bazalgette, 1999). While print literacy is deeply entrenched in our culture, the technological shift spearheaded by new ICTs is both welcome and overdue: 'I believe that while the rapidly increasing use of visual modes of communication has a complex set of causes, the simultaneous development and the exponential expansion of the potentials of electronic technologies will entrench visual modes of communication as a rival to language in many domains of public life' (Kress, 1998: 55). Children would undoubtedly relish this shift. One focus group we conducted, with a class of working-class boys aged 15–16, vividly illustrated their preference for screen over print media:

Interviewer:	Games console, Play Station?
Tom:	Electric.
Blake:	Good.
Charlie:	Exciting.
Lee:	Your hair's sticking up.
Interviewer:	Shelf of books?
Charlie:	Boring.
Blake:	Boring.
Lee:	Literature.
Blake:	Dumb.

Screen media are multimodal and within this the visual is prioritised; they are also increasingly fast-paced and interactive. Even when faced with competing sources of information, screen media are broadly preferred to books, as explained here by a group of middle-class 9-year-old girls:

Justine:	Computers you can learn like. You can do all sorts of interesting things on it – you can like have countryside things on it, and you just learn off them.
Lucy:	And some computers you can go to the Internet.
Justine:	Yes.
Interviewer:	Why can't I just do that from a book?
Annabel:	Well, because when it's on a computer, it's like showing you all what you can do on it, but in a book you're just reading it and it gets a bit boring.

For today's young people, it is television that provides a good story, and the computer that provides all the information one could ever want; for neither reason would many young people turn to a book. Given the frequency with which children reject books as 'boring' in our interviews, and the widespread turning away from reading for pleasure evident from teenage years onwards (chapter 2), a diversification of modes of engaging with knowledge representation might be judged beneficial. Yet this might prove a trap for those who desert the traditional forms if elite producers and users of knowledge continue to eschew such changes, retaining the stress on linear, print-based forms, this itself being probable given the link between linearity and authority. Notwithstanding the many and interesting experiments in creative writing, many of which challenge the conventions of linearity and authority in books, 'the conventions of print have already been socially negotiated … [while] the single most attractive feature of hypertext is that it has none' (Douglas, 1998: 160). While not all would agree with this 'attractive' feature, the implicit challenge to adult conventions of expertise and authority is indeed part of what makes new media appeal to young people.[17]

Kress takes the case for the visual turn further, arguing not only that the image is 'winning' over writing or linear verbal text, but also that writing itself is undergoing transformation. He notes that 'writing is thus doubly spatial: once metaphorical, through the order of syntactic hierarchy, and once actual, through the visual display on a surface' (Kress, 1998: 71). In the new media environment, the former spatiality is becoming impoverished, with the journalist's conventions of short declarative sentences and simple syntax coming to the fore; but the latter spatiality is of ever greater complexity. With the increasing manipulation of fonts, colours, arrangement on the page and integration with images, writing is ever more visual. Undoubtedly, in this latter sense of visual, young people take pleasure in writing, playing with the visual nature of writing not only in email and chat, but also in homework assignments. At the same time, they reject text, online and offline, that eschews such an aesthetisation of the visual aspects of print, seeing it as outdated, unattractive and, in consequence, uncommunicative. In this, they are in tune with the message producers.

Today's newspapers, advertisements and web sites all push 'writing to the margin' (Kress, 1998: 62), reversing the familiar pattern whereby language is seen to express everything there is to be expressed while the visual merely illustrates it. Rather, the expressive mode of these and other media — increasingly including educational texts — embody the assumption that 'writing is *no longer* the vehicle for conveying all the information, and … that some things are best done by using writing, and others are best done by using images' (Kress, 1998: 63).[18] The situation is one of both/and rather than either/or, with the relationship between written and visual text transformed from one of information/illustration to one in which both are informative, albeit in increasingly specialised ways. Written language, as Kress points out, is good for narrating, for commanding, for pointing at images, for sequencing, narrating and expressing causality, and hence for certain kinds of describing, explaining and classifying. Images are good at displaying, attracting and focusing attention, identifying components and showing their arrangement, or their part–whole relations. Both written and visual texts can be concrete or generalised; both can be realistic or abstract.

> Both modes [visual and written] produce semiotic objects – messages, textual forms. If texts are metaphors of the organisation of the world, then the two modes produce quite distinctly different takes on the world, different images of that world, and different dispositions by their users ... towards the world. The shift I have described here could be characterised ... as a move from *narrative to display*. (Kress, 1998: 72, original emphasis)

While it seems clear that young people welcome this shift, it is less obvious that the education system is prepared to accommodate it as yet, still tempted to contrast media (i.e. books and screen), rather than conceiving of the shift from one model of literacy to another.[19]

Hypertext and the End of Linearity

A second claim for a transformation of knowledge rests on the centrality of hypertext to many of the new media, particularly the world wide web. Hypertext is 'a structure composed of blocks of text connected by electronic links, it offers different pathways to users. ... The extent of hypertext is unknowable because it lacks clear boundaries and is often multi-authored' (Snyder, 1998a: 126–7). Mass media texts hitherto, whether printed, audiovisual or indeed audio, have been generally linear, supporting a particular form of literacy on the part of users: 'the conventions of reading, like those of writing, have grown out of the structure of sentences flowing into paragraphs, paragraphs flowing into pages, pages followed by other pages' (Burbules, 1998: 106). Such a familiar, linear, logical, hierarchical form of knowledge establishes standards for literacy and hence for cultural value.[20] Traditionally, 'printed texts are by nature selective and exclusive ... hypertexts on the Web are by nature inclusive' (Burbules, 1998: 103). Hence, in the world wide web, relations among elements are more often rhizomatic than logical, based on bricolage or juxtaposition, thus supplementing rather than simply replacing, more familiar linear structures.

> In general, then, hypertext seems to *add* dimensions of writing, and to that extent may encourage new practices of reading as well: ones that might prove more hospitable to alternative, non-traditional points of view and more inclusive of cultural difference. (Burbules, 1998: 107, original emphasis)

More than with linear media, therefore, the 'role of the reader', to use Eco's (1979) term, is under-specified by the text, with meaning realised as joint construction of text and reader, dependent on the interpretative paths followed from among a range of possibilities (Flichy, 2002). This is not always creative, however, for the potential for 'going wrong' seems also commensurately greater. As children observe in relation to the Internet, if you don't know what your purpose is or just where you want to go, you easily get lost. This 14-year-old is not alone in saying, of the supposed new world of information, 'It's annoying, you spend ages and ages trying to look for something and then you don't get it in the end' (Livingstone and Bovill, 1999). On the other hand, to the extent that 'writing has been the most valued means of communication over the last few centuries – the one that has regulated access to social power in Western societies' (Kress, 1998: 59), there is surely an interesting shift in the potential, if not yet the actual, forms of knowledge and communication now available to this and other ordinary teenagers. Hence, other children can say of the Internet, with equal justification, 'It's just a big world. ... You're in control. ... There's a lot of choice that you have. ... It's like an alternative life' (middle-class 12-year-old boys).

Whether or not hypertext actually 'works' for its users is crucially a matter of implementation and skill on the part of designers and users. But also, and more problematic for the 'end of linearity' argument, is the critique of hypertext developments from a political economy viewpoint. Joyce (1998), among others, identifies some of the ways in which the world wide web remains more hierarchical than hypertextual, pointing out how the home page is dominant, how movement through the web is constrained by design so that one must keep going 'back'. He is particularly critical of meta-sites (the best of, the top 100, all the lists), for these are generally hierarchically organised according to commercially driven principles invisible to the user. Rather as if we read only the card-index catalogue or the book spines in the library but never open the books, Joyce worries that many of the hypertextual possibilities of the Internet are never realised, while the many editorial decisions over content, and the interface tools which collate, filter, prioritise and re-present the outputs of those decisions as a series of menus, buttons and hotspots, represent ways of reasserting the power of established interests. In a manner strongly reminiscent of the early doubts about television (Boddy, 1985), he fears that the user suffers from 'a constant hunger for newness without a taste for detail. The eye gets tired of watching passing patters and we settle into a commercial glaze. We are so used to thinking something new will come, and so tired of seeing only patterns, that we never really see or settle into the particularity of where we are' (Joyce, 1998: 167).

From Roots to Routes

Yet interestingly, the particularity of where we are is also, from the viewpoint of those advocating a transformation in knowledge, open to critique. To discuss the third characteristic of new forms of knowledge mediation, I shall make a brief detour back to the offline world, using the work of Clifford (1997) to characterise a key dimension of the new forms. Clifford contrasts two conceptions of culture, arguing for a reversal of the assumption that culture and identity are best understood in term of roots or rootedness in a locale, and attempting to shift the frame so as to make visible the many journeys or routes that, for diverse and interesting reasons, together constitute the daily life of many communities. In focusing on the significance of travel to an understanding of culture, he thus critiques the assumption that 'authentic social existence is, or should be, centred in circumscribed places'. Methodologically, as he suggests, 'ethnography … has privileged relations of dwelling over relations of travel' (Clifford, 1997: 22), seeing the native (and home) as the taken for granted and the traveller (and the borders he or she crosses) as the exotic in need of explanation.

If we apply this analysis to the construction of identity and cultural representation on the Internet, there is evidently a tension between these two models. In the 'roots' model, the home page is paradigmatic of the relationship between identity and place. This model fits those sites designed to be self-contained so as to catch and keep the user within the site. For children, the 'walled garden' is the model which, like the garden at home, offers a safe place to play among the pleasures thoughtfully provided by the owner of the garden, though there may be no way to the fields or roads beyond. Whether the motivation is commercial (to maximise user exposure to the site and hence to the brand or to advertising) or public (to support children's activities within a safe and child-appropriate space) or both, this model contrasts with the 'routes' model of the world wide web, captured more strongly by the surfing metaphor. Here the user rarely pauses in any particular place but rather finds satisfaction from traversing a path across the crests of the waves, identity inhering in the nature of the journey rather than in the main places inhabited along the way.

The critic of the 'roots' model stresses the constraining aspect of familiar places, their invisible walls and behind-the-scenes guards or protectors. The critic of the surfing analogy is likely to observe that the ocean largely guides the surfer and, moreover, that the surfer rarely discovers what lies beneath the surface except by accident. In relation to the world wide web, these debates must adjust as the web itself changes. As Clifford (1997: 31) notes, we may contrast 'travel, negatively viewed as transience, superficiality, tourism, exile, and rootlessness' with 'travel positively conceived as exploration, research, escape, transforming encounter', but which of these will gain acceptance in popular and critical views of the Internet remains to be seen. Interestingly, when children talk of the experience of control, of abundance, of individual choice in relation to the Internet, it is often this experience of travel, of routes, that seems predominant. And as the activity constructs the actor, so do the routes traversed through the world wide web seem as significant as the sites themselves, if not more so, in the construction of the child's identity.

For example, an 11-year-old boy proudly showed us his personal web site.[21] On a black background, coloured writing announced 'DANIEL'S COOL SITE, COOL IS THE MAGIC WORD', and under this were listed three URLs with brief text appended, namely:

- *www.rmplc.co.uk*
  Visit the rm eduweb to get the best out of fun. And use it to help you with your project.
- *www.askjeeves.co.uk*
  The best ever search machine. You can ask any question that comes to mind.
- *www.encarter.msn.co.uk*
  Go beyond your encarter encyclopedia by searching online.

If we read this web site for its content in terms of 'roots', it is sparse indeed, for Daniel has written nothing about himself and has merely directed the visitor onwards to further sites of interest. For anyone seeking a place to stay, there is little reason provided here. But if we read the site in terms of its links, quite a different interpretation emerges.

By positioning himself in relation to his three selected web sites, chosen meaningfully from a potentially huge array, Daniel's site tells us several significant things about himself. First, he prioritises educational uses of the web, anticipating a user who, like him, faces the challenge of searching the web for specific information of interest or importance to him or her. Through his accompanying text, he declares that he is serious about learning but ready to have fun, and that he is active in searching, indeed, creative in his thinking and questioning, and adventurous in going beyond the limitations of Encarta, currently the mainstay of many children's informal learning environment at home. More tenuously, Daniel attempts to create a symbolic connection between himself, just one small boy in a suburban town in the UK, and three of the most popular commercial organizations on the web, implying that through this link he himself may provide value to others and perhaps gain value himself by the association.

In the 'routes' model of the world wide web, then, the link has become central. Indeed, once subordinated in the form of a footnote or a citation, for some sites (search directories being the obvious example) the link is more or less all there is. In his analysis of online texts, Burbules (1998: 103–5, original emphasis) invites a critical reading of the 'link' using an argument that parallels Clifford's:

> My hope is to invert the order of how we normally think about links and information points, nodes or texts; usually we see the points as primary, and the links as mere connectives; here I suggest that we concentrate more on links – as associative relations that change, redefine, and enhance or restrict access to the information they comprise ... [for] links do not only express semic relations but also, significantly, establish pathways of possible movement within the Web space: they suggest relations, but also *control access to information* (if there is no link from A to B, for many users the existence of B may never be known – in one sense, the link *creates* B as possibility).

A critical focus is crucial of course: while Daniel simply offered his favoured links as a matter of personal preference, for commercial web sites inclusion and exclusion are big business, with companies paying for priority in the listings. From the standpoint of a political or ideological analysis, similarly, the effect of juxtaposing two texts through establishing a link is to transform the meaning of both texts, and the significance in semiotic terms of that which is omitted may be as great as that which is included.

Thus it is not only valuable to read links and routes as well as sites and pages, but it is also imperative to decode the apparent naturalness or taken-for-granted nature of the link, recognising that 'links *create* significations themselves' (Burbules, 1998: 110) for they are 'rhetorical moves that can be evaluated and questioned for their relevance. They imply choices; they reveal assumptions; they have effects – whether intentionally or inadvertently' (1998: 117).[22] One may say that much of this holds also for the printed book, but there it is more apparent to the naïve reader that selections have been made, and that these reflect both the choices of the author and the anticipated interests, accurate or not, of the reader. In the apparently free, apparently open, apparently vast world of the web, however, decisions regarding inclusion and exclusion are far from obvious, the very existence of a producer or author may not be recognised, and it is generally the wide availability of information, rather than the closing down of options, which is most frequently commented on.[23]

NEW MEDIA, NEW LITERACIES

Each of the claims discussed above addresses the nature and future of the text in a changing information and communication environment, and each identifies some perhaps rather utopian possibilities. However, notwithstanding the radical potential of ICT in transforming processes of learning, literacy and pleasure, it may be argued that the slower-to-change, far-from-disinterested contexts of use tend to under-exploit or undermine such a potential. To the extent, however, that we are indeed witnessing a transformation in the notion of the text, one must ask whether there are parallel changes in the user (or reader)? And if so, are such changes in young people's ways of knowing to be encouraged?

The three features of new media texts considered above (multimodal, hypertextual, processal) are central to electronic and online games: one argument is that we should learn from how children have fun with ICT in order to understand how they might also learn from it. As explored below, this involves a shift from a rule-based model of education to the more immersive 'learning by doing'. Far from representing an irrelevant or even problematic alternative to 'serious' uses of computers, it might be argued that playing electronic games generates the kinds of skills and competencies that matter most for ICT use. This suggests a further step, of broadening the concept of literacy so as to unpick our cultural prioritisation of print literacy and to encompass a more plural and diverse range of literacies important in the new media and information environment.

From Rule-based Learning to 'Learning By Doing'

In gaining familiarity with new technological formats and interfaces, one key mode of engagement provides an entry point for children and young people, namely games-playing – favoured for work or play, alone or in company, as part of learning or relaxing. Johnson-Eilola (1998) argues that young people's orientation to and facility with computer games is the key to any educational and informational benefits on offer from computers and the Internet, while Snyder (1998b) claims that teachers and educators must confront the phenomenon of computer games or be further marginalised. Yet although computer games are big business, associated with huge advertising budgets and profits (Beavis, 1998), research on games-playing as an activity is sparse, certainly by comparison with the funding available for researching educational uses of ICT, even though it is games-playing which represents young people's primary mode of ICT engagement.

Unfortunately also for our present purposes, more research has been conducted on the content of computer games than on their users. In analysing video games at an early point in their mass market success, Skirrow (1986) characterises them as presenting as a virtue their lack of originality or autonomy regarding content; the video game represents 'a pastiche of borrowings from other forms of popular culture [and] inter-textuality is incorporated into the surprise mechanisms' (1986: 119). Arguably, electronic games have always combined technological newness of form with a strong link to familiar, and favoured earlier popular culture narratives and meanings – combining past pleasures in war games, board games, simulation games and fantasy novels with an enduring fascination with the occult, magic, futurology and the exploration of nature (especially of space, science, prehistory). Whether a game about Dracula, the Hobbit, the evil overlord, the menacing dinosaurs or the intergalactic struggle, these themes long preceded video games and it seems that no new big cultural themes have yet emerged.[24] Despite the familiarity of these themes, parents and onlookers tend not to be reassured, perhaps explaining the paucity of research on games and game-playing:

> Even if they admit that these games involve the traditional themes which they remember from their own childhood – victory of the forces of good over evil, subterranean powers against celestial ones, the aggressiveness of disgusting and perverted dragons against beautiful and innocent princesses – they still persist in their belief that these games convey negative values and that the battles are more brutal or more trivial than 'in our day'. (LaFrance, 1996: 305)

Indeed, although any harmful impact of such violent games remains unproven, there are many grounds on which games are criticised, not just in terms of content but also in terms of the demands made of the players; for in these games, as LaFrance (1996: 308) notes, 'flexibility and original ideas are generally not rewarded'.[25] However, it can be argued that games are crucial to understanding the new media context more as a mode of engaging with ICT than because of their particular contents. Indeed, in the new media environment, contents can be associated with any and all media, through what Kinder (1991) calls the 'transmedia intertextuality' of children's culture. Pokémon, Barbie, Power Rangers, Manchester United, Winnie the Pooh, these increasingly globalised and highly commodified products provide content for old and new media (as discussed in Chapter 3). In consequence, fandom becomes *par excellence* the mode of relating to media generally (Jenkins, 1992): whether framing television preferences, stimulating reading, guiding the purchase of software titles, or providing search terms for accessing the web, fandom offers a strategy to select information, individuate lifestyles, construct common (sub)cultures, and assert identity.

However, the form and mode of engagement with computer games can be seen as more original, by comparison with older media. A key consequence of interactivity is the radical shift in the positioning of the player – from the third person to the first. As Skirrow (1986: 126) argues for the video game, 'the reader has become a performer', unlike the third-person experience of spectatorship and identification in the cinema (or in some television), in the video game 'the first and third person are almost totally identified' (1986: 130) and so 'we do not identify with someone else's satisfaction, we expect to experience it' (1986: 128). LaFrance (1996: 306) agrees, drawing on Eco's notion of 'interpretative co-operation' to describe the relation between game creator and game player. But he goes on to caution that, in jumping 'onto the stage, destroying the symbolic separation between the stage and the public ... the individual takes command of the gameware and is himself subjected to its hold, just as the driver of a motor-race becomes a pilot constrained by the rules of the machine, the environment, the actions of others, and so forth'. Game-playing on the Internet, particularly with multiple players, clearly offers an expansion of such performance possibilities.

In interviews with children regarding their experience of screen entertainment culture, what is most noticeable is that when children talk about *computer games*, the words which appear over and over are 'control', 'challenge', 'freedom' (Livingstone, 2000). As a working-class girl aged 9 explained, 'I prefer games like Super Mario – you want to just control them and jump on the mushrooms. ... And I like Super Mario because it's just really like a challenge kind of thing.' Consider also these comments from a group of 15-year-old boys meeting to play games in a cybercafé:

It's first-person perspective, so you look through the eyes of a player.

One of my friends just calls himself God when he's playing. I have a lot of names, I mean usually I have, Inertia's my favourite.

Now I'm sort of more alive, more free to do what I want.

The comment here about computer games, unlike most other media, being experienced in the first person is especially revealing of the intensity and immersive nature of the experience (Laurel, 1993).[26] These and similar kinds of observation lead Johnson-Eilola (1998: 190) to conclude that 'far from being isolated, neutral objects, computer interfaces play out a range of assumptions, authorisations, and challenges to literacy practices'. He pursues this theme by analysing some of the ways of thinking and communicating encouraged by children's software, particularly drawing out how they value 'the ability to process multiple streams of information simultaneously, and the propensity to experiment in free-form, ill-defined problem domains' (Johnson-Eilola, 1998: 191).

The sense of control and freedom, the first-person immersive experience, the stress on flexible, parallel thinking – all these dimensions of games-playing are only now being built into the interface for more 'serious', informational uses of ICT. Hence, the skills that young people have developed within their leisure time are only now being recognised as, potentially, crucial for ICT literacy (or literacies) more generally. Commenting critically on formal education practices, Johnson-Eilola (1998: 186) worries that 'we are also trying to tie them [children] to a way of seeing the world, a way that is no longer feasible'. After watching his daughter play a computer game and attempt to explain to her father what the purpose and strategy of the game is, he notes that:

> To someone raised in an historical worldview – one valuing linearity, genealogies, tradition, *rules* – Carolyn's explanations of the game sound haphazard, unplanned and immature. But to someone familiar with global information spaces such as the World Wide Web, games such as these provide environments for learning postmodernist approaches to communication and knowledge: navigation, constructive problem-solving, dynamic goal construction. (Johnson-Eilola, 1998: 188)

The bewilderment which parents (but rarely their children) often express in understanding the games their children play on the home computer or, similarly, when faced with a new computer and no comprehensible rule-book for getting started, testifies to this shift in the mode of engagement with systems of representation. In comparing the literacy expectations of parents and children, Johnson-Eilola posits a generation gap in understandings of what constitutes a game, pointing out that 'where modernists are compelled to understand the rules before playing a game – or at best, must be able to discern simple, clear rules by trial and error – postmodernists are capable of working such chaotic environments from within, movement by movement' (1998: 195). For today's generation of children, it is important 'to understand things in multiple, contingent, spatial structures rather than in serial and chronological orders ... [and so] we will begin to see greater reliance on skills which modernists might dismiss as game-playing' (Johnson-Eilola, 1998: 202–3). Ask children how they work out what to do and where to go on the Internet, and they describe a combination of informal guidance from co-participants in front of the screen and a process of exploration and experimentation in the online environment itself (Livingstone and Bovill, 2001b). Their parents, by contrast, are more likely to use rule-books, help systems, and so forth, and yet may do less well with this approach.

For young people, then, it appears that 'learning by doing' fits their learning style more than formal rules-based approaches. In their study of young children's use of computer and video-game technology, Smith and Curtin (1998) confirm Turkle's (1995) observation that children 'just do it', figuring it out intuitively through trial and error, testing out hunches, 'just mucking around', and by drawing where needed on informal 'teachers' (relatives, friends) rather than beginning with the rules in the manual and then implementing them:

> With all these teachers the relationship is informal and the instruction experiential and 'just-in-time' (provided as required). This 'learning-by-doing' model contrasts with the teaching approach that attempts to provide a store of knowledge and skills before practice. (Smith and Curtin, 1998: 219)

Interestingly, 'learning by doing' is a model in tune with liberal approaches to early childhood education, but this is generally replaced as children get older with a rules-based approach. Yet it seems that, notwithstanding the poor fit with formal education, young people are ready to learn in ways less than familiar to the generation of their parents and teachers but which are particularly in tune with the model of the user embedded in new forms of ICT. If so, then games-playing within leisure time and domestic space cannot be dismissed as 'mere entertainment', but rather such an activity illustrates the deeper challenge posed to Western conceptions of literacy and, in consequence, to the institutions by which society regulates media use and promotes literacy among its young people.

Literacy and Empowerment

Underlying the traditional and alternative positions on the role of ICT in transforming knowledge lies an equally fundamental debate over the nature of literacy, often expressed through discussion of the cultural value of screen-based media. On the one hand, traditional cultural values are asserted, along with elite forms of knowledge and knowledge hierarchy, long-established (print-based) standards of literacy, and a clear separation between education/knowledge and entertainment/pleasure. On the other hand, we hear the assertion of multiple, context-appropriate conceptions of value, egalitarian or heterarchical specifications for knowledge, a plurality of literacies, and a blurring of boundaries between knowledge and entertainment, work and leisure, education and play.

There can be little argument that it is the former position that has underpinned the education system. In their attempt to reconstruct the home as an informal learning environment, parents similarly endorse such values in justifying their strategies for regulating the domestic environment, including their children's media use. Yet, in so far as new media technologies are heralded as potentially opening up new possibilities for knowledge, new forms of representation, new ways of engaging the user, these long-standing principles and value judgements are now thrown into confusion.

Caution is required lest one lapses into the often repudiated yet still pervasive assumptions of technological determinism,[27] for many factors, from politics to aesthetics, are as much if not more important than technological innovation in accounting for social change in practices of literacy, education and cultural knowledge. The past half century has witnessed debates over the nature of education, challenging assumptions regarding literacy and knowledge, attacking class-based forms of privilege and inequality, and responding to the growth of multiculturalism, all of which have served to relativise traditional conceptions of value. This chapter concludes by reflecting on some of the challenges currently facing the policy environment for young people's media use. In so doing, more questions are raised than can be resolved, given the current state of both evidence and practice, for what initially appears to be a set of specific questions regarding the introduction of ICT into the school and home rapidly unpacks into a more complex agenda.

Despite the public prominence of debates over literacy, the term 'literacy' remains difficult to define and is the subject of many myths. This is partly because it is incorporated into such a breadth of cultural and moral discourses, partly because of a series of empirical difficulties noted by historians and anthropologists in attempting to demarcate literacy/illiteracy boundaries, and partly because literacy is at times conceptualised as a feature of a technology, a culture and/or an individual.

> Literacy artifacts – the alphabet, the pen, the book, the computer – become metaphors for the diverse uses of literacy and its vague promise of 'enlightened

progress'. The term literacy is shorthand for cultural ideals as eclectic as economic development, personal fulfilment, and individual moral fortitude. To be 'illiterate' is a powerful social stigma. (Tyner, 1998: 17)

Print, oral and digital literacy link different historically and culturally contingent technologies with the capacity to represent, use and communicate knowledge in particular ways. In her overview of literacy research, Tyner characterises the emerging consensus to be arguing for many literacies generally co-existing in any one culture, no one literacy being superior to others (though some may be more culturally valued than others), and with multiple paths to literacy (of which school is, generally, more culturally valued than others). Just as we argued earlier in this volume that new media supplement rather than replace older media, so too are literacy scholars arguing that digital literacy practices add to rather than simply displace older notions of print or oral literacy, albeit that these latter are transformed in the process.[28] Thus literacy becomes diversified, with multiple literacies including technology literacy, information literacy, visual literacy, critical literacy, media literacy and network literacy (Beavis, 1998; Kellner, 2002; Tyner, 1998).[29]

Media literacy, still the preferred term to cover these literacies, has in the past been predominantly conceptualised narrowly, in protectionist terms, teaching children to critique popular culture and recognise the merits of high culture, thereby inoculating them against putative media harms. In relation to both traditional and new media, the debate is shifting so as to conceptualise literacy in terms of its enabling or empowerment capacity. The notion of critical literacy especially, founded on questioning rather than on skill, on critiquing rather than on affirming traditional hierarchy and authority (notably as in Freire and Macedo's (1987) notion of 'reading the world'), opens up a more exciting notion of literacy. Debates over the pedagogic role of the computer and, particularly, its role in the inter-penetration of educational and entertainment activities, are today centrally caught up in the latest version of these debates.

If it is agreed that optimal use of ICT in education is, at least potentially, not simply a matter of giving children encouragement in their studies while they gain a technical facility with the so-called tools of the future, but more significantly about facilitating a transformation in the nature of knowledge and the learning process, then there follow some notable implications for education. Certainly, there are many calls for a transformation of education policy, accompanied by dire warnings of the consequences if we as a society fail to rise to this challenge. Some calls are grand if vague, as with America's technology literacy challenge,[30] a proposal to make young people 'technologically literate', based on the assumption that it is on screen-based media, rather than print media, that knowledge, and hence employment, increasingly depend.[31] For Smith and Curtin (1998), the shift from print literacy to multiple literacies is contributing to a generational shift in which teachers and their pupils are inevitably caught up. In this reversal of traditional authority relations, it is children who are making the running:

> Young children are the first generations to live in an all-encompassing electronic habitat … to deal with this complex habitat, children develop forms of cognitive and attitudinal organisation that enable them to interpret the world and perform in it. In so doing, children help to shape and change the social world they live in, at both the individual and cultural levels … [while] conventional school curricula and pedagogical procedures are out of step. (Smith and Curtin, 1998: 212)

Indeed, many call for a period of radical rethinking, as when Kellner (2002: 90) argues that 'in a period of dramatic technological and social change, education needs to cultivate a variety of new types of literacies to make it relevant to the demands of a new millennium'. Similarly, evaluating the early attempts to use ICT in the classroom, Schroeder (1995) argues that although it can be shown to result in a more interesting, independent and enjoyable learning experience for pupils, there is a failure of imagination at the heart of the project. Without a creative rethinking of the curriculum, it remains unclear what pupils can learn and much time is wasted, and the new technology is likely to be reduced to either a distracting gadget or a way of playing games outside more traditional lessons. This failure of imagination translates also into a failure thus far of the policy agenda to move on from questions of diffusion or access to questions of use. As Tyner (1998: 71) somewhat wryly observes, 'until the culture of schooling, classroom pedagogy, and curricular issues are addressed in conjunction with technology access, it is not at all certain that high-tech tools would be used to benefit student performance, even if every student had unlimited access to information technologies'.

So what might this alternative model of teaching and learning involve? Snyder (1998a: 135–6) suggests that:

> If teachers are prepared to transfer to students much of the responsibility for accessing, sequencing and deriving meaning from information, hypertext can provide an environment in which exploratory or discovery learning may flourish [although teachers must] develop and extend their students' ability to think critically and make connections between discrete bodies of information.

If we unpack this claim, it involves several components:

- The move away from a *transmission* model of learning, as the teacher becomes less responsible for the transfer of information from expert to pupil and less reliant on dictation and other linear methods of transmitting information otherwise unavailable to pupils, towards a model which values searching, critiquing, integrating and connecting.[32]
- The move away from a *hierarchical* authority relation between teacher and learner, given that 'authority about what is most worthwhile culturally and the means to get it have slipped away from the traditional gate-keepers and cultural transmitters – schools, teachers, universities, books, libraries' (Smith and Curtin, 1998: 225).
- The move away from learning information to learning how to find information '*just-in-time*', important in so far as 'information' itself is acknowledged to be overwhelmingly abundant and subject to rapid change, so that a more effective strategy than learning 'the facts' is that of learning how to find them as and when needed.[33]
- The move away from discrete institutional contexts for learning towards a recognition that, as learning can and should occur anywhere, more attention is needed to the construction of *informal learning environments* and to the process of *learning by doing* (Johnson-Eilola, 1998).[34]

Now that 'computer technologies make it possible for students to learn what they want, when they want, how they want, without schools' (Smith and Curtin, 1998: 228), the spatial, temporal and social contexts of learning (and, by implication, being at leisure) are transformed. Crucially, there is also a cognitive shift central to a model of learning based on multiple literacies for an information-rich environment, and this concerns the growing importance of *critical literacy*. More than ever before, children and young people will require critical understanding, skills in argument, making distinctions, imagination, critical analysis, and a questioning approach. Learning increasingly occurs under conditions of information overload, much of the information available being of questionable quality. Hence, high-quality procedures for searching, critiquing and arguing become crucial. Such a position leads Quinn (1997) to define that much abused term 'empowerment' as neither the provision of adult or predigested information to children nor simply as the opening up of free access to information. Rather, he (and others) value the provision of an interactive context in which children feel able to do what they can do best – such as thinking as creatively or logically or critically as they can – and in which their activities are legitimated through peer and adult attention. Hence, the adult's role is that of carefully responding, feeding back to the child their understanding in an explicit and readily verbalisable form so that they can reflect upon it and, when appropriate, have ready access to such knowledge again.

Applying these expectations to the Internet, it is immediately apparent that the form of empowerment offered by the Internet is far from this, being instead a more limited encouragement towards 'right-answer' learning, notwithstanding the vast array of information from which to select. Rarely does the Internet invite children to judge for themselves the truth or value of the information it offers them, and rarely also do web sites provide either the information or the criteria by which such an evaluation might be conducted. Rather, web site design may be seen to adopt a set of strategies to encode what Hall (1980) called the preferred reading (frequently asked questions, recently asked questions, top ten lists, fact of the week, our favourites, etc.). As Eco noted, in his analysis of textual closure, the text which attempts to address a great diversity of actual readers by providing them with a uniformly satisfying and appropriate message, is precisely the one which runs the greatest risks of satisfying no one, for 'they seem to be structured according to an inflexible project. Unfortunately, the only one not to have been "inflexibly" planned is the reader. These texts are potentially speaking to everyone ... it is clear that they can give rise to the most unforeseeable interpretations' (Eco, 1979: 7). Moreover, the many questions and answers on an Internet site typically add up to a collection of facts which bear little structural relation to one another (offering neither an argument nor a narrative, but rather a patchwork of disparate items intended to provide an appealing variety). The questions are generally highly straightforward – rarely is one moved to say of web site content, 'that's an interesting question', though in face-to-face conversation this is a valued response, as is learning to recognise 'a good question' (meaning one which is precisely not of a standardised format).[35] At present, therefore, if children and young people are to approach ICT in a critically literate manner, the adult support they receive for developing such a literacy must be coming from in front of, rather than on, the screen. Doubtless, interface and web site design in the future could also foster critical literacy if this were given the priority it deserves.

Literacy, Learning and Regulation

It would seem perverse to argue against the empowerment of children through ICT, if empowerment means guiding children towards the newly accessible abundance of diverse information and communication possibilities. But there is an argument against the regulation of such a process, in so far as it extends the power of the state over the informal, leisure occupations of childhood conducted in the privacy of the home. The consequences of such an extension of power are, perhaps, what lie beneath the not insignificant anxieties expressed by parents as they invest in and come to grips with ICT at home, knowing that with the likely rolling back of national regulation for media, regulation will increasingly become the responsibility of parents.[36]

Such concerns represent the latest stage in a long history of inter-dependence between regulation and education. Luke (1989: 9) adopts a Foucauldian approach to the history of the idea of childhood in Europe[37], arguing that 'print, literacy, and education must be viewed as historically concomitant phenomena', within which 'the child was an intrinsic component – an important object of attention – of these discourses since it was seen that the possibility for reform lay with the proper training of children' (1989: 44). Thus she links the emerging discourse of child-rearing and childhood to both the invention of the printing press in the late fifteenth century and the 'birth of the school' by the middle of the sixteenth century:

> Public schooling would standardise what and how all children should be taught; it would provide all children with basic literacy skills and simultane-ously facilitate the mass transmission of centrally selected and controlled knowledge. The organisation of children in schools also would permit more systematic and uniform socialisation; prolonged mandatory school attendance would provide an extended and legally sanctioned opportunity for school and church authorities to shape the attitudes, values, and beliefs of future genera-tions. The uniform organisation of schools, teachers, and students according to (textually) identical school ordinances distributed to all schools in pro-Lutheran territories and principalities eventually would have, or so Luther had hoped, a socially and religiously unifying effect on German society. (Luke, 1989: 5)

Through the development of schools in the sixteenth century, 'learning had been removed from the home, the streets, or the community and had been replaced by an organised and regimented institutional setting where rewards, punishments, and the ideas and skills to be learned were pro-vided by an authority other than the more familiar and personal author-ity of family and community members' (Luke, 1989: 131). Today we see a reversal of this trend: the policy discourse stresses putting learning back into the home and community, and hence the challenge is to co-opt family and community members into more institutionalised roles of reward and punishment, transmission of ideas and skills which were originally developed for the school. Both the removal from, and then the reinsertion into, the home of education (and socialisation) may be seen as part of the same larger trend, however, namely the institutionalisation of childhood, the incursion of the state into the realm of family life, and the repositioning of children from being the private property of families into a public, civil discourse (Luke, 1989). If the twentieth-century discourse of children's rights represents the most positive side of this trend, the growth of state regulation over parents, children and the home may be seen as the downside.

When does social change merit the label 'revolution'? The first book was produced in Europe in 1450 and just fifty years later about 20 million books, representing some 10–15,000 different texts, had been printed (Luke, 1989: 45). Such rapid technological change was accompanied by both a significant spread of literacy among the general population and also by a series of struggles on the part of religious authorities and the state to restrict or direct the kinds of text, and hence knowledge, available. Whether or not historians will later look back on the start of the twenty-first century as undergoing an equivalent social and technological 'revolution', the parallel between the introduction of books and computers into society is thought-provoking. Given that the fundamental link between education, literacy and print has dominated the past half millennium, it is hardly surprising that the present discourse about computers worries about the supposed threat to printed books and book learning. Indeed, curiously, that long-past revolution of the printing press is newly visible four hundred years later, as the often-polarised debates over ICT take the form of arguing the merits of print literacy versus multiple/ screen literacies, these debates mapping old versus new onto printed page versus electronic screen, linear versus hypertext, authority versus anarchy. Luke (1989: 42) notes that today 'computers are locked into a struggle with traditional print on the epistemological field for dominance over the coding, storing, and distribution of knowledge; there is accordingly a correlative epistemological shift from humanist to technicist discourses'. And much of the current academic and pedagogic scepticism of the ICT 'revolution' can be read as an attempt to reassert a humanist agenda in the face of technicist hype, while, as we have seen, the extent to which computers introduce a radically new mode of engagement between text and reader remains contentious.

However, it is not simply technology that is responsible for revolutions in literacy. Luke is careful to remind us that, in the case of the printing revolution, 'the political and socioeconomic conditions of sixteenth-century central and northern Europe … were oppressive and intolerable for the masses and cannot be overlooked as antecedent conditions ripe for radical change' (Luke, 1989: 78). The interesting question, then, is how one regards the conditions of young people's lives today, in accounting for the appropriation of ICT into everyday life. Oppressive and intolerable is too strong, but as we have seen in earlier chapters, social research highlights considerable challenges facing young people in the realms of family, employment and education, as well as the new challenge of constructing a satisfying life project (Giddens, 1991). Divorce within the home, lack of consensual family values, loss of strong community, heightened educational and material expectations, decline of jobs for life, delayed entry into the job market, new forms of expressing sexuality and gender relations, all represent challenges for young people over the past few decades. In this context of uncertainty and difficulty, the media represent both an escape – a realm of undemanding and shared pleasure – and a means for dealing with this context – a realm of advice, images of diverse life strategies, a sphere for considering and contesting alternative viewpoints. While adults wish children would gain from the encyclopaedic knowledge resources of the Internet, their children play fantasy games or follow their favourite television and sports stars, or discuss their lives – cautiously, playfully or controversially – in chat rooms. While this may or may not prove 'beneficial', perhaps those adult observers who consider this an inappropriate or risky form of activity should instead turn their attention to those social conditions which serve to make new media so attractive to young people.

The ways in which ICT contributes to the changing cultural and pedagogic environment for children and young people continues to be hotly debated, and rightly so. The history of these complex linkages between childhood, education and print technologies shows us how the anxieties which they arouse are central to that history – framing and guiding policies regarding pedagogy, parenting and commerce. To develop a policy for information technology in education is simultaneously to espouse, whether or not explicitly, a particular view of childhood, of the role of parents, of the relation between home and school. To offer advice to parents has immediate implications for children's access and use of technologies and hence for their orientation towards the classroom. To express worries about technological change is to raise questions of values, standards and aspirations for children and families. And so forth.

We are witnessing a historical shift away from the assumption that the home can remain private, outside state regulation. Rather, as learning, work and public participation are increasingly conducted at home, facilitated by ICT, a detailed understanding of the nature and diversity of domestic practices surrounding the media becomes crucial to policy formation. Given the privacy and individuality accorded to the home and family, this requires, in turn, a shift in the form of regulation, from one primarily based on direct and enforced state intervention towards the management of a climate of social norms.[38] The scope for regulation depends significantly on the everyday activities and perceived responsibilities of ordinary people. For example, if parents regulated what their children viewed on television as the state might wish, there would be little need for content ratings, legal restrictions on broadcasting or technical means of control. Similarly, if the state did or could take on the full burden of educating children for their future workplace, what need would there be for parents to invest in ICT equipment and know-how at home?

It has been argued that ideas of a proper home, well spent leisure, the supportive parent, traditional values, all suggest the increasing – although far from new – inclusion of people's personal or private lives within the disciplinary purview of both commerce and the state. On the other hand, there are limits to the effectiveness of any system of discipline, and it may be that the blurring of work and leisure, education and entertainment, discussed in this book represents an overreaching, a vulnerability to loss of control or a collapse of sustainable classifications and regulatory practices. Ang's (1991) account of 'desperately seeking the audience', tracing how the broadcasting industry reaches – through population measurement technologies – ever further into our private and personal lives in order to classify viewing activities, may be read both as the effortful, commercially motivated attempt to extend the reach of such disciplinary knowledge, but also as the failure of that industry in grasping its goal as ordinary life evades such efforts at measurement. Although this does not necessarily add up to any kind of resistance, the evasion itself is a challenge of sorts, a distinct unmanageability in response to institutional power.

In many ways, particularly in relation to children and young people, media regulation has tended to be restrictive in aim, framed in terms of oppositions between market and pedagogic concerns, needs and wants, freedom and protection, and focused on the enforcement of rules, in effect seeking to limit children's mediated exposure to the world.[39] An alternative conception of regulation, centred on social norms, could be framed in the positive terms of seeking to guide and expand children's experience of the world. For example, while parents and teachers are attempting to regulate the learning/fun boundary, this might perhaps be seen as misguided once one recognises a place for learning through fun. Surely efforts would be better spent regulating the boundary between public and commercial contents, encouraging participatory as well as receptive engagement, and contents that challenge rather than underestimate children's intelligence. The point is that, unlike the learning/fun and learning/fun boundary, the task of developing a case for challenging and participatory contents shifts the regulatory focus from a negative or restrictive orientation to one of positive regulation, defined in terms of goals rather than dangers, part of the current interest in defending public service (and the public good), children's rights to cultural expression[40] and consumer empowerment.

Arguably, the present state of research suggests that we are witnessing a hiatus in the practice of disciplinary power, this being a period of interesting uncertainty regarding the changing media and information environment. Much is made, rightly (see Chapter 2), of the gap between access, use and consequences. But the gap is not simply a gap in practice but rather a systematic and widespread failure of vision. While the policy agenda pushes forward with the apparently straightforward goal of universal access, supposedly vital for an IT-literate, internationally competitive workforce, research on use raises more contentious questions reflecting the confused, elusive and ambivalent nature of everyday life. There must also be space in public debate to ask other questions. What are we losing as we rush towards an 'information society'? What counts as good use of a computer? How is literacy changing and what critical literacy skills should be taught? How, if at all, are ICTs empowering? From what, exactly, are the have-nots excluded? From what, exactly, do children need to be protected? And so forth. Crucial questions which are, at present, unresolved. While the debates regarding negative regulation are familiar ones, the debates over positive regulation – identifying the kinds of contents, modes of engagement, skills and literacies, and fora for participation that we as a society wish to encourage and enhance – are as yet underdeveloped. These remain, therefore, as a pressing challenge for all those concerned with the lifeworld and life prospects of today's children and young people.

NOTES

1 The analysis here draws on the comparative European perspective reported in Livingstone (1998a) and Livingstone and Bovill (2001a).

2 As discussed in Chapter 1, the 'active audience' literature has identified empirically a variety of ways in which, in their everyday lives, people

engage with different genres, from the comparatively direct (including developing parasocial relationships with key televisual figures or sending feedback to producers or stars; Horton and Wohl, 1956; Stacey, 1994), to the more interpretative, centred on the culturally-situated variability in reception facilitated by the polysemy, or structured indeterminacy, of the media text (Livingstone, 1998b). Perhaps the diversification of modes of engagement facilitated by the diversification of new technological forms of information and communication necessitates a terminological shift in focus from 'audiences' to 'users' of media or technologies (Lievrouw and Livingstone, 2002), but nonetheless much of what has been learnt regarding audiences can and should find a valuable application in the field of new ICT. Such an approach reminds us that, as analysts we must be careful not to underestimate the discrepancy between text and user. For example, Calvert (1999: 186) describes, in approving terms, the Sim Series software as teaching children 'about pollution, city planning, and the creation of healthy environments'. Having observed children gleefully playing such games 'against the grain' (destroying the town, encouraging varieties of urban destruction, etc.), this optimism rings hollow, and of course such 'perversity', in adult terms, is central to children's play.

3   For work on newly emerging formats and genres, see LaFrance (1996) and Buckingham (2002) on computer games, Gauntlett (2000) on the world wide web, Frenette and Caron (1995) on designing age-appropriate interactive materials, and Star and Bowker (2002) on interface design.

4   Of course, even user-to-user interaction is frustratingly difficult to manage. Knobel et al. (1998) describe a small study with a group of trainee teachers which attempted to benefit from email by improving communication among the students and with the teacher. Instead, the study illustrated the difficulties of making the technology 'work' in terms of the hoped for educational and social benefits. Over 14 weeks, the 28 students sent 279 messages as follows: 70% comprised the mandatory weekly learning logs; the remainder included 31 messages clarifying assessment requirements, 21 containing draft seminar outlines, 9 asked questions about the curriculum, 7 concerned problems with email, 6 concerned the timetable, 5 test messages, 4 notification of new email addresses, 3 comments on grades, 2 responses to the lecturer's 'welcome' message, and a miscellany of requests for additional references, professional development requirements, resource information, hints on converting file attachments, etc. Clearly the messages were mainly functional in nature, most (97%) were sent to the lecturer alone and, crucially, 'none of the students introduced topics for discussion on this network, despite being encouraged and shown how to do so' (1998: 45). If the potential for non-hierarchical, creative communication exists, the social experience and conditions of the users may prevent its realisation.

5   Specifically, wanting to research the purchase of a hamster for her friend, Megan asks Jeeves: 'What breed of hamster is friendlier than Russian

hamsters?' Jeeves answers: 'How do I say a word in Russian?' And, on a different attempt: 'Where can I determine the sex of my hamster?' (Livingstone, 2001a).

6   When critical educator Quinn (1997: 7) comments, 'I often see children faced with activities which have excessive expectations of them academically, whilst the intellectual expectations are laughably low', he might have been talking not of the classroom but of 'educational' software or web sites designed for children's use. Further, when children discuss the 'world of information' available on the Internet, the impression given is of a mountain of information with which one is supposed to become familiar (encouraging a 'right answer' orientation to learning) rather than of a set of challenges to be thought about. Indeed, if 'education is more about questioning answers than about answering questions' (Quinn, 1997: 54), then the Internet is as yet poorly adapted as an educational tool.

7   As Hill and Tisdall (1997) note, there is a tension between the development of human potential and the maximising of an efficient future workforce. Discussions of the benefits of ICT point up just this tension, being incorporated both into a discourse of empowerment, a discourse in which equality is primary, and into one of training for workplace skills, a discourse based on equipping a generation with the ICT literacy for a competitive national economy which must have losers as well as winners.

8   In 1997, the UK Government announced its plan for the National Grid for Learning, requiring the introduction of the Internet into all schools by 2002 (see *Connecting the Learning Society: A National Grid for Learning*. Green paper (1997), Department for Education and Employment). A period of rapid expansion has followed. Thus while in 1998 only 17% of UK schools were connected to the Internet, this figure had risen to 86% by 2000, with an average of 60 computers connected to the Internet per secondary school (Survey of Information and Communications Technology in Schools, England, 2000, Department for Education and Employment).

9   The best-known example is that of *Sesame Street*, a heavily researched educational programme (Fisch and Truglio, 2001) which did much to undermine knowledge gaps: poor and well-off children were just as likely to watch, maternal co-viewing was equivalent for both groups, as was learning from the programmes (see Calvert, 1999). Still, some researchers argue that television and other screen media undermine children's imagination while books stimulate it: in one study, for example, children who watched television in place of reading books or listening to the radio were found to offer fewer creative responses when asked to generate a novel response to the end of a story (Valkenberg and van der Voort, 1994). Perhaps research findings in relation to television are not indicative of likely trends for newer media. Books, unlike television or radio, allow children to go back and re-read until a passage is understood and,

interestingly, unlike broadcast media, the newer screen media from videos to the Internet support just this function of repetition and self-pacing. (Indeed, observation of children's uses of the Internet suggests that the 'forward' and 'back' functions are the first learned and most heavily used; Livingstone and Bovill, 2001b.)

10 The introduction of computers into education continues to be controversial, partly because many players are involved in what appears to be a straightforward educational issue: 'Vying for position in such disputes are not only educators but also publishers, commercial hardware and software producers, parents, governments, and the telecommunications players of the corporate world' (Hawisher and Selfe, 1998: 3; see also Facer et al., 2001 and Loveless and Ellis, 2001).

11 For a detailed report of these interviews, see Livingstone and Bovill (1999). Again, the difficulties facing an analysis of the educational potential of the computer parallel those of television (see, for example, Jordan and Woodard, 1997, for their discussion of how broadcasters redescribed existing programmes, generally those with pro-social entertainment content, as 'educational' in order to meet the requirements of the US 1990 Children's Television Act). Experts struggle with this concept as much as do parents, it seems. In attempting to define what is 'educational' content, Calvert (1999: 185) provides a list of eleven features: most concern the avoidance of impediments to learning (comprehensible language, age-appropriate content, etc.); several concern features important for all effective programmes for children, educational or not (familiar settings, fun, interactive, special effects); and only one is specifically educational, namely that 'each show should emphasize a specific lesson', this being more tautological than enlightening.

12 For quotations from teachers, see Livingstone and Bovill (1999).

13 See Calvert and Littman (1996, reported in Calvert, 1999). This kind of research design is widely used. For example, in a similar study, Bransford et al. (1988, reported in Calvert, 1999) presented a maths lesson to fifth and sixth grade children, using either a videodisc in which Indiana Jones faced a number of maths problems as part of the adventure narrative, or in a traditional, though more individualised, teaching method. Those who used the videodisc turned out to be better at solving these and other maths problems than those taught using traditional methods. CD-ROMs thus appear to offer an entertaining, interactive and effective teaching tool.

14 This should be qualified somewhat, as other research reviewed in Calvert (1999) shows this finding to hold more for boys than girls, suggesting that girls and women may learn more in a structured learning context than under conditions of informal use. This may reflect the greater confidence boys experience with computers, or it may reflect the way in

which informal contexts are subtly unfriendly to girls (as in computer clubs or even at home).

15 Rather than seeing the traditional and alternative approaches as in direct conflict, Knobel et al. (1998) regard each as typical of its time, distinguishing 'first generation claims', centred on the technical features of basic computer software (the advantage of spelling and grammar checking, for example) from the 'second generation claims' which recognise more innovative possibilities for ICT in education. Interestingly, Luke (1989: 144) notes that 'the first fifty years of printing reproduced the texts of the past': religious texts in the main, with also some domestic manuals, calendars, etc., but clearly this was followed by a huge diversity in printed materials. Translating this observation into today's rather familiar, often print-based, computer-based and online contents, we may surmise that current texts provide a poor basis for longer-term projections.

16 In the quest to understand computer games, Beavis (1998: 249) suggests that 'the closest parallel is not print text at all, but rather performance, where the play comes to life only by being acted/performed, and is subtly different every time'. The player must not only read, draw on intertexual knowledge, decode what is given, but also play, enter in, suffer the consequences of faulty strategies, take a position.

17 Many adult observers echo this excitement also. For example, Haywood (1995: 163) points out 'that 13 million people can hear an accurate account of the effect of contracting HIV via a popular television programme without the prior approval of a medical panel, while fewer than 5000 may read about it in a serious monograph', arguing that this 'is typical of the shift in information penetration that has taken place during the latter part of the 20th century'.

18 Thus 'the contemporary science textbook is no longer a book in that [traditional] sense at all; it functions as a packaged resource kit' (Kress, 1998: 65).

19 As Kress provocatively puts it, 'the single, exclusive, intensive focus on written language has dampened the full development of all kinds of human potentials' (Kress, 1998: 75).

20 Of course, print culture incorporates some hypertextual features (e.g. footnotes, digressions), but it retains the hierarchical nature of the text, treating these as subordinate to the dominant, linear flow. One must also beware assuming that a linear text is read in a linear fashion. Psychologists of reading have long known that people do not, in fact, read simply from left to right and top to bottom of a page (Coltheart, 1987). Rather, they scan back and forth over the page, returning to key points or definitions, checking earlier material in relation to new material, and so forth. Reading as an activity is structured by two main

factors – the structure of the text (narrative, explanatory, etc.) which guides the points of concentration or skimming, and prior knowledge, which defines what in the text is familiar, requiring less attention, and what is novel, requiring some re-reading and returning to understand. The linearity of television viewing, by contrast, is far more austere, and the viewers must hold the unfolding text in their minds' eye in order to have any hope of returning or recycling earlier material, while the cost is that of missing the currently broadcast material. Interestingly, through the structure of its texts, the Internet enhances just those reading strategies already common for the printed page. Scroll bars, forward and back buttons, hypertext links for further explanation or for missing out familiar details, all these are standard.

21 See Livingstone and Bovill (2001b).

22 Burbules (1998) consequently analyses world wide web links using the standard repertoire of rhetorical analysis – metaphor, metonymy, synecdoche, etc., this being highly appropriate to a medium which relies more on juxtaposition and bricolage than on logical or narrative relations of connection. More generally, it is clear that a variety of critical tools for analysing media texts can be applied to the analysis of the world wide web, including an 'agenda-setting' analysis of the use of ranking on 'sites of sites' (search directories etc.), a semiotic analysis of, for example, the way AOL announces its 'responsibility and civic sense' by putting 'parents/security' buttons on its home page, a preferred reading account (Hall, 1980) of how web sites render it comparatively easier to follow links already made for us than to create our own, and so forth.

23 At present, it seems that generally low levels of critical literacy are found among young users of the Internet. If, for Burbules (1998: 110), 'a thoughtful hyperreader asks why links are made from certain points and not others; where those links lead; and what values are entailed in such decisions', then in the 'Families and the Internet project' we met neither the child who meets this criterion, though it is a good one, nor the parent or teacher who is ready to support children in developing such critical judgement (Livingstone and Bovill, 2001b).

24 However, the forms of video games are evolving rapidly, although each earlier form also persists, resulting in a diversification as well as a growing sophistication of forms – from the Space Invaders of the early arcade games, through the emergence of strategy games to the present variety of adventure games – some faster action-oriented, some more strategic (Haddon, 1993).

25 Calvert (1999) reviews the psychological effects studies on playing video games, concluding that there is indeed evidence that playing these games is associated with increased hostility, but that there is no substantial evidence for aggressive effects (although see Roe and Muijs, 1998). On the

other hand, lest doubts about electronic games rest on an unrealistic view of the games they have superseded, Johnson-Eilola (1998) offers a critique of those old-fashioned games of chance that figure so strongly in our nostalgic memories of idealised childhood. 'For children, modernist games propel them relatively powerlessly along a gameboard according to the roll of dice or the spin of a wheel, learning to happily accept their position in a larger plan of historical progress' (1998: 194). By contrast, in contemporary computer games, 'the pace and structure of such games require children to accept chance and to learn to work with it, actively rather than passively' (Johnson-Eilola, 1998: 194).

26 Television programmes are rarely discussed in this way, though for favourite programmes, concentration can be intense.

27 See Chapter 1.

28 This trend has a long history. As Luke (1989: 71) observes, while 'the sixteenth century, then, unlike previous or subsequent centuries marked a transition period from oral/manuscript to print/book culture ... we might [also] argue that oral practices were, in fact, remade through the advent of print discourse'.

29 Beavis's (1998) notions of literacy are rather more specific, including multimedia authoring skills, multimedia critical analysis, cyberspace exploration strategies, cyberspace navigation skills, and the capacity to negotiate and deconstruct images.

30 *www.whitehouse.gove/WH/New/edtech/2pager.html* (15/2/1996).

31 There is a linguistic difficulty in characterising 'old' media, given that Internet texts are commonly characterised in terms of 'print' and 'pages'.

32 In mass communication research, the shift from a 'transmission' to a 'ritual' conception of the communication process has proved fruitful in generating new research questions (Carey, 1989). In education, critics of 'right-answer' teaching make a parallel case, attacking the tendency 'to define education in a child's mind as the transfer of information from the teacher's into the children's minds' (Quinn, 1997: 79), a model of education whose key verb is 'deliver'. Such a transmission view of communication and learning too easily omits questioning, critical analysis or awareness of alternatives, and ignores the ritual or symbolic processes through which such a relationship serves to perpetuate the unequal social position of its participants. The delivery model is also a consumer model, with teachers as producers, or perhaps only the distributors of information products, and the pupils as consumers, at best discerning ones but certainly not producers themselves. As Quinn points out, if we adopt the delivery model, the focus is upon the effectiveness of the delivery. Did the

pupil get the message? Can we demonstrate this through testing to produce a measure of effective delivery? What the pupil does with this knowledge and how well it serves them is outside the frame.

33 Without new strategies for searching, this 15-year-old boy's problem with the Internet will remain as commonplace as it is at present: 'The problem is there's too much on there. If you do a search over all the places in the world, over one thing, you normally come out with 3000 different places where you can go to, so you have to try and limit it down and that's where most of your time is spent' (Livingstone and Bovill, 1999).

34 This link between home and school is itself now central to educational policy, with UK Government policy for education explicitly stressing the importance of informal and lifelong learning (see the DfEE's green paper, *The Learning Age*. London: The Stationery Office (February, 1998)). The National Grid for Learning portal brings together a growing collection of sites that support education and lifelong learning (www.ngfl.gov.uk/). These include GridClub, which offers fun learning experiences for children, Parents Online and Parents Centre, which help bridge the gap between home and school, Inclusion, which catalogues online resources to support individual learning needs, as well as sites for teachers and on the National Curriculum. Since homes and schools generally share a community locale, the policy of establishing a link between them (whether fairly simply, through home–school email and web links, or more complex links such as schools making their ICT facilities and expertise open to the community) leads to the suggestion that 'any evaluation of future directions for the curriculum takes place in the larger context of the relationships between schools and society, and the role that schools are called upon to play in the formation and reformation of the community' (Beavis, 1998: 238).

35 Again, the link between technology and standardisation is not new. Discussing the spread of print and print literacy in the sixteenth century, Luke (1989: 61) argues that 'the systematization of ideas in more uniform linguistic categories and the materialization of those ordered ideas in books, helped to unify and fix sets of ideas within a given discourse. Furthermore, the mass distribution of standardized ideas systematized discourse by dispersing a material unit of ideas (i.e., a book or pamphlet) among a variety of readers, thus unifying them linguistically and, to a certain extent, in shared cultural knowledge.'

36 Indeed, with the benefit of hindsight it appears that the national regulation of media for children and young people was at its height precisely when there was least cause for concern. Today, as nationally the media environment is increasingly difficult to regulate, resulting in ever more expectations being placed on parents' shoulders, so too domestically it is less easy to supervise than before. Moreover, parents have come to rely on national regulators and wish to continue to do so (Livingstone, 2000).

37 See Foucault (1991), Gordon (1991).

38 Baldwin et al. (1998) distinguish three definitions of regulation: first, 'the promulgation of an authoritative set of rules, accompanied by some mechanism, typically a public agency, for monitoring and promoting compliance with these rules' (1998: 3); secondly, 'all the efforts of state agencies to steer the economy' (1998: 3); and thirdly, 'all mechanisms of social control – including unintentional and non-state processes' (1998: 4). For Baldwin et al., the all too common unintended consequences of regulation derive in part from a tendency to neglect the diversity of cultures and world views across which regulation operates, presuming instead a homogeneous and normative culture in which the consequences of regulation may be taken for granted.

39 Such policies are lucidly expounded in the final part of Singer and Singer (2001). For a critique of these approaches applied to the Internet, see Oswell (1998b, 1999).

40 See, for example, the United Nations Convention on the Rights of the Child (Hill and Tisdall, 1997) and, based on this, The Children's Television Charter (1996) (von Feilitzen and Carlsson, 1999).

APPENDIX: THE *YOUNG PEOPLE NEW MEDIA* PROJECT

This project began when the LSE research team, directed by Sonia Livingstone, was invited by a consortium of funders (see *Acknowledgements*) co-ordinated by the Broadcasting Standards Commission to conduct a wide-ranging empirical project exploring the place of new forms of media in the lives of young people aged 6–17. The purpose was to update the work of Himmelweit et al. (*Television and the Child*, 1958), a study of the introduction of television into British families forty years earlier. Published in 1999, the Young People, New Media (YPNM) report focuses on terrestrial and cable/satellite television, the personal computer (PC), the VCR, the CD-ROM, the TV-linked games machines, the Internet and email. It set out to achieve the following aims:

- To chart current *access and use* for new media at home (and, in less detail, at school)
- To provide a *comprehensive* account of domestic leisure and media activities
- To *understand the meaning* of the changing media environment for children and parents
- To map access to and uses of media in relation to *social inequalities* and *social exclusion*
- To provide a *baseline* for media use against which to measure future changes

The project adopted a cross-sectional, comparative approach, looking across media, children, households, cultures and time, arguing that this is vital to complement studies of particular media used by particular subgroups. The cross-national component, involving parallel studies conducted in each of 12 European countries (Belgium, Denmark, Finland, France, Germany, Israel, Italy, the Netherlands, Spain, Sweden, Switzerland and the United Kingdom) is published in Livingstone and Bovill (2001a). The national studies follow a common conceptual framework and methodology, incorporating both qualitative methods and a large-scale survey involving some 15,000 children and young people aged 6 to 16.

The present book draws primarily on the British YPNM project, for which the research methods, completed during 1997–8, were as follows (see Livingstone and Bovill, 1999, for further details):

Preparatory Phase

- A variety of pilot interviews with children in families and school
- Surveys of parents and children using the broadcasting industry's Television Opinion Panel

Qualitative Phase

- Group interviews in 13 schools (6 primary, 7 secondary) with approximately 6 same-sex children in each of 27 groups, totalling some 160 children
- Individual interviews with children and separately, with their parents, in 32 homes
- Interviews with Heads of IT teaching in 13 schools
- A booster sample of Internet users for qualitative interviews (21 in cybercafés and 15 in boarding schools)

Quantitative Phase

- A detailed survey questionnaire administered by the British Market Research (BMRB) in a face-to-face, in-home interview to a national 'random location' quota sample of 1303 young people aged 6–17 years across the UK
- A detailed self-completion questionnaire to the parents of those surveyed (achieved sample, n = 978)
- A time budget diary for one week from 334 of the young people in the survey, aged 9–10, 12–13 and 15–16

BIBLIOGRAPHY

Abrams, M. (1959). The teenage consumer, *LPE (London Press Exchange) Papers* (Vol. 5). London: The London Press Exchange Ltd.

Adam, B. (1995). *Timewatch: The Social Analysis of Time*. Cambridge: Polity Press.

Adorno, T., and Horkheimer, M. (1977). The culture industry: enlightenment as mass deception. In J. Curran, M. Gurevitch, and J. Woollacott (Eds.), *Mass Communication and Society*. London: Edward Arnold.

Alexander, A. (1994). The effect of media on family interaction. In D. Zillmann, J. Bryant, and A.C. Huston (Eds.), *Media, Children and the Family – Social Scientific, Psychodynamic and Clinical Perspectives* (pp. 51–57). Hillsdale, NJ: Lawrence Erlbaum Associates.

Allan, G. (1985). *Family Life: Domestic Roles and Social Organization*. Oxford: Blackwell.

Anderson, D.R., and Lorch, E.P. (1983). Looking at television: action or reaction? In J. Bryant and D.R. Anderson (Eds.), *Children's Understanding of Television: Research on Attention and Comprehension* (pp. 1–33). New York: Academic Press.

Andreasen, M.S. (1994). Patterns of family life and television consumption from 1945 to the 1990s. In J. Bryant and A.C. Huston (Eds.), *Media, Children and the Family – Social Scientific, Psychodynamic and Clinical Perspectives* (pp. 19–35). Hillsdale, NJ: Lawrence Erlbaum Associates.

Ang, I. (1991). *Desperately Seeking the Audience*. London: Routledge.

Ang, I. (1996). *Living Room Wars: Rethinking Media Audiences for a Postmodern World*. London: Routledge.

Annenberg Public Policy Center (1999). *Media in the Home 1999: The Fourth Annual Survey of Parents and Children*. Philadelphia, PA: University of Pennsylvania, The Annenberg Public Policy Center (Survey Series No. 5).

Aries, P. (1962). *Centuries of Childhood: A Social History of Family Life*. New York: Vintage Books.

Bachmair, B. (1997). Kinderfernsehen im Umbruch? In den kinderzimmern tnt sich was. *Television, 10*(2): 13–19.

Baizerman, M. and Magnuson, D. (1996). Do we need youth as a social stage? *Young, 4*(3): 48–60.

Baldwin, R., Scott, C., and Hood, C. (1998). Introduction. In R. Baldwin, C. Scott, and C. Hood (Eds.), *A Reader on Regulation* (pp. 1–55). Oxford: Oxford Unversity Press.

Ball-Rokeach, S. (2000). Metamorphosis Project White Paper Number One. *www.metamorph.org.*

Barker, M., and Petley, J. (Eds.) (1996). *Ill-Effects: The Media Violence Debate*. London, New York: Routledge.

Barwise, T., and Ehrenberg, A. (1988). *Television and its Audience*. London: Sage.

Bausinger, H. (1984). Media, technology and daily life. *Media, Culture and Society, 6*, 343–351.

Bazalgette, C. (1999). *Making Movies Matter: Report of the Film Education Working Group*. London: British Film Institute.

Beavis, C. (1998). Computer games, culture and curriculum. In I. Snyder (Ed.), *Page to Screen: Taking Literacy into the Electronic Era* (pp. 234–255). London and New York: Routledge.

Beck, U. (1992). *Risk Society: Towards a New Modernity*. London: Sage.

Becker, L.B., and Schoenbach, K. (Eds.) (1989). *Audience Responses to Media Diversification: Coping with Plenty*. Hillsdale, NJ: Lawrence Erlbaum Associates.

Beentjes, J.W.J., Koolstra, C.M., Marseille, N., and Voort, T.H.A. van der (2001). Children's use of different media: for how long and why? In S. Livingstone and M. Bovill (Eds.), *Children and Their Changing Media Environment: A European Comparative Study* (pp. 85–112). Mahwah, NJ: Lawrence Erlbaum Associates.

Bergh, B. van den, and Bulck, J. van den (Eds.) (2000). *Children and Media: Multidisciplinary Approaches*. Leuven-Apeldoorn: Garant.

Bijker, W.E., Hughes, T.P., and Pinch, T. (Eds.) (1987). *The Social Construction of Technological Systems*. Cambridge, MA: MIT Press.

Bingham, N., Valentine, G., and Holloway, S.L. (1999). Where do you want to go tomorrow? Connecting children and the internet. *Environment and Planning D: Society and Space*, 17, 655–672.

Biskup, M., Filias, V., and Vitanyi, I. (Eds.) (1984). *The Family and its Culture: An Investigation in Several East and West European Countries*. Budapest: Akademiai Kiado.

Blumler, J.G. (1992). *The Future of Children's Television in Britain: An Enquiry for the Broadcasting Standards Council*. London: Broadcasting Standards Council.

Blumler, J.G., and Katz, E. (Eds.) (1974). *The Uses of Mass Communications: Current Perspectives on Gratifications Research*. Beverly Hills, CA: Sage.

Blumler, J.G., Gurevitch, M., and Katz, E. (1985). REACHING OUT: a future for gratifications research. In K.E. Rosengren, L.A. Wenner, and P. Palmgreen (Eds.), *Media Gratifications Research: Current Perspectives*. Beverly Hills, CA: Sage.

Boddy, W. (1985). 'The shining centre of the home': ontologies of television in the 'Golden Age'. In P. Drummond and R. Paterson (Eds.), *Television in Transition*. London: British Film Institute.

Boethius, U. (1995). Youth, the media and moral panics. In J. Fornäs and G. Bolin (Eds.), *Youth Culture in Late Modernity* (pp. 39–57). London: Sage.

Bourdieu, P. (1984). *Distinction: A Social Critique of the Judgement of Tastes*. Cambridge, MA, and London: Harvard University Press and Routledge.

Bovill, M., and Livingstone, S. (2001). Bedroom culture and the privatization of media use. In S. Livingstone and M. Bovill (Eds.), *Children and Their Changing Media Environment: A European Comparative Study* (pp. 179–200). Mahwah, NJ: Lawrence Erlbaum Associates.

Brake, M. (1985). *Comparative Youth Culture: The Sociology of Youth Cultures and Youth Subcultures in America, Britain and Canada*. London: Routledge and Kegan Paul.

Brannen, J., and O'Brien, M. (Eds.) (1995). *Childhood and Parenthood: Proceedings of the International Sociological Association Committee for Family Research Conference 1994*. London: Institute of Education, University of London.

Bridgewood, A., Lilly, R., Thomas, M., Bacon, J., Sykes, W., and Morris, S. (1999). *Living in Britain: Results from the 1998 General Household Survey*. London: The Stationery Office.

Brown, J.D., Dykers, C.R., Steele, J.R., and White, A.B. (1994). Teenage Room Culture: where media and identities intersect, *Communication Research*, *21*(6): 813–827.

Bryce, J.W. (1987). Family time and television use. In T. R. Lindof (Ed.), *Natural Audiences: Qualitative Research on Media Uses and Effects* (pp. 121–138). Norwood, NJ: Ablex.

Buchner, P. (1990). Growing up in the eighties: changes in the social biography of childhood in the FRG. In L. Chisholm, P. Buchner, H.-H. Kruger, and P. Brown (Eds.), *Childhood, Youth and Social Change: A Comparative Perspective*. London: Falmer Press.

Buchner, P., Bois-Reymond, M., and Kruger, H.-H. (1995). Growing up in three European regions. In L. Chisholm (Ed.), *Growing Up in Europe: Contemporary Horizons in Childhood and Youth Studies* (pp. 43–59). Berlin: de Gruyter.

Buckingham, D. (1991). What are words worth? Interpreting children's talk about television. *Cultural Studies*, *5*(2), 228–245.

Buckingham, D. (1993). *Reading Audiences: Young People and the Media*. Manchester: Manchester University Press.

Buckingham, D. (2002). The electronic generation? Children and new media. In L. Lievrouw and S. Livingstone (Eds.), *Handbook of New Media: Social Shaping and Social Consequences* (pp. 77–89). London: Sage.

Buckingham, D., Davies, H., Jones, K., and Kelley, P. (1999). *Children's Television in Britain*. London: British Film Institute Publishing.

Burbules, N.C. (1998). Rhetorics of the web: hyperreading and critical literacy. In I. Snyder (Ed.), *Page to Screen: Taking Literacy into the Electronic Era* (pp. 102–122). London and New York: Routledge.

Byng-Hall, J. (1978). Family myths used as defence in conjoint family therapy. *British Journal of Medical Psychology*, *40*, 239–50.

Calvert, S. (1999). *Children's Journeys through the Information Age*. Boston, MA: McGraw-Hill.

Carey, J.W. (1989). *Communication as Culture: Essays on Media and Society*. New York: Routledge.

Caron, A.H., Giroux, L., and Douzou, S. (1989). Uses and impacts of home computers in Canada: a process of reappropriation. In J.L. Salvaggio and J. Bryant (Eds.), *Media Use in the Information Age: Emerging Patterns of Adoption and Consumer Use*. Hillsdale, NJ: Lawrence Erlbaum Associates.

Ceruzzi, P. (1999). Inventing personal computing. In D. MacKenzie and J. Wajcman (Eds.), *The Social Shaping of Technology* (2nd edn) (pp. 64–86). Buckingham: Open University Press.

Chaney, D. (1996). *Lifestyles*. London: Routledge.

Clifford, J. (1997). *Routes: Travel and Translation in the Late Twentieth Century*. Cambridge, MA: Harvard University Press.

Cohen, S. (1972). *Folk Devils and Moral Panics: The Creation of the Mods and Rockers*. Oxford: Basil Blackwell.

Cohen, S., and Young, J. (Eds.) (1981). *The Manufacture of News: Social Problems, Deviance and the Mass Media* (revised edn). London: Constable.

Cole, J. (2000 and 2002). *The UCLA Internet Report: 'Surveying the Digital Future'* (*www.ccp.ucla.edu*). Year One and Year Two. Los Angeles: UCLA Center for Communication Policy.

Coleman, J.C. (1993). Understanding adolescence today: a review. *Children and Society*, *7*(2), 137–147.

Coltheart, M. (Ed.) (1987). *Attention and Performance XII: The Psychology of Reading*. London: Lawrence Erlbaum Associates.

Compaine, B. (Ed.) (2001). *The Digital Divide: Facing a Crisis or Creating a Myth?* Cambridge, Mass.: The MIT Press.

Coontz, S. (1997). *The Way We Really Are: Coming to Terms with America's Changing Families.* New York: Basic Books.

Cordes, C., and Miller, E. (2000). *Fool's Gold: A Critical Look at Computers in Childhood. www.allianceforchildhood.com*: Alliance for Childhood.

Corner, J. (1991). Meaning, genre and context: the problematics of 'public knowledge' in the new audience studies. In J. Curran and M. Gurevitch (Eds.), *Mass Media and Society* (pp. 267–284). London: Methuen.

Corner, J. (1995). *Television Form and Public Address.* London: Edward Arnold.

Corrigan, P. (1976). Doing nothing. In S. Hall and T. Jefferson (Eds.), *Resistance through Rituals* (pp. 103–105). London: Hutchinson.

Corsaro, W.A. (1997). *The Sociology of Childhood.* Thousand Oaks, CA: Pine Forge Press.

Cunningham, H. (1995). The century of the child. In H. Cunningham (Ed.), *Children and Childhood in Western Society since 1500* (pp. 163–185). London and New York: Longman.

Curran, J., and Gurevitch, M. (1991a). Introduction. In J. Curran and M. Gurevitch (Eds.), *Mass Media and Society* (pp. 7–11). London: Edward Arnold.

Curran, J., and Gurevitch, M. (Eds.) (1991b). *Mass Media and Society.* London: Edward Arnold.

Davison, W.P. (1983). The third-person effect in communication. *Public Opinion Quarterly, 47*(1), 1–15.

Dayan, D., and Katz, E. (1992). *Media Events: The Live Broadcasting of History.* Cambridge, MA: Harvard University Press.

Desmond, R.J., Singer, J.L., Singer, D.G., Calam, R., and Colimore, K. (1985). Family mediation patterns and television viewing. Young children's use and grasp of the medium. *Human Communication Research, 11*(4), 461–480.

d'Haenens, L. (2001). Old and new media: access and ownership in the home. In S. Livingstone and M. Bovill (Eds.), *Children and Their Changing Media Environment: A European Comparative Study* (pp. 53–84). Mahwah, NJ: Lawrence Erlbaum Associates.

Dorr, A. (1986). *Television and Children: A Special Medium for a Special Audience.* Beverly Hills, CA: Sage.

Douglas, J.Y. (1998). Will the most reflexive relativist please stand up?: Hypertext, argument and realism. In I. Snyder (Ed.), *Page to Screen: Taking Literacy into the Electronic Era* (pp. 144–162). London and New York: Routledge.

Down, D. (2000). *Family Spending: A report on the 1999–2000 Family Expenditure Survey.* London: The Stationery Office.

Drotner, K. (1992). Modernity and media panics. In M. Skovmand and K.C. Schroeder (Eds.), *Media Cultures: Reappraising Transnational Media.* London: Routledge.

Drotner, K. (2000). Difference and diversity: trends in young Danes' media uses. *Media, Culture and Society, 22*(2), 149–166.

Duncan, S. (1998). Editorial: The spatiality of gender – and the papers in this issue. *Innovation, 11*(2), 119–128.

Durkin, K. (1995). *Computer Games: Their Effects on Young People.* Sydney: Office of Film and Literature Classification.

Eco, U. (1979). Introduction: the role of the reader. *The Role of the Reader: Explorations in the Semiotics of Texts.* Bloomington, IN: Indiana University Press.

Eldridge, J. (Ed.) (1993). *Getting the Message: News, Truth and Power.* London: Routledge.

Elliott, P. (1974). Uses and gratifications research: a critique and a sociological alternative. In J.G. Blumler and E. Katz (Eds.), *The Uses of Mass Communications: Current Perspectives on Gratifications Research*. Beverly Hills, CA: Sage.

Emler, N., and Reicher, S. (1995). *Adolescence and Delinquency: The Collective Management of Reputation*. Oxford: Blackwell.

Ennew, J. (1994). *Childhood as a Social Phenomenon: National Report – England and Wales* (Vol. 36). Vienna, Austria: European Centre for Social Welfare Policy and Research.

Facer, K., Sutherland, R., Furlong, R., and Furlong, J. (2001). What's the point of using computers? The development of young people's computer expertise in the home. *New Media and Society*, 3(2), 199–219.

Feilitzen, C. von, and Carlsson, U. (Eds.) (1999). *Children and Media: Image, Education, Participation*. Gothenburg: UNESCO/Nordicom.

Feilitzen, C. von, and Carlsson, U. (Eds.) (2000). *Children in the New Media Landscape*. Gothenburg: UNESCO/Nordicom.

Ferrari, M., Klinzing, D.G., Paris, C.L., Morris, S.K., and Eyman, A.P. (1985). Home computers: implications for children and families. *Marriage and Family Review*, 8(1–2), 41–57.

Fisch, S.M., and Truglio, R.T. (Eds.) (2001). *'G' is for Growing: Thirty Years of Research on Children and Sesame Street*. Mahwah, NJ: Lawrence Erlbaum Associates.

Fischer, C.S. (1994). Changes in leisure activities, 1890–1940. *Journal of Social History*, Spring, 453–475.

Flichy, P. (1995). *Dynamics of Modern Communication: The Shaping and Impact of New Communication Technologies*. London: Sage.

Flichy, P. (2002). Historical themes in new media development. In L. Lievrouw and S. Livingstone (Eds.), *Handbook of New Media: Social Shaping and Social Consequences* (pp. 136–150). London: Sage.

Flores, F., and Gray, J. (2000). *Entrepreneurship and the Wired Life: Work in the Wake of Careers*. London: Demos.

Fornäs, J., and Bolin, G. (Eds.) (1995). *Youth Culture in Late Modernity*. Beverly Hills, CA: Sage.

Foucault, M. (1991). Governmentality. In G. Burchell, C. Gordon, and P. Miller (Eds.), *The Foucault Effect: Studies in Governmentality* (pp. 87–104). Chicago: University of Chicago Press.

Freire, P. and Macedo, D. (1987). *Literacy: Reading the Word and the World*. South Hadley, MA: Bergin and Garvey.

Frenette, M., and Caron, A.H. (1995). Children and interactive television: research and design issues. *Convergence*, 1(1), 33–60.

Frith, S. (1978). *The Sociology of Rock*. London: Constable.

Furby, L. (1978). Possessions: towards a theory of their meaning and function throughout the life cycle. In P.B. Baltes (Ed.), *Life-span Development and Behavior*. New York: Academic Press.

Furnham, A., and Gunter, B. (1989). *Young People's Social Attitudes in Great Britain: The Anatomy of Adolescence*. London: Routledge.

Gadlin, H. (1978). Child discipline and the pursuit of self: an historical interpretation. In H.W. Reese and L.P. Lipsitt (Eds.), *Advances in Child Development and Behavior* (Vol. 12, pp. 231–261). New York: Academic Press.

Gauntlett, D. (Ed.) (2000). *Web.studies: Rewiring Media Studies for the Digital Age*. London: Arnold.

Giddens, A. (1991). *Modernity and Self-Identity: Self and Society in the Late Modern Age*. Cambridge: Polity Press.

Giddens, A. (1993). *The Transformation of Intimacy: Sexuality, Love and Eroticism in Modern Societies*. Cambridge: Polity Press.

Goffman, E. (1959). *The Presentation of Self in Everyday Life*. Harmondsworth: Penguin.

Goffman, E. (1961). *Asylums: Essays on the Social Situation of Mental Patients and Other Inmates*. Harmondsworth: Penguin.

Goodman, I.R. (1983). Television's role in family interaction: a family systems perspective. *Journal of Family Issues*, 4(2), 405–424.

Gordon, C. (1991). Governmental rationality: an introduction. In G. Burchell, C. Gordon, and P. Miller (Eds.), *The Foucault Effect: Studies in Governmentality* (pp. 1–51). Chicago: University of Chicago Press.

Graue, M.E., and Walsh, D.J. (1998). *Studying Children in Context: Theories, Methods and Ethics*. Thousand Oaks, CA: Sage.

Greenfield, P.N. (1984). *Mind and Media: The Effects of Television, Video Games and Computers*. Cambridge, MA: Harvard University Press.

Gunkel, D.J., and Gunkel, A.H. (1997). Virtual geographies: the new worlds of cyberspace. *Critical Studies in Mass Communication*, 14(2), 123–137.

Gunter, B., and McAleer, J. (1997). *Children and Television*. (2nd edn). London: Routledge.

Habermas, J. (1969/89). *The Structural Transformation of the Public Sphere: An Inquiry into a Category of Bourgeois Society*. Cambridge, MA: MIT Press.

Habermas, J. (1987). *The Philosophical Discourse of Modernity: Twelve Lectures*. Cambridge: Polity Press.

Haddon, L. (1988). The home computer: the making of a consumer electronic. *Science as Culture*, 2, 7–51.

Haddon, L. (1993). Interactive games. In P. Hayward and J. Wollen (Eds.), *Future Vision: New Technologies of the Screen* (pp. 123–147). London: British Film Institute Publishing.

Hall, S. (1980). Encoding/decoding. In S. Hall, D. Hobson, A. Lowe, and P. Willis (Eds.), *Culture, Media, Language*. London: Hutchinson.

Hall, S. (1996). Introduction: who needs identity. In S. Hall and P. du Gay (Eds.), *Questions of Cultural Identity*. London: Sage.

Hansen, M. (1991). *Babel and Babylon: Spectatorship in American Silent Film*. Cambridge, MA: Harvard University Press.

Hawes, J.M., and Hiner, N.R. (Eds.) (1991). *Children in Historical and Comparative Perspective: An International Handbook and Research Guide*. New York: Greenwood.

Hawisher, G.E., and Selfe, C.L. (1998). Reflections on computers and composition studies at the century's end. In I. Snyder (Ed.), *Page to Screen: Taking Literacy into the Electronic Era* (pp. 3–19). London and New York: Routledge.

Haywood, T. (1995). *Info-Rich–Info-Poor: Access and Exchange in the Global Information Society*. London: Bowker Saur.

Hendry, L.B., Shucksmith, J., Love, J.G., and Glendinning, A. (1993). *Young People's Leisure and Lifestyles*. London and New York: Routledge.

Hill, M., and Tisdall, K. (1997). *Children and Society*. London and New York: Longman.

Hillman, M., Adams, J., and Whitelegg, J. (1990). *One False Move … A Study of Children's Independent Mobility*. London: Policy Studies Institute.

Himmelweit, H. (1996). Children and television. In E.E. Dennis and E. Wartella (Eds.), *Ammerican Communication Research – The Remembered History* (pp. 71–83). Hillsdale, NJ: Lawrence Erlbaum Associates.

Himmelweit, H.T., Oppenheim, A.N., and Vince, P. (1958). *Television and the Child: An Empirical Study of the Effect of Television on the Young*. London and New York: Oxford University Press.

Hobsbawm, E., and Ranger, T. (Eds.) (1988). *The Invention of Tradition* (5th edn). Cambridge: Cambridge University Press.

Hodge, R., and Tripp, D. (1986). *Children and Television: A Semiotic Approach.* Cambridge: Polity Press.

Hoggart, R. (1957). *The Uses of Literacy.* London: Chatto & Windus.

Holland, P. (1992). *What is a Child? Popular Images of Childhood.* London: Virago Press.

Home Office (1994). Children as victims of crime, by type of crime 1983 and 1992 (i.e. abductions and gross indecency). *Central Statistical Office: Special Focus on Children, 1994.* London: The Stationery Office.

Horton, D., and Wohl, R.R. (1956). Mass communication and para-social interaction. *Psychiatry, 19,* 215–229.

Howard, S. (Ed.) (1997). *Wired Up: Young People and the Electronic Media.* London: UCL Press.

Iser, W. (1980). Interaction between text and reader. In S.R. Suleiman and I. Crosman (Eds.), *The Reader in the Text: Essays on Audience and Interpretation.* Princeton, NJ: Princeton University Press.

James, A., Jenks, C., and Prout, A. (1998). *Theorising Childhood.* Cambridge: Cambridge University Press.

Jenkins, H. (1992). *Textual Poachers: Television Fans and Participatory Culture.* New York: Routledge.

Johnson-Eilola, J. (1998). Living on the surface: learning in the age of global communication networks. In I. Snyder (Ed.), *Page to Screen: Taking Literacy into the Electronic Era* (pp. 185–210). London and New York: Routledge.

Johnsson-Smaragdi, U. (1983). *TV Use and Social Interaction in Adolescence: A Longitudinal Study.* Stockholm: Almqvist and Wiksell.

Johnsson-Smaragdi, U. (2001). Media use styles among the young. In S. Livingstone and M. Bovill (Eds.), *Children and Their Changing Media Environment: A European Comparative Study* (pp. 113–140). Mahwah, NJ: Lawrence Erlbaum Associates.

Jordan, A.B., and Woodard, E. (1997). *The 1997 State of Children's Television Report: Programming for Children over Broadcast and Cable Television.* Philadelphia, PA: University of Pennsylvania, The Annenberg Public Policy Center.

Joyce, M. (1998). New stories for new readers: contours, coherence and constructive hypertext. In I. Snyder (Ed.), *Page to Screen: Taking Literacy into the Electronic Era* (pp. 163–182). London and New York: Routledge.

Kamptner, N.L. (1989). Personal possessions and their meanings in old age. In S. Spacapan and S. Oskamp (Eds.), *The Social Psychology of Aging.* Newbury Park, CA: Sage.

Katz, E., Gurevitch, M., and Hass, H. (1973). On the use of the mass media for important things. *American Sociological Review, 38*(2), 164–181.

Kellner, D. (1995). *Media Culture: Cultural Studies, Identity and Politics between the Modern and the Post-Modern.* London: Routledge.

Kellner, D. (2002). New media and new literacies: reconstructing education for the new millennium. In L. Lievrouw and S. Livingstone (Eds.), *Handbook of New Media: Social Shaping and Social Consequences* (pp. 90–104). London: Sage.

Kelly, M.J. (1998). Media use in the European household. In D. McQuail and K. Siune (Eds.), *Media Policy: Convergence, Concentration and Commerce* (pp. 144–164). London: Sage.

Kinder, M. (1991). *Playing with Power in Movies, Television and Video Games: From Muppet Babies to Teenage Mutant Ninja Turtles.* Berkeley, CA: University of California Press.

Kinder, M. (Ed.) (1999). *Kids' Media Culture*. Durham, NC: Duke University Press.

Kline, S. (1993). *Out of the Garden: Toys, TV, and Children's Culture in the Age of Marketing*. London and New York: Verso.

Knobel, M., Lankshear, C., Honan, E., and Crawford, J. (1998). The wired world of second-language education. In I. Snyder (Ed.), *Page to Screen: Taking Literacy into the Electronic Era* (pp. 20–50). London and New York: Routledge.

Kress, G. (1998). Visual and verbal models of representation in electronically mediated communication: the potentials of new forms of text. In I. Snyder (Ed.), *Page to Screen: Taking Literacy into the Electronic Era* (pp. 53–79). London and New York: Routledge.

Krotz, F., and Hasebrink, U. (2001). Who are the new media users? In S. Livingstone and M. Bovill (Eds.), *Children and Their Changing Media Environment: A European Comparative Study* (pp. 245–262). Mahwah, NJ: Lawrence Erlbaum Associates.

Kubey, R., and Larson, R. (1990). The use and experience of the new video media among children and adolescents. *Communication Research*, *17*(1), 107–130.

LaFrance, J.P. (1996). Games and players in the electronic age: tools for analysing the use of video games by adults and children. *Reseaux (The French Journal of Communication)*, *4*(2), 301–332.

Lagree, J.-C. (1995). Young people and employment in the European Community: convergence or divergence? In L. Chisholm, B. Buchner, H.-H. Kruger, and M. Bois-Reymond (Eds.), *Growing Up in Europe: Contemporary Horizons in Childhood and Youth Studies* (pp. 61–72). Berlin: de Gruyter.

Lakoff, G. (1980). *Metaphors We Live By*. Chicago: University of Chicago Press.

Lasswell, H.D. (1948). The structure and function of communcation in society. In L. Bryson (Ed.), *The Communication of Ideas*. New York: Harper and Brothers.

Laurel, B. (1993). *Computers as Theatre* (Vol. 2). New York: Addison-Wesley.

Lemish, D., Liebes, T., and Seidmann, V. (2001). Gendered media meanings and uses. In S. Livingstone and M. Bovill (Eds.), *Children and Their Changing Media Environment: A European Comparative Study* (pp. 263–282). Mahwah, NJ: Lawrence Erlbaum Associates.

Lieberg, M. (1995). Public Space: lifestyles and collective identity. *Young*, *3*(1): 19–38.

Liebes, T. (1991). A mother's battle against TV news: a case study of political socialisation. *Discourse and Society*, *2*, 203–222.

Lievrouw, L. (2000). How fast is fast? *ICA Newsletter*, *28*(2): March 6–7.

Lievrouw, L., and Livingstone, S. (2002). Introduction: the social shaping and consequences of ICTs. In L. Lievrouw and S. Livingstone (Eds.), *Handbook of New Media: Social Shaping and Social Consequences* (pp. 1–15). London: Sage.

Lin, C.A. (1988). Exploring personal computer adoption dynamics. *Journal of Broadcasting and Electronic Media*, *42*(Winter), 95–112.

Livingstone, S. (1992). The meaning of domestic technologies: a personal construct analysis of familial gender relations. In R. Silverstone and E. Hirsch (Eds.), *Consuming Technologies*. London and New York: Routledge.

Livingstone, S. (1996). On the continuing problems of media effects research. In J.G. Curran and M. Gurevitch (Eds.), *Mass Media and Society*. London: Edward Arnold.

Livingstone, S. (1997). Changing audiences, changing media: a social psychological perspective. In T. van der Voort and P. Winterhoff-Spurk (Eds.), *New Horizons in Media Psychology: Research Cooperation and Projects in Europe*. Opladen, Germany: Westdeutscher Verlag.

Livingstone, S. (1998a). Mediated childhoods: a comparative approach to young people's changing media. *European Journal of Communication*, *13*(4), 435–456.

Livingstone, S. (1998b) *Making Sense of Television: The Psychology of Audience Interpretation* (2nd edn). London: Routledge.

Livingstone, S. (1998c). Audience research at the crossroads: the 'implied audience' in media theory. *European Journal of Cultural Studies, 1*(2), 193–217.

Livingstone, S. (1999a). New media, new audiences. *New Media and Society, 1*(1), 59–66.

Livingstone, S. (1999b). From audiences to users? Doing audience research in a new media age. In G. Bechelloni and M. Buonanno (Eds.), *Audiences: Multiple Voices.* Fiorenze: Edizioni Fondazione Hypercampo.

Livingstone, S. (1999c). Les jeunes et les nouveaux medias: Sur les leçons à tirer de la télévision pour le PC. *Reseaux, 92–3,* 101–132.

Livingstone, S. (2000). Thoughts on the appeal of 'screen entertainment culture' for British children. In T. Lees, S. Ralph, and J.L. Brown (Eds.), *Is Regulation Still an Option in a Digital Universe?* (pp. 43–64). Luton: University of Luton Press.

Livingstone, S. (2001a). Children on-line: emerging uses of the internet at home. *Journal of the IBTE* (Institute of British Telecommunications Engineers), *2*(1), 1–7.

Livingstone, S. (2001b). Children and their changing media environment. In S. Livingstone and M. Bovill (Eds.), *Children and Their Changing Media Environment: A European Comparative Study* (pp. 307–334). Mahwah, NJ: Lawrence Erlbaum Associates.

Livingstone, S., Allen, J., and Reiner, R. (in press). The Audience for Crime Media 1946–91: A Historical Approach to Reception Studies. *Communication Review,* 4(2): 165–192.

Livingstone, S., and Bovill, M. (1999). *Young People, New Media: Final Report of the Project, 'Children, Young People and the Changing Media Environment'.* An LSE Report. London: London School of Economics and Political Science, *http://psych. lse.ac.uk/young_people.*

Livingstone, S., and Bovill, M. (Eds.) (2001a). *Children and Their Changing Media Environment: A European Comparative Study.* Mahwah, NJ: Lawrence Erlbaum Associates.

Livingstone, S. and Bovill, M. (2001b). *Families and the Internet.* A Report to British Telecommunications plc. London: London School of Economics and Political Science.

Livingstone, S., Bovill, M., and Gaskell, G. (1999). European TV kids in a transformed media world: findings of the UK study. In P. Löhr and M. Meyer (Eds.), *Children, Television and the New Media.* Luton: Televizion/University of Luton Press.

Livingstone, S., d'Haenens, L., and Hasebrink, U. (2001). Childhood in Europe: contexts for comparison. In S. Livingstone and M. Bovill (Eds.), *Children and Their Changing Media Environment: A European Comparative Study* (pp. 3–30). Mahwah, NJ: Lawrence Erlbaum Associates.

Livingstone, S., and Gaskell, G. (1997). Children and the television screen: modes of participation in the media environment. In S. Ralph, J.L. Brown, and T. Lees (Eds.), *Tune In or Buy In?: Papers from the 27th University of Manchester Broadcasting Symposium, 1996* (pp. 7–24). Luton: John Libbey Media.

Livingstone, S., Holden, K.J., and Bovill, M. (1999). Children's changing media environment: overview of a European comparative study. In U. Carlsson, U. and C. von Feilitzen (Eds.), *Children and Media: Participation and Education – Yearbook from the UNESCO International Clearinghouse on Children and Violence on the Screen* (pp. 39–59). Gothenburg: UNESCO/Nordicom.

Livingstone, S., and Lemish, D. (2001). Doing comparative research with children and young people. In S. Livingstone and M. Bovill (Eds.), *Children and Their Changing Media Environment: A European Comparative Study* (pp. 31–50). Mahwah, NJ: Lawrence Erlbaum Associates.

Lohr, P., and Meyer, M. (Eds.) (1999). *Children, Television and the New Media.* Luton: University of Luton Press.

Loveless, A., and Ellis, V. (Eds.) (2001). *ICT, Pedagogy and the Curriculum: Subject to Change*. London: Routledge.

Loyd, B., Loyd, D., and Gressard, C. (1987). Gender and computer experience as factors in the computer attitudes of middle school students. *Journal of Early Adolescence*, 7, 13–19.

Luke, C. (1989). *Pedagogy, Printing and Protestantism: The Discourse on Childhood*. Albany, NY: State University of New York Press.

Lull, J. (Ed.) (1988). *World Families Watch Television*. Newbury Park, CA: Sage.

Lull, J. (1990). *Inside Family Viewing: Ethnographic Research on Television's Audiences*. London: Routledge.

Mackay, H. (1995a). Patterns of ownership of IT devices in the home. In N. Heap, R. Thomas, G. Einon, R. Mason, and H. Mackay (Eds.), *Information Technology and Society: A Reader* (pp. 311–340). London: Sage.

Mackay, H. (1995b). Theorising the IT/society relationship. In N. Heap, R. Thomas, G. Einon, R. Mason, and H. Mackay (Eds.), *Information Technology and Society: A Reader* (pp. 41–53). London: Sage.

MacKenzie, D., and Wajcman, J. (Eds.) (1999). *The Social Shaping of Technology* (2nd edn). Buckingham: Open University Press.

Madigan, R., and Munro, M. (1999). 'The more we are together': domestic space, gender and privacy. In T. Chapman and J. Hockey (Eds.), *Ideal Homes? Social Change and Domestic Life* (pp. 61–72). London: Routledge.

Marvin, C. (1988). *When Old Technologies Were New: Thinking about Electric Communication in the Late Nineteenth Century*. Oxford: Oxford University Press.

Maslow, A.H. (1970). *Motivation and Personality*. New York: Harper & Row.

Matthews, H. (1998). Research briefing on children and young people's views on and use of the street. *Children 5–16 Research Programme*. Hull: Centre for the Social Study of Childhood, University of Hull.

McLuhan, M. (1994). *Understanding Media: The Extensions of Man*. Cambridge, MA: MIT Press.

McMillan, S.J. (2002). Exploring models of interactivity from multiple research traditions: users, documents, and systems. In L. Lievrouw and S. Livingstone (Eds.), *Handbook of New Media: Social Shaping and Social Consequences* (pp. 163–182). London: Sage.

McQuail, D., Blumler, J.G., and Brown, J.R. (1972). The television audience: a revised perspective. In D. McQuail (Ed.), *Sociology of Mass Communications: Selected Readings*. Harmondsworth: Penguin.

McRobbie, A., and Garber, M. (1976). Girls and subcultures. In S. Hall and T. Jefferson (Eds.), *Resistance through Rituals: Youth Subcultures in Post-War Britain*. London: Hutchinson.

Mead, M. (1978). *Culture and Commitment: The New Relationships between the Generations in the 1970s*. New York: Columbia University Press.

Meyrowitz, J. (1985). *No Sense of Place: The Impact of Electronic Media on Social Behavior*. New York: Oxford University Press.

Meyrowitz, J. (1993). Images of media: hidden ferment – and harmony – in the field. *Journal of Communication*, 43(3), 55–66.

Miles, I., Cawson, A., and Haddon, L. (1992). The shape of things to consume. In R. Silverstone and E. Hirsch (Eds.), *Consuming Technologies: Media and Information in Domestic Spaces*. London: Routledge.

Miller, D. (1987). *Material Culture and Mass Consumption*. Oxford: Blackwell.

Moores, S. (1988). The box on the dresser: memories of early radio and everyday life. *Media, Culture and Society*, 10, 23–40.

Moores, S. (1993). *Interpreting Audiences: The Ethnography of Media Consumption*. London: Sage.

Moran, C., and Hawisher, G.E. (1998). The rhetorics and languages of electronic mail. In I. Snyder (Ed.), *Page to Screen: Taking Literacy into the Electronic Era* (pp. 80–101). London and New York: Routledge.

Morley, D. (1986). *Family Television: Cultural Power and Domestic Leisure*. London: Comedia.

Morris, M., and Ogan, C. (1996). The internet as mass medium. *Journal of Communication*, 46(1), 39–51.

Morrow, V., and Richards, M. (1996). The ethics of social research with children: an overview. *Children and Society*, 10, 90–105.

Moyal, A. (1995). The feminine culture of the telephone: people, patterns and policy. In N. Heap, R. Thomas, G. Einon, R. Mason, and H. Mackay (Eds.), *Information Technology and Society: A Reader* (pp. 284–310). London: Sage.

Muncie, J., Wetherell, M., Langan, M., Dallos, R., and Cochrane, A. (Eds.) (1999, first printed 1993). *Understanding the Family*. London: Sage and the Open University Press.

Murdock, G., Hartmann, P., and Gray, P. (1995). Contextualizing home computers: resources and practices. In N. Heap, R. Thomas, G. Einon, R. Mason, and H. Mackay (Eds.), *Information Technology and Society: A Reader* (pp. 269–283). London: Sage.

Murray, J.P., and Kippax, S. (1979). From the early window to the late night show: international trends in the study of television's impact on children and adults. In L. Berkowitz (Ed.), *Advances in Experimental Social Psychology* (Vol. 12). New York: Academic Press.

Neuman, S.B. (1988). The displacement effect. *Reading Research Quarterly*, 23(4), 414–440.

Neuman, S.B. (1991). *Literacy in the Television Age: The Myth of the TV Effect*. Norwood, NJ: Ablex.

Neuman, W.R. (1991). *The Future of the Mass Audience*. Cambridge: Cambridge University Press.

Newhagen, J.E., and Rafaeli, S. (1996). Why communication researchers should study the internet: a dialogue. *Journal of Communication*, 46(1), 4–13.

Nurmi, J.-E. (1998a). Conclusions and perspectives. In J.-E. Nurmi (Ed.), *Adolescents, Cultures and Conflicts: Growing Up in Contemporary Europe* (pp. 243–247). New York: Garland.

Nurmi, J.-E. (Ed.) (1998b). *Adolescents, Cultures and Conflicts: Growing Up in Contemporary Europe*. New York: Garland.

Osgerby, B. (1998). *Youth in Britain since 1945*. Oxford: Blackwell.

O'Sullivan, T. (1991). Television memories and cultures of viewing 1950–65. In J. Corner (Ed.), *Popular Television in Britain: Studies in Cultural History* (pp. 159–181). London: British Film Institute Publishing.

Oswell, D. (1998a). Early children's broadcasting in Britain, 1922–1964: programming for a liberal democracy. *Historical Journal of Film, Radio and Television*, 18(3), 375–394.

Oswell, D. (1998b). The place of 'childhood' in Internet content regulation. A case study of policy in the UK. *International Journal of Cultural Studies*, 1(1), 131–151.

Oswell, D. (1999). And what might our children become? Future visions, governance and the child television audience in postwar Britain. *Screen*, 40(1), 77–105.

Øyen, E. (1990). The imperfection of comparisons. In E. Øyen (Ed.), *Comparative Methodology: Theory and Practice in International Social Research*. London: Sage.

Palmer, P. (1986). *The Lively Audience: A Study of Children around the TV Set*. London: Allen and Unwin.

Pasquier, D. (2001). Media at home: domestic interactions and regulation. In S. Livingstone and M. Bovill (Eds.), *Children and Their Changing Media Environment: A European Comparative Study* (pp. 161–178). Mahwah, NJ: Lawrence Erlbaum Associates.

Pasquier, D., Buzzi, C., d'Haenens, L., and Sjöberg, U. (1998). Family lifestyles and media use patterns: an analysis of domestic media among Flemish, French, Italian and Swedish children and teenagers. *European Journal of Communication*, 13(4), 503–520.

Pearson, G. (1983). *Hooligan: A History of Respectable Fears*. London: Macmillan.

Pollock, G. (1997). Individualization and the transition of youth to adulthood. *Young*, 5(1): 55–68.

Poster, M. (1997). Cyberdemocracy: Internet and the public sphere. In D. Porter (Ed.), *Internet Culture* (pp. 201–218). New York: Routledge.

Postman, N. (1992). *The Disappearance of Childhood: How TV is Changing Children's Lives* (2nd edn). New York: Viking.

Prout, A., and James, A. (1990). A new paradigm for the sociology of childhood? Provenance, promise and problems. In A. James and A. Prout (Eds.), *Constructing and Reconstructing Childhood – Contemporary Issues in the Sociological Study of Childhood* (pp. 7–34). London: Falmer Press.

Putnam, R.D. (2000). *Bowling Alone: The Collapse and Revival of American Community*. New York: Simon & Schuster.

Putnam, T. (1990). Introduction: design, consumption and domestic ideals. In T. Putnam and C. Newton (Eds.), *Household Choices*. London: Futures Publications.

Quinn, V. (1997). *Critical Thinking in Young Minds*. London: David Fulton.

Qvortrup, J. (1994). *Childhood Matters: Social Theory, Practice and Politics*. Aldershot: Avebury.

Qvortrup, J. (1995). Childhood in Europe: a new field of social research. In L. Chisholm (Ed.), *Growing Up in Europe: Contemporary Horizons in Childhood and Youth Studies*. Berlin and New York: de Gruyter.

Radway, J. (1988). Reception study: ethnography and the problems of dispersed audiences and nomadic subjects. *Cultural Studies*, 2(3), 359–76.

Reimer, B. (1997). Texts, Contexts, Structures: Audience Studies and the Micro–Macro Link. In V. Carlsson (Ed.), *Beyond Media Uses and Effects*. Gothenburg: Nordicom. pp. 41–59.

Reimer, B. (1995). Youth and modern lifestyles. In J. Fornäs and G. Bolin (Eds.), *Youth Culture in Late Modernity*. London: Sage.

Ribak, R. (2001). 'Like immigrants': negotiating power in the face of the home computer. *New Media and Society*, 3(2), 220–238.

Roberts, D.F., Foehr, U.G., Rideout, V.J., and Brodie, M. (1999). *Kids and Media @ the New Millennium*. Menlo Park, CA: Henry J. Kaiser Family Foundation.

Rochberg-Halton, E. (1984). Object relations, role models, and the cultivation of the self. *Environment and Behavior*, 16(3), 335–369.

Roe, K., and Muijs, D. (1998). Children and computer games. *The European Journal of Communication*, 13(2), 181–200.

Rogers, E.M. (1995). *Diffusion of Innovations* (Vol. 4). New York: Free Press.

Rojek, C. (1995). *Decentring Leisure: Rethinking Leisure Theory*. London: Sage.

Rompaey, V.V., and Roe, K. (2002). Families' organisation of space and the allocation of information and communication technologies (ICT) in the home. In A. Schorr, B. Campbell, and M. Schenk (Eds.), *Communication Research in Europe and Abroad: Challenges of the First Decade*. Berlin: de Gruyter.

Rose, N. (1990). *Governing the Soul: The Shaping of the Private Self*. London: Routledge.

Rose, N. (1999). *Powers of Freedom: Reframing Political Thought*. Cambridge: Cambridge University Press.

Rosengren, K.E., Wenner, L.A., and Palmgreen, P. (Eds.) (1985). *Media Gratifications Research: Current Perspectives*. Beverly Hills, CA: Sage.

Rubin, A.M. (1984). Ritualized and instrumental television viewing. *Journal of Communication*, 34(3), 67–77.

Scannell, P. (1988). Radio times: the temporal arrangements of broadcasting in the modern world. In P. Drummond and R. Paterson (Eds.), *Television and its Audience: International Research Perspectives*. London: British Film Institute.

Schoenbach, K., and Becker, L.B. (1989). The audience copes with plenty: patterns of reactions to media changes. In L.B. Becker and K. Schoenbach (Eds.), *Audience Responses to Media Diversification: Coping with Plenty*. Hillsdale, NJ: Lawrence Erlbaum Associates.

Schramm, W., Lyle, J., and Parker, E.B. (1961). *Television in the Lives of Our Children*. Stanford, CA: Stanford University Press.

Schroeder, K.C. (1994). Audience semiotics, interpretive communities and the 'ethnographic turn' in media research. *Media, Culture and Society*, 16, 337–347.

Schroeder, R. (1995). Virtual reality in the real world: history, applications and projections. In N. Heap, R. Thomas, G. Einon, R. Mason, and H. Mackay (Eds.), *Information Technology and Society: A Reader* (pp. 387–399). London: Sage.

Sefton-Green, J. (Ed.) (1998). *Digital Diversions: Youth Culture in the Age of Multimedia*. London and Bristol, PA: UCL Press, and Taylor and Francis.

Segalen, M. (1996). The Industrial Revolution: from proletariat to bourgeoisie. In A. Burguiere, C. Klapisch-Zuber, M. Segalen, and F. Zonabend (Eds.), *A History of the Family: Volume II: The Impact of Modernity* (pp. 377–415). Cambridge, MA: Harvard University Press.

Seiter, E. (1999). *Television and New Media Audiences*. Oxford: Clarendon Press.

Shotter, J., and Gergen, K.J. (1988). *Texts of Identity*. London: Sage.

Silverstone, R. (1994). *Television and Everyday Life*. London: Routledge.

Silverstone, R. (1996). From audiences to consumers: the household and the consumption of communication and information technologies. In J. Hay, L. Grossberg, and E. Wartella (Eds.), *The Audience and its Landscape*. Boulder, CO: Westview Press.

Silverstone, R. (1999). *Why Study the Media?* London: Sage.

Silverstone, R., and Hirsch, E. (Eds.) (1992). *Consuming Technologies: Media and Information in Domestic Spaces*. London and New York: Routledge.

Silverstone, R., Hirsch, E., and Morley, D. (1991). Listening to a long conversation: an ethnographic approach to the study of information and communication technologies in the home. *Cultural Studies*, 5(2), 204–227.

Simmel, G. (1990). *The Philosophy of Money*. London: Routledge.

Singer, D.G., and Singer, J.L. (Eds.) (2001). *Handbook of Children and the Media*. Thousand Oaks, CA: Sage.

Skirrow, G. (1986). Hellivision: an analysis of video games. In C. MacCabe (Ed.), *High Theory/Low Culture: Analysing Popular Television and Film* (pp. 115–142). Manchester: Manchester University Press.

Smith, M.R., and Marx, L. (Eds.) (1994). *Does Technology Drive History? The Dilemma of Technological Determinism*. Cambridge, MA: MIT Press.

Smith, R., and Curtin, P. (1998). Children, computers and life online: education in a cyber-world. In I. Snyder (Ed.), *Page to Screen: Taking Literacy into the Electronic Era* (pp. 211–233). London and New York: Routledge.

Snyder, I. (1998a). Beyond the hype: reassessing hypertext. In I. Snyder (Ed.), *Page to Screen: Taking Literacy into the Electronic Era* (pp. 125–143). London and New York: Routledge.

Snyder, I. (Ed.) (1998b). *Page to Screen: Taking Literacy into the Electronic Era*. London and New York: Routledge.

Spigel, L. (1992). *Make Room for TV: Television and the Family Ideal in Postwar America*. Chicago: University of Chicago Press.

Stacey, J. (1994). Hollywood memories. *Screen*, 35(4), 317–335.

Stafford, L., and Dainton, M. (1995). Parent–child communication within the family system. In T.J. Socha and G.H. Stamp (Eds.), *Parents, Children and Communication: Frontiers of Theory and Research* (pp. 3–21). Hillsdale, NJ: Lawrence Erlbaum Associates.

Star, S.L., and Bowker, G.C. (2002). How to infrastructure. In L. Lievrouw and S. Livingstone (Eds.), *Handbook of New Media: Social Shaping and Social Consequences* (pp. 151–162). London: Sage.

Star, S.L., and Ruhleder, K. (1996). Steps toward an ecology of infrastructure: design and access for large information spaces. *Information Systems Research*, 7, 111–134.

Steele, J.R., and Brown, J.D. (1994). Studying media in the context of everyday life. *Journal of Youth Adolescence*, 24(5), 551–576.

Stone, L. (1977). *The Family, Sex and Marriage in England 1500–1800*. New York: Harper & Row.

Street, E. and Dryden, W. (Eds.) (1988). *Family Therapy in Britain*. Milton Keynes: Open University Press.

Suess, D., Suoninen, A., Garitaonandia, C., Juaristi, P., Koikkalainen, R., and Oleaga, J.A. (1998). Media use and the relationship of children and teenagers with their peer groups: a study of Finnish, Spanish and Swiss cases. *European Journal of Communication*, 13(4), 521–538.

Suoninen, A. (2001). The role of media in peer group relations. In S. Livingstone and M. Bovill (Eds.), *Children and Their Changing Media Environment: A European Comparative Study* (pp. 201–220). Mahwah, NJ: Lawrence Erlbaum Associates.

Tapscott, D. (1997). *Growing Up Digital: The Rise of the Net Generation*. New York: McGraw-Hill.

Teune, H. (1990). Comparing countries: lessons learned. In E. Øyen (Ed.), *Comparative Methodology: Theory and Practice in International Social Research*. London: Sage.

Thomas, R. (1995). Access and inequality. In N. Heap, R. Thomas, G. Einon, R. Mason, and H. Mackay (Eds.), *Information Technology and Society: A Reader* (pp. 41–53). London: Sage.

Thompson, J.B. (1995). *The Media and Modernity: A Social Theory of the Media*. Cambridge: Polity Press.

Tichenor, P.J., Donohue, G.A., and Olien, C.N. (1970) Mass and media flow and differential growth of knowledge. *Public Opinion Quaterly*, 34, 159–170.

Tisdall, K., and Hill, M. (1997). *Children and Society*. London and New York: Longman.

Tomlinson, J. (1999). *Globalisation and Culture*. Chicago: University of Chicago Press.

Turkle, S. (1995). *Life on the Screen: Identity in the Age of the Internet*. New York: Simon & Schuster.

Turow, J. (1999). *The Internet and the Family: The View from Parents, the View from the Press*. No. 27 in Report Series. Philadelphia, PA: The Annenberg Public Policy Center, niversity of Pennsylvania.

Tyner, K. (1998). *Literacy in a Digital World*. Mahwah, NJ: Lawrence Erlbaum Associates.

Valkenburg, P., and Voort, T. van der (1994). Influence of TV on daydreaming and creative imagination: a review of research. *Psychological Bulletin*, 116(2), 316–339.

van der Voort, T.H.A. (1991). Television and the decline of reading. *Poetics*, 20, 73–89.

van der Voort, T., Beentjes, J., Bovill, M., Gaskell, G., Koolstra, C.M., Livingstone, S., and Marseille, N. (1998). Young people's ownership and uses of new and old forms of media in Britain and the Netherlands. *European Journal of Communication*, 13(4), 457–477.

Varenne, H. (1996). Love and liberty: the contemporary American family. In A. Burguiere, C. Klapisch-Zuber, M. Segalen, and F. Zonabend (Eds.), *A History of the Family: Volume II: The Impact of Modernity* (pp. 416–441). Cambridge, MA: Harvard University Press.

Wartella, E., and Reeves, B. (1985). Historical trends in research on children and the media: 1900–1960. *Journal of Communication*, 35(2), 118–133.

Widdicombe, S., and Wooffitt, R. (1995). *The Language of Youth Subcultures: Social Identity in Action*. New York: Harvester Wheatsheaf.

Wigley, K., and Clarke, B. (2000). *Kids.net Wave 4*. London: National Opinion Poll Family. (Updated on www.nop.co.uk;16/8/01).

Williams, R. (1974). *Television: Technology and Cultural Form*. London: Fontana.

Willis, P. (1977). *Learning to Labour*. London: Gower.

Willis, P. (1990). *Common Culture*: Milton Keynes: Open University Press.

Winner, L. (1999). Do artefacts have politics? In D. MacKenzie and J. Wajcman (Eds.), *The Social Shaping of Technology* (2nd edn). Milton Keynes: Open University Press.

Winston, B. (1998). *Media Technology and Society: A History, from the Telegraph to the Internet*. London: Routledge.

Woolgar, S. (1996). Technologies as cultural artefacts. In W.H. Dutton (Ed.), *Information and Communication Technologies: Visions and Realities* (pp. 87–102). Oxford: Oxford University Press.

Ziehe, T. (1994). From living standard to life style. *Young: Nordic Journal of Youth Research*, 2(2), 2–16.

AUTHOR INDEX

SUBJECT INDEX